ONLY WHEN I STEP ON IT

ONE MAN'S INSPIRING JOURNEY TO HIKE THE APPALACHIAN TRAIL ALONE

A Memoir

PETER E CONTI

ISBN: 978-1-7370490-1-2 (Hardback)
ISBN: 978-1-7370490-0-5 (Paperback)
ISBN: 978-0-692-84545-5 (Kindle)

I've altered the names of some places and people as well as edited timelines to protect the innocent. This indulgence allows me to share every part of my journey without maligning or disturbing the many interesting characters I met along the way.

Book Cover Design: Najdan Mancic
Interior Layout: Najdan Mancic and Henrietta Sampson
Developmental Editing: Phyllis Parker
Copy Editing: Claire Molk
Proofreading: Karina Monesson
Front Cover Photo—McAfee Knob, the most photographed spot on the Appalachian Trail

Published in the United States of America on June 17, 2021

Adversity Press
www.AdversityPress.com
Peter@AdversityPress.com

This book is dedicated to all the seriously injured people that I've met over the past eight years. I know that each of you is challenged every day to make the most of your new normal. If this book helps you to feel a little bit better or perhaps distracts you from the pain that may continuously demand your attention, even for a moment, then I will consider this writing to be a success.

For it is in that split second, when you are first able to "not notice" the pain, that a window in your soul opens up to give you that first spark of hope, a hint of possibility for a better life to come.

This adventure would not have been possible without mountainous amounts of encouragement, support, and understanding from my beautiful wife, Joanna.

TABLE OF CONTENTS

PROLOGUE

Somewhere on the Appalachian Trail

My fingers were beginning to cramp up from holding onto the rock face in front of me. I hadn't seen anyone all day. I'd spent the entire morning clambering up the mountainous pile of rocks, using my hands and feet like a chimpanzee.

Now I tried and missed for the umpteenth time to swing my leg up to a toe hold that would allow me to push up and grab onto the tree root that was just beyond the reach of my right arm.

What the heck am I doing here? I can't do this!

The aching, burning sensations in my leg reminded me of why I was there. I guess you could call it a mission. I was determined to heal myself.

I wanted to get moving so I could warm up, but I'd been stuck there for half an hour.

I looked around, searched for other options, and finally decided to retreat down after finding none. Using my bum leg, I tried to feel around below for a place to step, but all I could find was the mountainside's smooth rock face.

And to think that a blind guy hiked the Appalachian Trail.

That's when the rain came pouring down.

1

1

PLEASE STOP THE PAIN

For Those That Look at The
Reasons Why You Cannot Do
Something, Perhaps You Are
Looking at it The Wrong Way.
Consider Why You Must.

My wife, Joanna, and I were having lunch at the Park Tavern with Tom, a friend of hers who had been paralyzed ten years ago. It had been 18 months since I had been injured and I was doing my best to keep it together. My foot and leg were hurting so much that I couldn't sit still.

Tom, the poor guy, had been working as a ski patrol when he caught an edge coming down the bunny hill, of all places.

His accident had left him paralyzed from the waist down with, as he described it, "intense pain in my butt."

Joanna brought him up to speed on how I had gotten injured and explained that I was still on opioid pain medications.

"He needs to get off that stuff. It's not good for him, and his memory is getting really bad," she said.

My mind wandered, occasionally focusing long enough to think, *she can say whatever she wants. I'm not getting off Oxycontin. At least not until they give me something else to take this never-ending pain away.*

"I didn't want to be on pain killers, so somehow I found a way for me to just not think about it," Tom said.

"What? How do you do that?" I asked. *He must be delirious. He couldn't possibly have dealt with pain like I have, could he?*

"I tried to notice a moment when I wasn't thinking about it," he said. "Once I realized that I could do that for a few seconds, it opened the door to be able to go for longer periods of time. It doesn't always work, especially when I get tired at the end of the day. But if I have a hard day, then I go to bed at night knowing that tomorrow will be a better day."

I didn't believe him. I figured that maybe that worked for him, but it certainly wouldn't work for me. My leg and foot were hurting every single second of the day, and that was *with* all the pain medications that I was on. I'm a bit ashamed to admit that I sat there pretending to listen while assuming such an outlandish idea would simply never work.

In hindsight, I can see that he had planted a tiny little seed of possibility in my mind that day. I desperately wanted a way to fix my life. Things had gotten out of control. Every day was never-ending pain. I had to find a way out.

Over the next few months, I continued to feel like chronic pain had kidnapped my life. I wanted it back. Instead of getting out and doing things, I lived each day sitting on the couch watching Netflix to try and distract myself from the searing sensation in my leg.

By this point, I'd been to twenty-three different doctors searching for a way to reduce the pain, hoping for a solution that would allow me to heal. With each new doctor, book, and web search, my hopes rose as I envisioned myself getting back to normal within a matter of weeks or, worst case, within a few months.

Having raced motocross when I was much younger, I had plenty of experience with injuries and broken bones. When I was initially injured, I expected that my shattered hip and crushed nerve in my leg would take several months, maybe a little longer, to heal up most of the way. When I was much younger, after an injury I'd wear a cast for six weeks or so, my damaged body part would be sore for a few months and then I'd be all healed up. Not such a big deal.

The truth is that breaking bones is bad, but damaging nerves is a whole new ballgame.

I had tried everything from morphine, opioids, and a bunch of nerve medications to physical therapy, walking in pools, hanging upside-down, and various anti-depressants and anti-convulsants that were supposed to help reduce nerve pain. I couldn't move my left leg below my knee for the first year, so my muscles had atrophied away. I had to wear a clunky foot brace to keep from tripping over my own foot.

I went to a neurologist who ran some tests only to tell me, "I'm sure they told you it could have been much worse. You shouldn't expect to get any better than you are now."

Oh really? %*$# you, I thought while trying my hardest not to cry. *I'm not going to believe that!* I went to get a second opinion. But the other neurologist told me the same thing. "Sorry, but your lower leg isn't getting any nerve signals. Whatever you were able to get back in the first year is all that most people can expect."

What if it really wasn't possible for me to overcome this constant pain? That thought was too much to deal with, so I pushed it off to the side. One thing was certain: I wasn't going to live the rest of my life this way. Suicide wasn't really an option, although to be honest, I had considered it at one point. Maybe I'll share that story with you when we're sitting around the campfire sometime. For now, I'd reached a point where I knew that I wanted my life back, but I couldn't find a way to make it happen.

Five months later, I was sitting at City Dock Coffee, one of my favorite coffee shops where I live in Annapolis, Maryland, writing in my journal. I like to write down all kinds of thoughts and ideas and have found that this can sometimes lead to practical answers or solutions. I'll write out a question and then mentally step out of my limited viewpoint by pretending to be the wise old sage who has answers to everything.

So, here's what I wrote:

- I need to find a way to embrace my injury and quit this life of avoiding it because it sucks!

- How can I make my injury an advantage?

- How can I become surrounded by people who cheer me on to challenge this and overcome my injury?

I checked in with the wise old sage but wasn't able to come up with any answers. I've found that sometimes bigger challenges take more time. I let this sit, trusting that God, my mind, or whatever would eventually come up with something for me to try.

A few weeks later, my wife and I saw the movie "Wild" where Reese Witherspoon's character hikes the Pacific Crest Trail. There's a scene where her hiking boots go over the edge of a cliff, leaving her in the middle of the wilderness with no apparent way out. I could relate to this because I didn't see any way out from the pain that had haunted me every day for the past twenty-three months.

After seeing the movie, I read David Miller's book *AWOL on the Appalachian Trail* and a few others written by people who'd thru-hiked the Appalachian Trail. To become a thru-hiker, you must complete all 2,189 miles of the trail within a year. Most people attempt this by leaving everything else in their life behind and taking about half a year off to hike the whole way from Georgia to Maine.

Thru-hiking the entire Appalachian Trail is no easy feat. It's roughly the distance between Los Angeles and Washington, D.C. A thru-hiker will experience 464,500 feet of elevation change, or sixteen climbs up Mount Everest and back down to sea level. Thousands of people attempt an Appalachian Trail thru-hike every year, yet only one in four hikers finish the journey. They typically take five to seven months to complete the entire trail, according to the Appalachian Trail Conservancy.

Officially it's called the Appalachian National Scenic Trail, but most people know it as the Appalachian Trail or simply the AT. I had been introduced to the AT many years ago by reading *A Walk in The Woods* by Bill Bryson. At the time I had thought hiking the AT would be fun to do but figured I'd never have the time to do it.

After reading a few more books about the Appalachian Trail I thought, *I wonder if I could do that?*

I knew that I couldn't run or even ride a bike, but I could walk as long as I had my cane. And I figured that hiking couldn't be that much more demanding than walking.

And then I thought, *if I were to hike 2,000 miles, then my foot and leg would have to be better.* And after thinking about it some more, I decided that I would do it. I would start my hike on March 3rd, the two-year anniversary of the day I was injured. This anniversary was significant to me because I *never expected I'd still be hurting two whole years later. It was a point that I thought I'd never reach. What better time to set off on an adventure that I hoped, dreamed, and prayed would finally solve the seemingly inescapable trap I'd fallen into.

If I were going to head off into the wilderness for five or six months, the first challenge would be to find a way to warm my wife up to the idea. We've always supported each other during our twenty-plus years of marriage. Both of us have started and run various businesses. Joanna founded an international non-profit and even ran for U.S. Congress at one point.

The next day, I managed to casually mention to her that I was thinking of hiking the Appalachian Trail. She smiled and said, "Oh, that's nice, honey. Maybe that's something that you could work up to."

I don't think that she really believed me and, to be truthful with you, I had major doubts myself. My boastful claim to hike several thousand miles to heal my leg wasn't based on any experience or even reality, for that matter. With all the pain I was in, I was hesitant to take the dog down the street for a walk, much less hike over 2,000 miles through fourteen different states.

Since I hadn't ever backpacked before, I started watching YouTube videos and reading what I could online along with every hiking book that I could get my hands on to find out what type of supplies and gear I might need if I were going to go on a long hike like this. Each book or article that I read would mention two or three other new things that I thought I might need to take with me.

I discovered that long-distance hiking was a whole different ball of wax compared to taking the kids car camping. I would have to get into shape, buy freeze-dried food, energy bars, and other supplies that would need to be organized into "resupply boxes" that could be shipped to towns along the trail.

I would also need a tent, sleeping bag and pad, a water filtration system, portable cookstove, cold weather gear, raincoat, rain pants, and a whole bunch of other stuff. I quickly figured out that I would need to carry all this stuff in my pack. Therefore, I also needed to purchase the lightest possible version of each item.

I drove out to our local REI store to look at some gear and figure out how much all of this would set me back. I looked at some of the basics and could see right away that this wasn't going to be cheap. As I wandered around the store, I discovered all kinds of handy-looking camping stuff, most of which I didn't even know existed. While all of this looked enticing, I was hesitant to buy a bunch of gear until I was sure that I would be able to actually go hiking.

My concern was alleviated once I discovered that REI has a lifetime "no questions asked" return policy. Despite this liberal policy, I was hesitant enough to limit myself to getting just a set of hiking poles. I figured with the poor balance I had with my injured leg, I'd for sure need those. Besides, how much could they cost? Thirty or forty bucks?

I went over to the hiking-poles section to see what they had available. I focused on a pair that appeared to be lightweight and folded up nicely. That must be an advantage—why else would they make them that way?

I looked at the tag to see what the price was. It said $139.00, but that must be a mistake. Maybe a clerk had meant to put $39.00 and accidentally hit an extra digit. I checked the price tag on all the other sets.

$139.00 for hiking poles?

I put them back down and walked away, asking myself, *am I really going to do this?* Then I pictured myself back at home, sitting on the sofa with my leg killing me. I picked the poles up, paid for them, and drove home.

The next day, although I still had quite a bit of concern over my abilities, I confidently announced to Joanna, "I've decided that *I am* going to hike the Appalachian Trail."

Joanna had a puzzled look on her face and didn't say anything.

I spoke up and added, "I'm starting in three weeks, on March 3rd."

"Okay . . . Do you have anyone you can go with?"

"Ah . . . No. I'm going by myself."

"You're going alone? ALL ALONE?"

"Well, I, uh . . . might meet some people on the trail."

"What happens if something goes wrong?"

"I'll be fine!" I insisted. "What could possibly go wrong?"

"And you're starting March 3rd?"

"Yup, that's the plan."

"That's in three weeks."

"Uh . . . yeah, I guess so."

"And you're going to be down in Georgia by then?"

"Yeah. I was thinking of taking the train."

"Well, I'd feel a lot better if you found someone you could go with."

While it was pretty clear that she didn't think this was a good idea, I took her response as tacit approval since she didn't explicitly say no. The truth was, I really had no idea if I could hike or not.

The next night at dinner, I said, "I've been thinking about what you said about hiking and I've come up with a good solution."

"Oh, what's that?"

"Let's get an RV, and then you can meet me each night at the next trailhead with dinner all cooked up. I could get cleaned up and sleep in it, too."

"Ha, ha, ha, ha," she replied. "That's not going to happen."

Oh, well. I didn't think she would go for that, but it didn't hurt to ask. When she tells this part of the story, she says, "And then he wanted me to hike in each night to *bring his* dinner to the shelter! Isn't that crazy?"

After researching some more, I made another trip out to the REI store. While getting a pack and a pair of hiking boots, I discovered even more stuff that looked like it might be helpful to have while I was out in the woods. In addition to what

I found on my own, I ended up having long conversations with the friendly staff about things that I'd already purchased, like the lightweight tent I'd ordered online.

"Oh, you don't want a tent. What you really need is one of these hiking hammocks. It's lighter, and you don't need a flat spot to set it up. All you need is a couple of trees."

"Can I stay dry and warm enough?"

"Oh, that's no problem, as long as you have this tarp, under quilt, suspension system, and bug netting.

"What does all that cost?"

"Oh, it's only $520."

After several hours of this, I'd spent another five or six hundred dollars and brought home eight or ten other things to add to my growing collection of camping gear. Then there were all the boxes arriving daily from Amazon. Mountain House freeze-dried meals, peanut butter crackers, Pop-Tarts, trail-mix, Peanut M&Ms, Snickers bars, protein bars, cotton balls, Q-Tips, and a first aid kit.

My plan at this point was to have my wife send me boxes of freeze-dried food and other hiker chow to some of the towns and hostels along the trail. I had no idea how many peanut butter crackers I might need to hike 2,000 miles, so I ordered plenty to make sure that I didn't run out.

Now that I had my pack, I was eager to go out and see if I could hike with a heavy load on my back. I put most of the gear I'd purchased so far into my new backpack and then added a few hand weights to get it over 30 pounds.

Then I laced up my new hiking boots, put a leash on Snickers, my Yorkie, put my pack on, and grabbed my new hiking poles to go on a test hike around the neighborhood.

I planned to hike around a four-mile loop that, despite being perfectly flat, would give me an idea of whether or not I'd be able to pull off this crazy idea.

I felt a little silly hiking along the side of the road with my backpack and poles. I wondered if the neighbors thought I was running away from home. I wasn't used to walking with hiking poles, and I found it hard to sync them as I walked. On top of this, Snickers was running back and forth, sniffing everything, and getting his leash tangled up in the poles.

I did okay for the first 10 or 15 minutes, but then the pain in my leg started to flare up. As I walked along in my hiking boots, I did my best to ignore this, hoping—willing the pain to go down. When I was first injured, I hoped I'd be completely healed within a few months or so. Once I reached 90 days, I moved my goal out to 6 months. I told myself and others, "Surely I'll be better in time for my daughter's wedding." At 6 months' time, I was still limping around using a cane, so I pushed my goal out to a year. Then the one-year mark came and went. I'd been searching for a way to get better for almost two years. I felt like this was my final chance. I knew that if I could hike the Appalachian Trail, then I'd finally get better.

I continued to nudge myself along, pushing mentally and physically against the growing pain in my leg. *I'll just ignore it,* I told myself, as I kept walking. The pain resisted this idea by hurting even more, almost as if it were saying, "*How about THIS.*" I tried shouting out some affirmations.

"I can do this!"

"I am a champion!"

"I *am* going to hike the Appalachian Trail!"

These mental gyrations worked just well enough that I was able to make it another quarter mile. Meanwhile, the pain in my foot and leg was growing stronger and stronger until it took over all my mental capacity. It was as if my brain and foot were having a shouting match, bouncing the unwanted pain back and forth against each other.

I knew at this point that I could force myself to go a little bit further, but there was no way that I was going to be able to make it around the four-mile loop. Snickers and I had made it just over a mile. I considered calling my wife to come and get us, but the idea of calling my hiking adventure off so soon was embarrassing. I pushed the pain aside long enough to give my brain a moment to decide if I could walk back home.

No. That's not happening. My leg was killing me.

I pulled out my cell phone and called Joanna to come pick us up with the car. I made up a story about how Snickers was having a hard time, but I'm pretty sure she saw right through that. She was sweet to not say anything about whether she thought I'd be able to hike the Appalachian Trail.

Even though my test hike failed completely, I was still bound and determined to start hiking the Appalachian Trail. If anything, I was more determined than ever. There was no way that I was going to admit to Joanna or myself that I wasn't in condition to hike through fourteen different states. I ignored all the indications that I wasn't ready for this great adventure and doubled down on my preparations. I did extra physical therapy at home, climbed up and down seven flights of stairs at the hospital twice a week, and walked in the therapy pool every other day.

Emily, my physical therapist, was excited about the idea and provided encouragement. She had hiked parts of the Appalachian Trail in Maryland with her father and was familiar with it. She made a sign for me that said, "You Can Do It!" I had plenty of doubts, but what other options did I have? Just sitting at home hurting day after day wasn't the life that I wanted to be living.

Most people who earn the title of an Appalachian Trail thru-hiker complete the entire journey within four to five months. By starting in March, I'd have seven months to finish and reach Mt. Katahdin in Maine before the mountain is closed due to weather, which usually happens by October 15th.

Shortly after choosing my start date, I got a call from Mona, the widow of my best friend Brian, who had unfortunately died from a brain tumor about six months earlier. When I told Mona about my plans to hike the AT, she said, "Oh my goodness!" She then explained that Brian had hiked the Appalachian Trail in 1994 and asked her to spread his ashes along the trail after he died. She also said that Brian discovered his illness on March 3rd, and she couldn't believe that I was starting on that date.

Here's the letter she wrote me:

Dear Peter,

I am struggling to find just the right words to express the gratitude for carrying the remains of Brian to fulfill one of his wishes to have some of his remains rest at the beloved Appalachian Trail.

Brian walked the AT the summer of 1994 as he contemplated next steps in his life. He was unhappy in software and in a relationship going nowhere. His time on the AT helped him explore possibilities and come up with some answers.

He decided on law school and was grateful because of the career and meeting me. He'd often say it was the best decision he'd made and credited the AT for enabling him to get to that decision.

I wish you tremendous hope on your journey, however long it may be, for this isn't a simple walk in the woods. This is your journey into reclaiming your life after your accident and recovery. Brian loved you. No better person could take him back to the AT right now.

Much love from all of us,

Mona H
Golden, CO

At this point, I knew and believed with all my heart that if I could hike 2,000 miles, my leg would have to be better.

2

A WOLF IN THE DARK

ONE DAY THIS PAIN WILL
MAKE SENSE TO YOU

One of my worst traits is my tendency to put off final preparations until the last minute. As far as I can tell, this started in Mr. Blase's English class in 7th grade. I can't blame him for this, nor would I want to, as he was an excellent teacher. I think this was because he believed in us and treated us like young adults. He expected us to excel, and we knew it.

Every Tuesday, we had a vocabulary test. The bell would ring, and we always took the test first thing. I discovered that if I got to class ten minutes early, I could pull out the list of words that Mr. Blase had given us the week before and, without any practice at all, I'd run through the list twenty times and ace the test. This worked for the test but I'm not sure how many words I still knew a week later.

I continued this tradition of last-minute preparation when I raced motocross as a teenager. I'd wait until Saturday night to start preparing my bike for the next day's race. After going to a race one weekend and discovering that my motorcycle wouldn't start, I initiated a ritual that exemplified the traditional teenager–parent relationship. No matter how late it was on Saturday night, sometimes near midnight, I'd fire up my dirt bike and take it for a run up the street and back. My poor parents later told me that they would lay awake knowing that it was coming; they just didn't know when. I'm not sure what the neighbors thought of me, but I probably wasn't too popular.

After the outright failure of my neighborhood test hike with my dog, I started walking slowly on the treadmill and stretching each day to see if I could improve my ability to hike. I determined that the best place for a second test would be on the Appalachian Trail itself, a section of which runs through Maryland about an hour's drive from my house. I'd picked an 18-mile section that ran from Turner's Gap on US 40 down to Harper's Ferry. I figured that if I could complete six miles a day, I could make it in three days.

My wife asked me how I thought that I'd be able to go six miles a day when I couldn't make it more than a mile on flat ground the week before. I didn't have an answer for that or all the other questions she was asking me like, "Is there cell service on the trail? What are you going to do if you get hurt?" I tried to brush her concerns aside. I figured there was only one way to find out.

I had planned to leave early in the morning, but of course waited until that day to get all my gear ready. If you've never gone hiking out in the wild before, the tendency is to try and bring everything. As I've mentioned earlier, I'd never backpacked before. I didn't even know how to dress in layers. All I knew was that it was the middle of February, and it was going to be cold.

It was late in the day, with the sun already low in the sky when I pulled into the parking lot at Turner's Gap. I thought for a moment that perhaps I should wait until the next morning to start into the woods but decided to press on. Joanna had asked me to find a hiking partner, but after searching some web forums, I couldn't find anyone, so I decided to go by myself.

As I was tightening down the straps on my pack, I thought about my wife's concerns. *What if something did happen to me and I didn't have cell service? In this cold weather, that could be dangerous.* I called Joanna to let her know that I had changed my plans and was just going to hike a few miles into the woods to reach the first shelter, spend the night there, and then head back out. She was happy to hear this news and I felt somewhat relieved as well.

I put on the full-body fleece I had along with a sweater and my biggest LL Bean down coat. By the time I put on my fur-lined hat, I looked like I was ready to go to the Arctic Circle. My pack was bulging at the seams. I used the straps on the outside to hold onto a big bulky foam sleeping pad I used when I'd taken the kids car camping. I had a couple of flashlights, including a recent purchase with a hand crank on the side to generate electricity while I was out hiking in the dark.

The trail had been covered with snow and previous hikers had packed this down to create an icy, slippery surface with occasional rocks poking out. I, of course, didn't have any kind of traction device, so I did my best to be careful by going slowly over the slippery parts while thinking, *can I really do this?*

I took a selfie and sent it to my kids. "Hey, look at me. I'm hiking the Appalachian Trail!" My big smile in the photo didn't reveal the thoughts that continued to bother me. *You're going to be out here in the woods, the dark Appalachian Trail woods, with no one else around for miles and miles.* I'd have been surprised to know that I'd eventually learn to love being alone in the wilderness, so much so that I missed it once I stopped hiking.

It was rather dark by the time I saw the sign pointing down a side trail to Rocky Run Shelter. I'd been using one of the two flashlights I was carrying to see my way for the last mile or so. The shelter looked almost brand new, and like many shelters on the AT, it had one side completely open to the elements. I was the only one there, so I decided to go up the ladder to the upper level just in case any bears came by to check on me during the night.

Because I hadn't known how to layer my clothes, I had overdressed, and the fleece bodysuit was soaking wet. I took it off, hung it up to dry, got into some dry clothes, and rolled out my old foam sleeping pad. I pulled out my sleeping bag and plumped it up.

I climbed into the sleeping bag and lay there shivering as I tried to warm up as quickly as possible. Since it was so cold, I decided to go ahead and eat my dinner of protein bars and trail mix right there rather than away from the sleeping area.

I had read this was important to do to avoid having a bear or other wild animal come into the shelter during the night.

I tried to send Joanna a text letting her know that I had made it to the shelter safely, but I didn't have any service. I did my best to go to sleep while trying not to think about what might be out there in the darkness. I told myself, *I'm actually here. I'm on the Appalachian Trail… I'm doing it!*

It was so cold that before long, I was shivering and moving around trying to stay warm. I don't remember if I pulled the enclosures to draw the sleeping bag up tight around my face or not. That's the best way to keep warm at night. This likely was one of the hundreds of things I had left to learn.

So, it was pitch black out, I was freezing, and yes, I'm not too proud to let you know that I was scared of being out in the woods all by myself. I took a few deep breaths and told myself that it was too cold for bears to be out and that any other animals would have a hard time getting up the ladder to the top level of the shelter where I was trying to sleep.

And that's when the howling began.

At first, it was from far away. It was a sustained doleful cry. A "Yow, yow yow yowoooo!" Then it seemed to be coming closer. The shelter was a short way down a side trail from the Appalachian Trail. The main trail ran through a valley that contained and reinforced this howling much like a megaphone. "Yow, Yow Yow Yowooooooooo!"

Coming closer . . .

"Yow, Yow Yow Yowooooooooo!"

Now getting louder...

"Yow, Yow Yow Yowooooooooo!"

The hair on the back of my head stood straight up, and

I could feel my heart pounding inside my chest. I thought about getting up to grab my hiking poles so that I could defend myself but thought, *No. Don't move. It might hear you.*

"Yow. Yowwwwl…Yup…Yowwwwwl.."

From the sounds of this creature, it had to be a wolf, and it was approaching. *Would it be able to smell the Snickers bars that I had right next to me in my pack?*

I thought about looking for my flashlight, but no matter how hard I tried, I couldn't move. I was frozen with fear. I held my breath as the wolf howled non-stop, making its way down the trail and past the shelter to the south. The howling continued its frequency, but the volume receded as the wolf ran further and further down the valley to the south.

I finally was able to breathe again and tried my best to go to sleep despite the cold. Then, about an hour later, I heard it again. It faded in at first but got louder and louder as the wolf returned up the valley heading north.

"Yow, Yow Yow Yowoooooooooo! Yow, Yow Yow Yowoooooooo!"

Although I couldn't see anything out in the pitch black of the night, I vividly envisioned a wolf running with big muscular legs, its mouth hanging open with a bit of slobber dripping off the side of a long pink tongue that was flapping in the breeze. It wasn't hard to track since it was yowling non-stop. Once again, it came right down the main trail and past the shelter. Then the yowling slowly faded away again as the wolf moved further and further up the valley.

Between all the excitement and the fact that it was rather cold out, I can't say that I felt rested in the morning. Happy to be alive was more like it. I looked out to see that a light dusting of snow had fallen overnight. I made breakfast, hiked the two miles back to my car, and then drove over to say hi to my folks who live nearby in Frederick, MD. I shared this story with them and a few other people, but no one seemed to believe that it was a wolf.

I looked online to see that wolves will howl like this to communicate to other wolves about their territory, their way of saying, "stay away." I also found that the gray wolves who used to roam Maryland have been extinct since the mid 1800s.

Then I learned that there's a refuge for wolves seventy miles north of where I was near Harrisburg, PA. *Maybe I should call them to see if they've had an escapee.*

Whatever it was scared the dickens out of me during my first night out on the Appalachian Trail.

3

A GOOD TIME TO BEGIN IS NOW

TALK IS CHEAP, HEADING
NORTH IS PRICELESS

During my final week of preparations, I made numerous trips to REI and two other outfitters to scour their shelves for any other items that I might need. The kitchen looked like a tornado had gone through with opened boxes of food resupply items stacked in odd piles against the wall, and all sorts of cold-weather gear was strewn about. The table had stacks of random backpacking components that I was doing my best to sort through.

I was using a food scale to weigh everything. I cut my toothbrush in half to save a few grams. I removed some of the extra straps from my pack and cut all the labels out of my clothes. I looked at all the stuff and tried to figure out if I really needed things like a folding cup, a multi-wipe towel, or an egg carrier. *Should I take the large medical kit, the medium-sized one, or the small, "survival only" version?* (Yes, I had bought all three.)

The problem was that since I hadn't hiked before, I didn't know what I truly needed. I was concerned about being out there in the wild and figured it would be better to have a bit too much stuff rather than getting stuck out there without, say, a snake bite kit when you really need it. But my pack was only so big, and at about the exact moment I realized this, my lovely wife danced by and said, "I hope the inside of that pack is bigger than the outside because you're going to have a hard time fitting everything in."

The Hiker Hostel called on Friday to confirm that I'd be arriving at the train station in Georgia the next morning. I looked at everything strewn about and realized that I'd planned on getting to the Hostel two days before my scheduled start date of March 3rd.

"Actually, could you pick me up one day later on Sunday morning?" I asked.

"Sure thing! Josh will be there to get you at 8:30 when the train arrives."

Whew! That gave me an entire extra day to figure all of this out. I started going through everything one by one and putting things into one of three piles: must have, would be nice to have, and I'm okay leaving this behind. Using every bit of the extra day to sort all that out (and make one last trip to REI), I finally got everything stuffed into my pack with about fifteen minutes to spare before we had to leave for the train station.

By the time my wife dropped me off at the Amtrak station, it was starting to get dark. I had her take a picture of me standing there in my hiking boots wearing my pack. The train would take me from Baltimore and head south through the night, arriving in Gainesville, Georgia at 8:30 the next morning.

I had fond memories of Amtrak as I had taken a few of my kids on trips for some good one-on-one time. I found that it was a great way to get away from everything. Traveling by train is a different experience. You get to meet quirky people, everyone from budget travelers to those afraid to fly on airplanes. My favorite quotes from Amtrak employees are, "That's not bad, we're only six hours late" and "We can't possibly help you with that."

I went out on the platform and saw the train pulling into the station. I waited in line and then used my arms to pull myself up onto the train. I walked down through a few cars and chose two open seats, hoping to keep them to myself. I had tried the sleeping cars on Amtrak before, but the fold-down bunks just didn't work for me. Every time the train hit a little bump, I'd wake up thinking that it might be going off the tracks.

I put my pack up in the luggage rack, leaned my seat back, and took some time to allow everything to soak in. *I'm doing it! I'm really on my way to start hiking the Appalachian Trail!*

After I settled in a bit, I reached up to my pack to pull out some dental floss, a sewing needle, my headlamp, and wool hat. I used the needle and floss to sew the headlamp onto the front of my hat. I'd seen this online as a way to cut some extra weight by getting rid of the headlamp band.

As the train made its way down through Washington, DC and over the Potomac River, I closed my eyes and decided to get some sleep. It proved difficult, however, because in the seat behind me there was a lady with two kids who was yapping on the phone. I've found that when using public transportation, it's helpful to be able to ignore characters like this, those who obviously have no regard for anyone else around them.

No worries, I told myself. *I'm sure she'll be off the phone soon.*

An hour later, she was still talking, in her louder than usual cell phone voice, of course.

"Uh Huh. Really? You Don't Say!"

Surely, she's going to be done soon, I thought to myself.

"Yap, yap, yap . . ."

Another hour went by.

And then, another.

At this point, my ability to ignore the lady had run its course, and I was getting pretty darn annoyed. With nothing left to talk about, she was now asking for a play-by-play of whatever her friend was doing on the other end of the call.

"Okay, now what are you doing? Uh, huh. Really? I wouldn't do it that way. Blah blah blah blah blah blah!"

I was exhausted and just wanted to go to sleep. I thought about saying something to her, but I had become so angry that I realized if I said anything, it wouldn't come out very well. I was ready to bite her head off. *Certainly, she was going to hang up soon!* It was almost 2:00 AM.

I don't know why, but instead of getting up and moving, I just sat there getting more and more annoyed. It's not like we had assigned seats or anything. I think this was one of those situations where I stubbornly insisted on sticking to my initial decision—in this case, to wait until she got off her call. Instead of getting up and moving, I'd count to a hundred. Then another hundred. *I'm SURE she's almost done.* I counted to a hundred again. Thinking back on this, I'm wondering if some part of me *likes* having someone or something to be mad at. That wouldn't be a healthy way to go through the world, would it? But why else would I continue to sit there?

I knew I hadn't ever been that thoughtless or insensitive. Or have I? I did drive my wife crazy one time when we were driving to Florida. I called anyone and everyone that I knew just to stay awake for the fifteen-hour drive. Come to think of it, she was ready to wring my neck when we finally arrived. Maybe I shouldn't complain so much.

When the train screeched to a stop in Charlottesville, Virginia, I could see the remnants of a recent snowstorm. Big banks of snow were piled up alongside the loading platform. One of my sisters lived here with her husband and she had called the week before to let me know she was worried about my heading out all on my own into the cold weather.

"Oh, I'll probably be fine," I said. "There are other people hiking the trail and maybe I can find someone to hike with me."

While March 3rd made sense as the anniversary of my injury, it probably wasn't the best time to start a thru-hike. If I'd done more research, I would have found that generally, and depending on the year, hikers beginning in March or even April are quite likely to experience snowy and cold conditions in Georgia and the higher elevations found in the Smoky Mountains.

So, there I was. I hadn't hiked before, other than the

terrifying overnight test a week ago. I had no experience or much of any clue about how to stay warm and safe in cold, icy conditions. Why was I so bull-headed and intent on hiking the Appalachian Trail?

Reason number one was the physical pain I was in and the hope that this endeavor would release me from it. The second reason was more of an emotional one. I've always been pretty active, riding motorcycles, bicycles, and running. I even flew sailplanes for about ten years. I wanted to run and jump and be myself rather than the disabled, hurting person that I had become. I ultimately wanted to be healed, but the immediate need was to *do* something. I wanted to take charge of my recovery rather than hoping for someone else to magically make the pain go away and fix my life. That's why I was hiking the Appalachian Trail, and that's what I had told my wife when she asked why I was doing this.

"Honey, if I can hike over 2,000 miles then my leg will *have to* be healed up."

I'm not sure how much sleep I got, if any. What I do know is that the sun was coming up when the nice lady behind me finally got off her phone. When we arrived in Gainesville, I got up, pulled my pack down from the overhead, and stepped down from the train. Josh, who owned the Hiker's Hostel with his wife, was there waiting for me. I realized that he could tell who I was because I was the only one with a big pack and hiking poles. I tossed my stuff into the back of his big Suburban, and he drove us up to the hostel in Dahlonega.

After thru-hiking the Appalachian Trail in 2000, Josh and Leigh Saint decided to open a hostel that would encourage and support hikers such as myself who wanted to hike the trail. It was a thirty-mile drive from the train station to the hostel in Dahlonega. The place looked squeaky clean and appeared to be well run. Leigh showed me around and told me that breakfast would be at "8:00 AM sharp."

I spent part of the day napping to help recover from my overnight trip on Amtrak. When I woke up, I got to know some of the other hikers, with the usual conversation consisting of "Where are you from?" and "Why did you decide to hike the Appalachian Trail?"

We had our own kitchen downstairs, which included a hiker-box. A hiker-box is a cardboard or plastic box where hikers can leave extra food, equipment, or clothes they don't need. While pretty much anyone can show up and help themselves to the hiker box, the unwritten rule is that the contents are reserved for thru-hikers.

I found some spaghetti in the hiker box to cook up for lunch and ordered a pizza for dinner. After dinner, Josh offered to do a pack shake-down demonstration for all the hikers. One of the female hikers volunteered to have her pack contents reviewed.

As she pulled everything out, one at a time, Josh would put each item into one of three piles. The first pile was essential things to keep, the second was for optional things that she should consider removing from her pack, and the third pile was for things that Josh said she should get rid of. This was interesting because I'd struggled with this same process before leaving home.

The pile of essential things included the basics like a tent, sleeping bag, and pad. Her little cookstove and fuel also went in the essential pile, but Josh said they ended up getting rid of their stove when they were thru-hiking so they could be as light as possible once they got up to New Hampshire and Maine.

The second pile had things that you could bring depending on how you felt. Josh explained that while everyone carried a raincoat and rain pants, "If you wear these, you're going to sweat and be soaked. If you don't wear them, you're going to be soaked. As long as the temperature is above 40 degrees or so, you'll be ok without them."

The third pile was for things that, in Josh's opinion, shouldn't be carried on the trail. Items that went into this category included a compass ("You don't need this on the AT"), a huge medical kit, and an extra cooking pot. Josh explained that hikers tend to show their fears by what's in their packs.

"One girl a few weeks ago had seven different flashlights in her pack." I could relate to this, remembering the two flashlights I took on my overnight test hike.

Having never backpacked before, I found this very helpful with my ongoing process of getting my pack's weight down as low as possible. Despite this, I still held onto plenty of stuff that I'd end up getting rid of later. One good example was a mini-iPad. I'd weighed it and discovered that it was lighter than a single paperback book. I didn't know yet that I'd be too tired to read much of anything at night.

Josh explained that "Grams turn into ounces and ounces turn into pounds. You want your pack to be as light as possible." He went on to tell us that on the Appalachian Trail, you were—for the most part—always within a day or two's walk from a road or a town. In addition to this, at least down south in Georgia and the Carolinas, you could expect to see many other hikers along the trail. If you really needed something, then chances are another hiker may either have what you need or be able to send help your way. "Here in Georgia, there is plenty of water along the trail, so you don't really need to carry more than about a liter or so at any one time."

I planned to stay at the hostel the next day, figuring I could talk with hikers and finish any last-minute preparation. Since I had all day, I took my time getting upstairs to breakfast only to find that "8:00 AM sharp" didn't mean 8:25. Most of the good stuff was already gone. This was my first introduction to the importance of rules, which varied from one hostel to the next. From then on, I paid attention and showed up on time for breakfast.

I wished all the hikers who were heading out to start their AT journey good luck and spent a good part of the day trying to finish up some work for one of my consulting clients. This was hard to do on the older hostel computer with a slow internet connection. I mentally kicked myself a few times for not getting this done before I had left home.

In the evening I watched two other pack shakedowns, which gave myself and the other hikers the advantage of hearing a broad spectrum of advice.

"I don't use hiking boots; trail runner shoes are the only way to go."

"I hiked the entire AT and never used a bear bag once. I slept with my food right in my tent."

If you don't know what a bear bag is, you use it to hang your food from a tree branch where it's supposedly impossible for a bear to reach. This last piece of advice seemed to contradict everything I had heard so far. I soon discovered that opinions about gear, food, and how to hike varied quite a bit from one "expert" to the next.

I finished my final day at the Hiker Hostel with another pizza dinner before spending the remaining time putting a few finishing touches on my pack so that I'd be ready to leave for the trail right after breakfast in the morning.

I woke up excited the next morning and got up with enough time to give my pack yet another final look over before heading upstairs *on time*. The table bustled with other hikers, all of whom shared the dream of hiking the Appalachian Trail. The wet and foggy weather outside didn't seem to dampen my spirits or those of the other hikers who were all eager to hit the trail.

After a hearty breakfast of eggs, bacon, potatoes, and pancakes, I stepped out on the front porch and hung my pack on a scale to see how well I'd done at getting the weight down. I was surprised to see that my gear, along with a few days of food and two liters of water, came in at 36 pounds. *Whew!* I'd slimmed down a bit by donating a few items to the hiker box, but I'd hoped to keep it below 30 pounds, *Oh, well!*

Josh surveyed how many of us needed a ride to each of the two possible starting points. The southern terminus of the Appalachian Trail is the summit of Springer Mountain in Georgia. The first decision you need to make is whether to start at Amicalola Falls State Park and hike mostly uphill for 7.8 miles to the Summit of Springer or start where Forest Service Road 42 crosses the trail one mile north of Springer and hike backwards one mile south. I, of course, chose the forest road so I could get as close as possible.

When we left the Hiker Hostel, the van was packed full of excited, hopeful, and energetic thru-hikers. Each of us took turns sharing our reasons for taking on the trail as the van made its way up the long and bumpy forest road. The twenty-mile trip took us an hour and a half, and Josh finally dropped our group off at the dirt parking lot one mile north of the official starting point. We all smiled, took some pictures, and then wished each other well.

It was with two opposing forces of *"Yes, I can"* and *"No, you're nuts"* battling inside my head that I stepped into the woods and headed towards Springer Mountain. To be honest with you, I didn't know if I could even make it the one mile to Springer and back.

Many portions of the trail are mostly flat dirt with plenty of room for someone with a disability like mine to make their way. Not this part though. I was surprised to see that the trail was littered in places with rocks that varied from football-sized to some as big as a large suitcase. These required me to step on angled surfaces with my injured leg and foot. Something that happens to most people who have a consistently painful injury is the tendency to avoid using that part of their body, so they favor the stronger side.

I was no exception. The two-year vacation for my injured side resulted in a floppy marionette foot. The only exercises that I had done were during my physical therapy appointments twice a week. On top of this, the nerve damage rendered the communication channel from my brain to my foot almost nonexistent. I'd been taking nerve growth supplements and willing my nerves to regrow, but it was taking forever. As a result, even with all the physical therapy, my foot and lower leg muscles had become so atrophied that even after I started to get some nerve signals back, I wasn't able to control my foot.

All the muscles that used to help me keep my balance, land softly, and push off with each step were basically useless at this point. I couldn't control or slow down the motion of my foot to keep it from banging into and matching the angle of the surface I was stepping on. On top of this, my proprioception was lousy on my injured side. This meant that I didn't have a good idea of exactly where my foot was unless I looked right down at it. All I could do was try to find a flat place to flop my foot down. I used my poles to help, of course, although with all the weight that I was putting on my hands, before long, they began to hurt.

For someone who was already dealing with chronic pain like I was, it wasn't even the boost in suffering that concerned me at this point. I figured that I could deal with that, for the day at least. But I couldn't help from worrying about how this would add up over the next 2,189 miles. I wondered if I'd end up making my foot worse instead of healing it as I had hoped.

Within fifteen minutes, everyone else had moved past me and before long, I met hikers who weren't from our group, that were coming back from the top of Springer Mountain.

"Are you a thru-hiker?"

"Yup, I'm going to Maine. Mt. Katahdin, here I come!"

Pretty much everyone I met that day seemed just as thrilled as I was about hiking the entire trail despite the truth that most of us wouldn't make it that far. Rather than sharing my own doubts, I did the same as everyone else. I was overly positive and optimistic to make up for the fact that I had serious doubts about my own ability to make it.

I kept expecting to reach Springer Mountain's summit only to find that the trail kept going. *Certainly, I've gone a mile by now.*

Finally, a hiker coming the other way said, "It's just ahead! You're almost there,"

And there it was. A large clump of rocks with a brass plaque dated 1934. It described the Appalachian Trail as "A footpath for those who seek fellowship with the Wilderness."

I was suddenly overcome with emotion. All my frustrations and efforts over the past two years had somehow led me here—the beginning of the Appalachian Trail. This misty, slightly rainy morning seemed a match for the mix of feelings swirling around in my head.

Then I remembered Brian's ashes. I didn't really know what to do with them. My first thought was to put some here and then carry the rest to the top of Mt. Katahdin. Then I realized that if something happened to me or I didn't make it all the way, I'd have this as an unfinished task. So, I looked around and found an appropriate spot with a view looking out across the valley and tucked Brian's ashes between a couple of rocks.

A few minutes later, another hiker arrived, and I asked him to take a photo of me standing optimistically in front of the plaque. Then I found a metal box that held the trail register mounted to the side of the rock. I pulled out a simple coil-bound notebook protected by a large Ziplock bag. It looked like the spiral binders I used back when I was in school.

I thought for a few minutes and then wrote this:

I'm here to celebrate the life + joy of my incredible friend Brian Hart. He was here + hiked the AT with the same passion that he carried with him every day, Godspeed Brian!

Peter—FLASH—Conti

P.S. Thanks to my wife + kids who encouraged me and all of you who said I couldn't or shouldn't do it. It's because of all of you that I'm here.

I put the register back into the metal box, took a deep breath, and took my first step northward. *Katahdin, here I come.*

I noticed a tree with a white blaze on it which confirmed I was on the Appalachian Trail. White blazes are six inches high and two inches wide. They are painted on trees or rocks to guide you from Georgia to Maine. The distance between blazes varies. I'd learned that if you hadn't seen a blaze in a while, you should retrace your steps until you locate one, so you don't end up wandering off the trail. I made my way back to the forest road where I'd started and then crossed the road to continue following the white blazes. I was delighted to see that the pathway flattened out and, in some sections, looked like a dirt sidewalk wandering through the woods.

After I'd been hiking for a few hours, it hit me. I was actually hiking the Appalachian Trail! As I looked at the path that disappeared into the woods a few hundred feet in front of me, I thought about how the trail went from where I stood over 2,000 miles all the way to Maine.

I stopped to take a break and made a video sharing my thoughts and feelings about my friend Brian. I had met him eight years ago at the Turkey Trot run in our neighborhood. I had worn one of my bike riding jerseys with the hope of connecting with other bike riders. Brian was into riding bikes, so he came up and introduced himself.

We ended up doing a bunch of riding over the years along with getting our families together. Brian was quite the over-achiever. There was an annual 120-mile bike ride that went over three different mountain passes in Colorado called "The Triple Bypass." Brian would get up early and start from his house to ride an extra eight miles in the dark to get to the starting point.

Then the next year, he added a loop up to the top of the 14,000-foot Mt. Evans so that his ride became "The Quadruple Bypass." I remember one year where 95 percent of the riders, including myself, dropped out due to freezing rain and sleet. Brian ended up suffering most of the way with hypothermia but managed to finish. While walking along, I thought about all the fun times I had with Brian and made a note to remember his indomitable spirit if my hike ever got to be overly challenging.

I arrived at the Stover Creek Shelter at 2:30 PM and decided to call it a day. This was the second shelter along the trail, the first being near Springer Mountain's summit. There are 262 shelters along the 2,189 miles of the Appalachian Trail for hikers to sleep in. While some of them are built of rock, most are simple wooden structures placed an average of eight and a half miles apart. Some are closer, about six miles apart, while others can be as far apart as fifteen miles. Some shelters are located directly on the trail, while others are reached by taking a trail marked with blue blazes that can be anywhere from one-tenth to six-tenths of a mile off the AT.

As for structure, they are typically elevated a few feet off the ground and tend to have three wooden walls with the fourth side open to the elements. The shelters often have a slanted roof, like a lean-to, and most of them are tall enough to stand up inside. Many look like log cabins or a small barn. They usually have a picnic table outside to cook on, write in your journal, play cards, or layout clothes. There is also often a fire pit, a nearby water source (stream, pipe in the ground, etc.), and a privy. Privies are like backcountry outhouses located around fifty yards from the shelter. In areas with high bear-density, there are bear boxes or bear cables to store your food along with anything else that may have a scent.

For my first day, I hiked a total of 3.6 miles, including the one mile south from Forest Service Road 42 to the summit of Springer Mountain. Although this was not very far at all, I was happy just to be there and have started my trek. While my foot and leg were hurting a fair amount, I proved to myself that I could make it over and around the various rocks and logs strewn across the trail.

I pulled out my sleeping bag and pad and laid them out against one wall to reserve a spot for me in the shelter. Before long, several hikers that I had seen earlier in the day arrived to spend the night at the shelter. They were, as Mom would say, "big boned."

Even though I was thirty pounds overweight myself, I'm ashamed to admit that I judged them thinking, *that couple is way overweight, they aren't going to last.* And when another hiker stopped by later, *this guy's pack is way too big and heavy—he's going to have a hard time.*

Of course, the reason I did this was because of all the

doubts I had about myself. When we find fault in others, it's often because of the concerns we have about our own abilities. That was certainly the case that day.

It's a little strange in the beginning because many of the hikers, like myself, have little to no experience hiking, living in the woods, or dealing with the variety of challenges that can come up during a long-distance trek on the Appalachian Trail. In fact, most hikers are quite freaked out by taking on a new experience not knowing what it's going to be like. When we began, none of us, me included, had any idea at all if we were going to be able to make it to Maine. *Are we going to like it? Is this monumental task we've committed to even possible?*

To compensate, I often heard myself and other hikers putting on overly confident airs, saying, "Yep, I'm going to Katahdin. Absolutely!" From what I observed, the net effect of this seemed to be that instead of boosting our confidence, all of us became even more worried about the immense task in front of us.

About twenty percent of hikers decide to quit within the first fifty miles. Reasons include, "I didn't know it would be so hard," "I'm lonely," "I got injured," and even, "I discovered that I don't enjoy hiking."

My motivation was three-fold. As I've said, I was sick and tired of living life feeling disabled and in constant pain. I wanted—no, I HAD—to do something, to get better. I knew that if I just sat around waiting to get better, the chances of overcoming my debilitating injury were slim to none.

The second reason for me was that I've always seemed to be motivated by a challenge. A former business partner of mine figured this out and would often motivate me to get stuff done by saying, "I don't think you can do this." To which I would respond, "Oh, yeah? I'll show you!"

It took me awhile to figure out that he was pushing this button of mine. The funny thing is, even after I called him out on it, he kept doing it. And though I knew exactly what he was doing, anything posed as a challenge continued to push me to complete the task at hand.

The third reason was harder for me to define. At this point, I realized that I somehow wanted or needed something more out of life. I'd been successful in real estate and business and had a happy family life, living in a nice house with an awesome wife and kids. Despite all this, I never seemed to feel completely content. I'd spent much of my life achieving things only to realize that each accomplishment provided only a short-term burst of satisfaction followed by the desire to look for something more. I didn't know if hiking the trail might help with this or not. I had read about people who said they changed their lives by hiking the Appalachian Trail. At the time, I didn't know what changes, if any, were in store for me.

As we huddled around the fire wearing our puffy down coats to help ward off the cold, I shared my first two reasons with other hikers. I didn't try to define this third thing since I hadn't figured it out yet.

The shelter filled most of the way up by the end of the day, with seven of us lined up in a row, and a few other hikers in their tents set up nearby. It was interesting to talk with everyone and find out where they were from and, of course, ask "the question." "Why did you decide to hike the AT?"

As I said hi to each person, I couldn't help but size them

up and think about whether I thought they might make it all the way to Maine. I didn't consider how many of these folks might be guessing about my ability to make it that far.

I slept well for my first night in a shelter with other hikers. One of my concerns before starting out was how I'd be able to go to the bathroom at night when sleeping in a shelter. I didn't want to wake up the other folks, and I was concerned that I might step on someone or fall because of my poor balance. I won't get into all the details here other than to say I found a good use for an empty Gatorade bottle that I had brought with me.

When I got up the next morning, I discovered that my foot was hurting and had gotten stiff overnight. I spent some time stretching it out while I used my nifty little camp stove to heat some oatmeal and make a cup of coffee. Before long, I was clumping my way along the trail.

One thing that I really like about hiking is that most everyone uses hiking poles. Before hiking the AT, I was still using a cane to get around. Using a cane made me feel old, so changing to using hiking poles allowed me to see myself in a better light. I was able to get the support I needed to walk without sticking out like a sore thumb.

After a couple of hours, I came to a side trail that led to Long Creek Falls. The people who've completed a thru-hike have told me to be sure to stop and see the attractions along the way, so I turned down a blue-blazed side trail a short way to get to the falls. I enjoyed watching the water pouring down over the rocks while listening to the pleasant roar that filled the air. I thought about how lucky I was to be out there by a beautiful waterfall on the Appalachian Trail. *Life is great!*

After taking some time to soak up the waterfall experience,

I decided to make a few videos and have my morning snack before leaving. Ninety minutes after arriving at the falls, I finally pulled my pack on so that I could get back to hiking. I was surprised that I didn't see any other hikers while I was here. *They aren't smart enough to enjoy the trail. Oops, there I go again, judging other people.*

One of the mantras that you'll hear along the trail is "Hike your own hike." This means that each person has their personal reasons and ways of doing things. I would learn over time to appreciate, understand, and accept the differences among hikers. I had plenty to learn and understand about myself.

By mid-afternoon, I'd progressed a total of five miles for the day and reached Hawk Mountain Shelter. I put my pack down and laid down on the wood floor to rest my legs. My foot still bothered me when I put it up, but it felt better than when I was walking on it.

I met several other hikers as they stopped for a break while others joined those of us who were spending the night. Two teenagers hiking with their mother were excited about all the coins they were finding at the shelters. It seems that hikers were dumping any change they had to help lighten their packs.

I woke up during the night due to the sound of snoring and looked out into the black forest. I had thought that I'd be scared of various wild animals, like that wolf or whatever it was that I'd heard on my test hike, but somehow, I felt at peace with the forest. This may sound strange to you, but it was like everything had its place in the world, and I felt like I belonged here in the wilderness.

The only way I can explain this is to say I knew that my ancestors had lived and traveled in the wild at some point many, many years ago. If you think about it, each of us is the result of a long line of ancestors that goes back tens of thousands of years. Part of me was right at home there in the woods. Using the red light on my headlamp to avoid bothering the other hikers, I dug out a set of earplugs to help me sleep through the rest of the night.

I took my time getting up and making my breakfast of oatmeal and coffee the next morning. I had called the Hiker Hostel yesterday and asked them to pick me up at 2:00 PM at Cooper Gap, only four miles from where I was. I wanted to make sure that I didn't overdo it the first week and decided that I'd head back to the hostel and take my first "zero." This is what hikers call a rest day because you're making zero progress along the trail.

Back at the hostel, I took a shower. It felt *great*. I checked out the hiker box, picking through unneeded food and gear other hikers had donated. I found the ingredients to make a dinner of spaghetti along with some yummy looking Little Debbie cupcakes for dessert. I figured that I'd end up losing weight with all the hiking I was doing, no matter what I ate. Besides, I was famished.

That evening I got to see yet another pack shakedown. This one was done by Layann, one of the helpers at Hikers Hostel. She talked another young woman into offering up her pack for inspection. Each shakedown helped me to become less attached to everything that I had in my own pack. Children are so often given a hard time for dragging around security blankets. Turns out adults are similarly prone, especially on an adventure with so many unknowns.

The next day at breakfast, the table was once again

surrounded with eager new hikers who were all excited to begin their adventure on the trail. I spent most of the day propping my foot up so that I could give it a rest. There was another hiker there who had sprained his ankle. He was optimistically thinking that he'd be able to get back out hiking after a few days of rest. His ankle was swollen, and I could tell that he was really hurting.

The next morning, it was the same routine of hurrying up to breakfast so I wouldn't miss out. I carried up a small daypack that Leigh from the hostel gave me to use so that I could "slackpack" for the day. This is where you leave your heavy pack behind and hike with just a few snacks, a lunch, and a raincoat.

Scott, another helper from the hostel, drove me back to Cooper Gap where I had stopped my hike two days earlier. After hiking for several hours, I realized I had to go to the bathroom, the kind where I needed an outhouse or a privy, not just a tree to step behind. While this felt both strange and difficult, I knew that this would be part of the adventure. I wasn't anywhere close to a shelter, so I went at least 200 feet off the trail, uphill and away from the stream, and dug a hole in the ground. I managed to complete my business, although I felt somewhat uncomfortable the entire time because I was doing an inside activity while I was outside.

During the day, I ran into about twenty other hikers. Well, actually they ran into me as I was hiking slower than they were. Each person I met was friendly, upbeat, and encouraging. At 3:30 in the afternoon, I arrived at Gooch Gap to see a white van with a blue tarp stretched out above a table with food, cold drinks, and a grill. *Fresh Ground*, a gregarious trail angel, offered me a couple of hot dogs on a bun with all the fixings.

Fresh Ground said, "Hiker must be hungry. Want some French fries with that?"

"Uh, yes please," I responded, unsure why this nice man was out here in the woods, cooking up food for me and the other hikers. *Fresh Ground* pulled out four big potatoes, sliced them up in less than a minute, and then dropped them into a five-gallon pot of hot grease that had a propane burner going underneath it. A few minutes later, he scooped out a big bunch of hot fries, salted them, and handed them over to me.

"There you go. Ketchup is right there. Anything else you want, you got it."

Trail angels are people who provide food, beverages, and other support to thru-hikers. A few of them, like *Fresh Ground*, do this through the entire hiking season, following the hiker bubble up the trail. A hiker bubble is a dense group of hikers moving up (North Bounders) or down (South Bounders) the trail, formed by people starting at about the same time each year. I wasn't sure whether to leave a donation, so I didn't. In hindsight, I wish I had as I don't know how else a full-time trail angel could manage to do this.

While slackpacking, I discovered that it was much easier for me to walk down the trail without my heavy pack slowing me down. Hiking seven miles without hardly any weight to carry was easier for me than hiking four miles with my pack on the day before. I thought about this as I walked along and decided that getting the weight of my pack down as low as possible would be critical to my making it to Katahdin. Just as

I arrived at the trailhead, Scott pulled up in the tired-looking Suburban truck. I was looking forward to getting back to the hostel to have a shower, eating pizza for dinner, and sleeping in a real bed again. The next morning, I followed the same routine getting up for breakfast and catching a ride out to the spot where I was picked up the day before.

During the day, I enjoyed talking with other hikers at the overlooks or when they passed me on the trail. After talking with other hikers and searching online, I'd learned that a one mile-an-hour hiking speed is considered slow with two miles an hour as average. If you can hike three miles an hour, then you're a fast hiker. With seven months to make it Mt. Katahdin in Maine before its October 15th closing date, I'd have to average fourteen miles each hiking day. This would allow for one zero each week to rest and resupply, as well as for some extra days off to visit my wife and family.

The problem was I was barely reaching one mile per hour as my hiking speed. At that point in March, we were only getting about twelve and half hours of daylight. This increased slightly each day, but even in June, the available daylight still isn't quite fourteen hours long. I was going to have to increase my hiking speed sooner or later if I was going to make it.

With all these calculations and discussion about increasing my hiking speed, let me say that I was happy at this point to even be able to make it down the trail. However, I had noticed blisters forming on my hands because I was using my poles to carry as much of my weight as possible. While I was able to take a good step with my right leg, I had to swing my left leg forward by using the muscles in my hip.

The other thing that really bothered me was that even with my hiking poles, I couldn't walk along without looking like someone who'd just sprained their ankle. When I came limping up to a shelter, I looked like I was really hurting because, well, I was. Other hikers always said, "Oh my goodness, are you okay? What happened to you?" I would respond by going into a detailed description of the accident along with details about my various attempts to heal myself over the past two years.

"Does it hurt?" they would invariably ask.

"Only when I step on it," became my response.

True to form, I was trying to add humor to the situation. But I was extremely angry at life (and myself) for getting injured. I knew that I should have listened to my wife as she had pleaded with me not to leave that fateful day.

It was nonetheless fun to sit around chatting with the other hikers as we made our freeze-dried dinners. My choice for my fourth night on the trail was Mountain House lasagna. I pulled out my Pocket Rocket stove and screwed it on top of a small gas cylinder to heat up water in a small lightweight pot. This little cookpot, which held two cups of liquid, was used to cook, serve, and doubled as a mug to hold hot chocolate or coffee in the morning.

I brought along an orange-colored plastic frozen yogurt spoon that I used as my one utensil for stirring and eating. It also served as a token of sorts to remind me of times when my oldest daughter and I used to get frozen yogurt together. It was lightweight, and the cost was right—free!

As we sat around the fire, I got to know more about the other hikers at the shelter with me that night. Many of the younger folks had carved out six months to hike either before, during, or after college. A few people in their 30s or 40s described how they were between jobs, which gave them time to get away. Then a handful of us in our 50s and 60s rounded out the bunch.

4

EVERYTHING CHANGES IN A SECOND

CHAMPIONS AREN'T MADE IN GYMS. CHAMPIONS
ARE MADE FROM SOMETHING THEY HAVE DEEP
INSIDE THEM. A DESIRE, A DREAM, A VISION.
THEY HAVE TO HAVE LAST-MINUTE STAMINA,
THEY HAVE TO BE A LITTLE FASTER, THEY HAVE
TO HAVE THE SKILL AND THE WILL. BUT THE
WILL MUST BE STRONGER THAN THE SKILL.

—MUHAMMAD ALI

When my son was 14 years old, we went on a fishing trip in Michigan where we had fun canoeing down a river for three days. My son even caught a few fish. We had an extra day before we needed to fly home, so we rented a couple of four-wheelers to ride. Michigan has excellent state-maintained trails, and I was in heaven as I rode along behind my son. My son told me recently that he also thought that day was a lifetime highlight. We had so much fun that I began to think of ways that we could do more riding together. I wonder if all fathers dream of their sons excelling in the same sports they did when they were younger. For me, it was trail riding motorcycles and racing motocross.

When I spoke to my wife about getting dirt bikes again, she was opposed to it.

"You're going to get hurt. Don't do it."

I stubbornly insisted over her protests that I could stay safe riding trail bikes with our son. It took me a month or two of badgering her until she finally gave in.

"Fine. Do what you want, but you have to agree to no racing," she said.

Her mandate came from knowing me and my history. I was sixteen years old when I entered my first motocross race at Big Berm Raceway in northern Maryland. Forty of us lined up at the start to see who could squeeze through the first turn where there was only room for four or five riders.

I went as fast as I could through the first few turns and ended up somewhere around mid-pack. The dust from the riders ahead of me reduced visibility to less than twenty feet. Suddenly, out of the middle of the cloud of dust, I saw another motorcycle lying sideways right ahead of me on the face of the next jump.

I had a split second to attempt to get my front wheel up and try to make it over this unexpected obstacle. I don't think

I succeeded because I launched up into the air and was then looking *down* at all the other riders. I'd seen this view before on TV, streaming from a helicopter filming a race. My ability to enjoy watching the race from this perspective lasted only a second or two before the ground rushed up. I slammed into the hard dirt track, and was run over by the remaining motorcycles.

I jumped up and was MAD! I brushed myself off, jumped back on the motorcycle, and finished the race as I tried to make up for all the places I'd lost by crashing. I was pretty darn sore for a few days but otherwise okay.

So, I made it through motorcycle racing when I was much younger, and a few other sports that got my adrenaline up—flying sailplanes, for example—without any of what I considered "serious" injuries. I experienced plenty of broken bones and four or five concussions, but I was always able to heal within a few weeks or months. I've never thought of myself as a risk taker, but I'm sure some people may disagree with me.

By the time I was 40 years old, I decided to take up racing motorcycles again. I went to three races but ended up in the hospital two different times after falling off and getting hurt. When I was younger, my reaction time must have been better because I remembered seeing everything that happened during a fall, almost as if time slowed down. But in these two accidents, I was riding along one moment, and then I was suddenly on the ground wondering, *what the heck just happened?* In a rare moment of wisdom, I decided that racing motorcycles was no longer safe at my age and promptly sold off my new motorcycle along with all my gear and supplies.

When Joanna put her foot down about racing now that I was in my fifties, after months of back and forth, we finally agreed on "trail riding only." I shook her hand, happy to have finally gotten her to allow this minor indulgence. I quickly went out and bought two used Honda CR230 trail bikes. I rode them with my son, daughter, and a business partner a number of times. To get to a place to ride, we had to load the bikes on a trailer and drive an hour and a half to a farm in southern Maryland. It had a small track and some trails through the woods.

The farm trips involved quite a bit of driving to ride for just a few hours, so I started looking around to see where else we might be able to go riding. That's when I found a hare scrambles race in New Jersey. I figured that instead of racing, I'd let everyone else go ahead of me with the idea that I could go around the eleven-mile loop, treating it like an organized trail ride instead of a race. The day before the race, when I casually mentioned that I was going on this "trail ride," my wife wasn't shy about expressing her opinion.

"Sounds like a race to me! Bad idea."

I, of course, ignored her protests.

So, the next day, March 3rd, when I went to the hare scrambles race to "not race," my wife made sure to take her cell phone with her just in case she got "the phone call." While I had fully intended to take it easy, once the other riders looped around and started passing me, my competitive spirit kicked in. I decided to try and keep up with them.

This was a monumental, life-altering mistake. I clipped a tree a few minutes later and was thrown over the handlebars, tumbling to the ground.

"Are you okay? Can you move at all?" It was a woman's voice.

I wasn't in pain yet, perhaps because I was in shock, but I had a good idea of what was going on. I knew I had a major injury and was lying on the ground unable, or perhaps simply unwilling, to move. I didn't even attempt to take my helmet off. Whether this was from my previous experiences with broken bones or another sense of self-preservation, I'm not sure.

"No, I'm not okay. I can't move. I think I may have broken my hip."

I became aware of several other riders who had stopped in the middle of their race to help. I heard them working together to move course markers off to one side to keep other riders from running into me. A few of them, including Blair, the first person who had stopped, stayed with me for over an hour while waiting for the medics to arrive. As it turns out, she was one of the organizers that I'd emailed back and forth to register for the event. In my email, I'd said, "Maybe I'll see you at the event." But I didn't expect to meet her like this.

After the medics arrived, they temporarily stopped the race and a bunch of riders helped carry me 100 yards on a stretcher to a waiting ATV. They did a great job, despite almost dropping me once. The medics used the four-wheeler to get me out of the woods, including one section where we went straight up a steep hill. After about twenty minutes on the ATV, we arrived at a dirt road where I was transferred into a waiting ambulance. As a result of being jostled around, my hip was starting to hurt.

After another twenty-minute ride in the ambulance, they told me I'd be transferred into a waiting flight-for-life helicopter. I told them I didn't think I needed a helicopter, but they ignored my advice. Joanna's cell phone rang at 2:06 PM, as they were loading me into the rescue helicopter. The medic said, "Your husband has been injured in a motorcycle race. Which hospital do you want us to take him to?"

My wife asked him two questions, "Which one would you take your spouse to?" and "Which one has the best trauma center?" They settled on Cooper University Hospital in Camden, New Jersey. Shortly after lifting off into the air, I received my first shot of morphine.

Thirty minutes later, we landed on the rooftop of the hospital, and I was carried into the emergency room and placed on an operating table surrounded by six or seven people in green scrubs. After cutting off my riding gear, they *straightened out my injured leg* and I started screaming at the top of my lungs.

"Stop screaming! Stop screaming! Stop Screaming!" the head doctor yelled back at me.

5

CARING ANGELS

EVERYONE DEALS WITH PAIN. THE PAIN
OF HAVING TO GO WORK AT A JOB YOU
DON'T LIKE. THE PAIN OF GROWING OLD
AND HAVING DIFFERENT PARTS OF YOU
HURT AT TIMES. THE PAIN OF A LOST
LOVE, OR A CHILD THAT'S STRUGGLING
TO FIND THEIR OWN WAY IN LIFE.

Two days after meeting *Fresh Ground*, I was steadily working my way uphill toward the summit of Blood Mountain. At 4,458 ft in elevation, this mountain is the highest on the trail in Georgia. I was looking at this as the first of many challenges I'd need to overcome.

I moved along at my slow, limping pace and set a goal to keep moving steadily up the trail without stopping until I got to the top of the mountain. I convinced myself that if I could get up the highest mountain in Georgia, it would somehow prove my ability to "make it," whatever that meant. I'm not sure who I was trying to prove anything to other than to myself.

When I finally made it to the summit, I was wiped out physically and emotionally. I tried making a celebration video to show how happy I was to have been able to make it to the top without stopping. Within seconds of beginning to talk, I was surprised to find that a tidal wave of mixed emotions washed over the joy I thought I was going to be sharing. I started crying. The video was already running, so I decided to open up and share my feelings. But then I thought I'd also try to make it funny. Let's just say the video didn't turn out well, as there's no way to use humor to hide the raw emotions that had risen to the surface. The AT had opened my mind up to a process where I'd have to learn to accept many things I'd kept hidden away.

I was looking for some way, *any* way to free myself from the never-ending pain that held me down as if a huge boulder were on top of me. Now that I'd made it that far, I had a sense that I *could* hike the Appalachian Trail. I *could* use this voyage as a pathway to heal and to reclaim my life.

As I started heading down the north side of Blood Mountain, I was surprised to see that the white blazes went straight down a sloped rock surface. Using my poles, I reached ahead of myself with each step to keep myself from falling headfirst down the mountain slope. If I had fallen there, it probably wouldn't have killed me, but it wouldn't have been a pretty sight either.

I noticed that my fear had caused the length of my steps to shorten considerably, so much so that each foot tentatively moved ahead about four inches at a time. As I did this, I saw a picture in my head of myself at 80 years old trying to make my way to the bathroom in a nursing home.

Twenty seconds later, two girls strolled past without any hiking poles. From my perspective, we were going down a 45-degree slope, although I'm sure it wasn't actually that steep. Yet they were chatting and walking along as if they were out for a stroll in the park. Meanwhile, I was worried that at any moment I might fall off the mountain and land in a big heap at the bottom of the hill. The difference in speed and agility didn't compute for me.

You see, for my entire life—that, is until my injury—I'd thought of myself as young, capable, and vibrant. When I went to my high school reunion, I felt I wasn't like the rest of those "old people" in my class. I always had the idea in my head that I was still in my 20s. Of course, this didn't make sense when my oldest daughter turned 30. But a stubborn part of me desperately clung onto the idea that I would somehow stay forever young.

As I continued down the steep face of Blood Mountain, I kept thinking about those two girls. *Was I old and slow but just didn't know it?* At the bottom of the mountain, I would be at Neel Gap where a good percentage of thru-hikers called it quits. *Was I fooling myself by being out here or did I really have a chance at making it?* I continued to make my way over, down, and around various physical rock obstacles, all while staving off the idea that I was middle aged and disabled. *That's not who I am,* I told myself. *I just need to heal this leg up a bit and I'll be fine.*

When I finally made it to the bottom and stepped out to the side of the road, it was with a measure of both satisfaction and fatigue that I looked across to see Mountain Crossings Outfitters, the famous "1st stop" on the Appalachian Trail. I also saw the legendary tree whose branches were filled with hundreds of pairs of hiking boots swinging by their laces. Supposedly everyone who gives up at this point tosses their hiking boots up into that tree. I limped my way up the rock walkway and opened the door, anticipating a place to warm up and get something good to eat.

"Hello, hiker! Welcome to Mountain Crossings," came the greeting from a heavy-set gentleman with long blondish hair. "Have a cup of coffee—no charge—and look around. Let me know if you need anything," he said with a welcoming smile.

"Thanks," I said before asking his name.

"Just call me Jack."

I didn't realize it at the time, but this was the legendary *"Baltimore Jack"* who had thru-hiked the Appalachian Trail a total of seven times. Jack was in charge of welcoming hikers coming into Mountain Crossings and advising them on gear and other hiking questions. He had an encouraging, upbeat attitude that was a warm welcome for cold, tired hikers like me who wandered in.

I thought *Baltimore Jack* oversaw the store or perhaps was the owner of Mountain Crossings. I later found out that he volunteered, worked, or traded work for food and lodging at various places along the trail to stay involved with and support hikers. I read an article online that talked about a man who was fascinated by Jack's lifestyle. He approached Jack in Shenandoah National Park, which the AT passes through about 900 miles north of Mountain Crossing.

"Well, this has been fascinating," Jack recalled the man saying. "This is a side of the world I never knew existed." The man continued by asking, "What do you do in the real world?"

"In the real world, I hike," Jack responded, and then he walked away.

Within the first few weeks of my adventure, I'd seen how Josh and Leigh Saint at the Hiker Hostel had turned their love of the trail into helping hikers get started at Springer Mountain. I'd met *Fresh Ground*, one of the most famous trail angels whose mission was to feed and support hungry hikers. And now I'd met this guy, Jack, who turned out to be the *Baltimore Jack*, another person who'd chosen to center his life around helping hikers on the Appalachian Trail.

I found this inspiring and extremely comforting. I had spent most of my life attempting to prove that I could do anything without any help from anyone else. Now, I was waging this physical and mental battle over whether I'd be able to hike the Appalachian Trail. Getting this boost of encouragement from *Baltimore Jack* helped me out when I needed it most. Making it over Blood Mountain boosted my confidence up a notch as well. I still didn't know if I'd be able to make it all the way to Maine, but at least I wasn't going to be one of the twenty percent that dropped out there at Neel Gap.

When I first started buying gear for this trip, a small part of me recognized that I might spend a bunch of money on hiking stuff only to find out that I wasn't really able to go hiking. I was now confident I'd be able to hike, but I was still concerned about how slow I was going. To help fix this, I figured it was time to start spending money on lighter gear. In the back room of Mountain Crossings, I met *Squirrel*, a thru-hiker from a few years ago who was eager to help me figure out the best way to lighten my pack.

When *Squirrel* hung my pack from the scale, I could see that it weighed just under thirty pounds. This included three days of food but no water. My goal was to get it down to twenty pounds or less. Why twenty pounds? The only reason I had was that it was a nice round number.

He told me to open my pack, pull everything out, and put all my stuff into a pile on the floor on the side of the room. We weighed the Osprey pack that I had gotten from REI, and it came in at five and a half pounds. After looking at a few different options, I chose the small version ULA pack which weighed two and a half pounds. I figured saving three pounds on my pack was a no-brainer and would get me almost a third of the way to cutting ten pounds. The ULA wasn't nearly as big as the Osprey, but I hoped that I could trim my stuff down so that everything would fit.

I spent the next hour or so looking at sleeping bags, zipping myself into them, and comparing various temperature ratings. I chose a yellow and blue Big Agnes twenty-four-degree bag which saved another couple of pounds compared to the ten-degree sleeping bag I was using. *Squirrel* assured me that this would probably be warm enough and if not, "That's when you start doing sit-ups to warm up."

I selected a lighter air mattress, a better quality down puffy coat, mittens with rain covers, and an inline water filter. I installed this last item in the water tube that came out of my Camelback water reservoir. This way I could filter water as I drank it while hiking along.

But I had a problem. No matter how many ways I tried, I couldn't get everything into the smaller ULA pack. I could have moved up to a bigger ULA pack, but the next size up weighed another half of a pound. I'm not sure what I expected him to say but I asked, "What can I do here, *Squirrel?*"

"You need to get rid of all this crap," he said, pointing to some of my stuff that was sitting in a small pile. I felt defensive, in part because I'd spent so much time and money finding lightweight versions of everything I was carrying. I didn't want to part with anything but knew that if I was going to have a chance to make it to Maine, I *had* to get the weight down.

I sat on the floor thinking and I realized that there had been plenty of other people on the trail so far. Whenever I stopped for a break, I'd see three or four other hikers. I decided that if I needed a knife, medical kit, or whatever else, then chances were pretty good that someone else would be along shortly and would have whatever I might need.

This probably sounds reckless, but it's what I did. I took my pile of "other stuff" and put it into a box to mail to my next resupply point. This is called a bounce box because it bounces up the trail with you. I figured that if I ended up needing something, I'd get it back out of the box in another week or so. I squeezed a few last remaining items into the new pack and hung it on the scale. *Hmm . . . twenty-two and a half pounds. That looks much better.*

Next up was trying out a pair of trail runners. I didn't know if my ankle on my injured side could make it without the support of hiking boots but based on all the opinions I'd heard lately, this seemed to be the way to go. I placed my hiking boots into the bounce box and addressed it to the lodge near Fontana Dam.

I put the Osprey pack and all the other things I had replaced with lighter versions of gear into another box to return to REI and paid the clerk at Mountain Crossings for the postage. I estimated that I'd get refunded $600, which would help offset the $790 that I had just spent.

By this time, it was getting late in the day, so I decided to stay at the Mountain Crossings Hostel. The Hiker Hostel in Dahlonega had been squeaky clean, like a nice bed and breakfast. But the hostel at Mountain Crossings was run by hiker volunteers and "cleaned" by hiker volunteers. I discovered that "cleaned by hikers" basically meant that it wasn't really cleaned, ever. After seeing four inches of black water on the shower floor, I decided to skip cleaning up.

To compensate for the mess, the hostel was full of other friendly, encouraging hikers. One in particular, *Minister*, told me that it was normal for my knees to be hurting at that point.

"Just stick with it and eventually your knees will stop hurting."

A local church was nice enough to drop off a piping hot lasagna dinner for everyone, and I had my fill before heading back into the bunk room to sleep. The bunk room had a low ceiling with bunk beds made from two-by-fours painted light green.

After waking up several times from the sound of snoring in the room, I pulled my earplugs out of my pack so that I might have a chance at getting a good night's sleep. Using them proved to be somewhat difficult. I wasn't used to having earplugs stuck in my ears, so I found them quite uncomfortable. The other problem was that one of the other hikers had severe sleep apnea, and even with my earplugs in, he was hard to ignore. He would snore and snort a couple of times before stopping breathing altogether. I lay there silently counting in my head to see how many seconds it was before he took another breath.

55, 56, 57, 58 . . .

"SNUUCK . . . SNUUG . . . SNOOOORE."

Whew. He's breathing again. I had planned to say something to this guy— "Uh . . . excuse me. Did you know that it sounded like you almost died last night?"—but he was already gone by the time I got up.

After I put my sleeping bag and other items back into my pack, I left the hostel and went back over to Mountain Crossing Outfitters to get a breakfast sandwich and a cup of coffee to start my day. I headed out the front door and turned north on the trail to go through the breezeway. This is the only place on the entire route where the Appalachian Trail goes through a building. I could feel the difference in weight from the gear that I had swapped out at the outfitters and was glad that I had found a way to lighten up my load.

Overnight the fog was thick enough that a small layer of ice had formed on the downwind edge of the tree branches and bushes along the trail. This frost, along with the still present misty fog and a dose of sunlight streaming down in a few isolated places through the forest, gave the morning a magical feeling.

On top of that, my new bright orange trail runners looked cool and felt easier to move along in compared to the heavier hiking boots that I'd been using previously. The bad news was that, within the first hour, my ankle started hurting every time I stepped on an angled rock or uneven ground. I did consider turning around and heading back to Neel Gap, but I pushed this thought off to the side and continued on my way north.

By mid-morning, my foot was throbbing, and by lunchtime, my entire foot and ankle were screaming with every step I took. *Bad idea*, I said to myself. *Why did I get rid of my hiking boots?* I sat down on a log to see what my options were. I needed to get off the trail to give my foot a break and change back into the hiking boots that I'd left behind at Mountain Crossings.

In the guidebook, I could see that Tesnatee Gap was another two miles up the trail. Out of the six or seven listings for cabins and motels, only one indicated they provided a shuttle service, so I gave them a call. Jason, the owner, answered and said he was happy to pick me up and that he could meet me at the trailhead in two hours. I gritted my teeth for the rest of the hike while mentally beating myself up for making a change when I already had boots that were working for me.

Once Jason picked me up, I asked if he'd be willing to drive the extra distance to loop back around to Neel Gap so I could try to get my hiking boots before they mailed them off to Fontana Lodge. It turned out that package had already been sent, so I picked out another pair of hiking boots to purchase, figuring that I'd need at least one more pair if I was going to hike the entire Appalachian Trail anyway. My new trail runners got packed into yet another box that I mailed home.

Jason then whisked me away to the Misty Mountain Inn and Cabins. It was a beautiful bed and breakfast that Jason and his wife had purchased a few months earlier. I took a photo of my leg propped up on the bed in the fancy B&B style room and sent it to my daughter, saying, "Here's a photo of my campsite." I spent a few days there resting up and enjoyed an incredible breakfast each day. While I enjoyed my time there, I hoped I wouldn't be staying in too many expensive places like that.

After four more days of hiking, my goal for the day was to make it to Helen, GA where I could rest up and purchase some food to resupply my pack. When I finally reached the trailhead, it was a little past one o'clock. I walked out to the road and reluctantly stuck my thumb out to try and hitch a ride into town. I managed to catch a ride in the back of a pickup truck along with a few other hikers. It was fun to see bright green leaves on the trees along the road and feel the wind rushing past as we made our way down the winding road into Helen.

As an old logging town that was in decline, Helen resurrected itself by becoming a replica of a Bavarian alpine town with a classic south-German style. In 1969, the residents mandated through zoning that every building, even the Huddle House and Wendy's, needed to look like it was in Switzerland.

The pickup truck slowed to a stop in front of the motel I had called a few days ago, and as I climbed out, I wished the other hikers well. I used my hiking poles for support as I made my way across the parking lot. The carbide tips clacked in protest against the pavement as they were accustomed to being on the softer dirt trail.

After checking in, I discovered that my room was on the second floor and I'd have to walk "all the way" across the parking lot to get to the stairs. This seemed annoyingly far away at the time, but it was actually only two or three hundred feet. I thought about going back into the office to request a closer, easier-to-get-to room but struggled with making this decision.

For one thing, I was too tired to even put the effort into making a decision. For another, it didn't make sense to me that an Appalachian Trail hiker who's going to be hiking thousands of miles would have a problem with walking across the parking lot. As I slowly limped my way across the black pavement, my mind tried to make sense of this dichotomy.

Why did they make my room so far away?
Now I have to climb up the stairs. Really?
I should have asked for a closer room.
You can't do that. You're hiking the Appalachian Trail!

My leg and foot were killing me. Yet because I was hiking the Appalachian Trail, I felt foolish about asking them to help me out by providing a closer room. When I was on the trail, every step, no matter how painful, counted towards my goal of making it to Maine. I had committed to making it to Maine and while dealing with the pain from my leg was unpleasant, I had accepted it as part of the journey. Once off the trail in town for a rest day, every step seemed to hurt three times as much. The satisfaction of advancing up the trail was lacking.

I paused at the bottom of the stairs, looking at the dreadful climb up the steps to my room. Then I saw one of the railing posts where the paint had worn away, leaving a spot that looked like a white blaze. Smiling, I slowly made my way up the stairs. Once in my room, I dropped my pack and flopped onto the bed like a sack of potatoes, too tired to even take off my boots.

I drifted in and out of sleep throughout the afternoon, finally deciding to get up and look for food when it started to get dark outside. I wandered over to the German restaurant next door, half-heartedly hoping that I could connect with some other hikers for dinner.

At 9:00 PM, I was one of few people in the restaurant and the only hiker. I ordered a beef roulade with mashed potatoes and sat there by myself, eating slowly because I was so drained, and so tired that I wasn't especially hungry.

Without anyone else to talk with, I was left to process my own thoughts. The loneliness, paired with all the doubts over my hiking capability, were exacerbated by my physical and mental exhaustion.

What the heck am I doing?

This is supposed to be fun!

I ate as much of my meal as I could and walked outside, across the parking lot and back up the stairs to my room where I fell asleep within seconds of hitting the bed.

The next day was another zero day for me. I'm not sure what time I woke up, but I do know that I spent the first half of the day in the same place I did the day before. Flat on my back, lying on the bed. I was completely out of energy. I lay there drifting in and out of sleep until afternoon when

I realized I had chores to do. I needed to go to the grocery store to resupply, as well as find a place to wash my stinky hiking clothes.

I searched on my phone and found the closest grocery store was over a mile away. It feels strange to write this out for you, but at the time, the thought of walking ANY extra miles that wouldn't count toward my goal of making it from Georgia to Maine was simply a no-go. I thought for a moment about trying to hitch a ride and decided to call a taxi instead.

During the taxi ride, I unhappily watched the meter count up the price I was paying to avoid walking to the store. It wasn't the money that bothered me as much as I felt I should be able to easily walk a mile in town on flat ground and back. *If I can't even do that, how can I possibly be out here hiking the trail?*

I picked up my food resupplies at the grocery store then walked to a nearby laundromat where I washed my hiking clothes. When I was finished, I reluctantly called the number the cab driver had given me so he could pick me up and return me to the motel. Back at the motel, I sorted my food out on the bed into portions for each day and then returned to the German restaurant for another meal. My only company, once again, was all of my doubts and concerns about my life and the hike.

After my zero day in Helen, the next morning I got a ride back to Unicoi Gap and continued my journey northward, hiking six miles further that day to spend the night at Tray Mountain Shelter. The views out across the valley were amazing to see, and I enjoyed sitting around sharing stories with other hikers, all of whom were likewise pursuing their goal to hike the entire trail.

The next day I got up and headed down the mountain intending to make it seven miles further to Deep Gap shelter. The muscles in my leg seemed to loosen up a bit during the day, and I decided to pick up the pace a bit to see if I could get my average speed up. It's not like I was breaking any records, mind you. I probably increased my average from one to 1.2 miles per hour.

Then while going up Kelly Knob, which was about 1,000 feet of climbing in elevation, I did my thing of not stopping until I got to the top. My rules were that I could slow down, but I had to focus on my breath and keep moving forward no matter what.

In hindsight, I couldn't explain why I was pushing myself like this. I think I was trying to overcome my doubts about being able to hike the entire trail by setting out mini challenges like this. *If I could make it up this mountain without stopping, then that would mean I'd be able to get all the way to Mt. Katahdin.* That type of thing.

But while I worked harder than usual that day, I didn't drink enough water. So, I was quite tired when I arrived at Deep Gap Shelter that afternoon. About eighteen other hikers were wandering about, cooking their Mountain House freeze-dried dinners, and engaged in typical hiker conversations. I heard people talking about how far they'd gone for the day, asking how much everyone's pack weighs and giving out unsolicited advice on the best brands of hiking gear to bring along.

On the Appalachian Trail, no one goes by their real names; rather, everyone knows you by a trail name. The adoption of a trail name indicates a walking away from everyday life, a new persona, an acceptance into the thru-hiker community, and maybe even a rejection of what went before. I had heard stories about hikers who'd made a mistake, or done something memorable to earn a trail name that was assigned to them by other hikers they were hanging out with.

I took the liberty of creating my own moniker and went with "*Flash*," an old nickname from when I played ice hockey as a kid. This trail name worked fine for a few days until I met another *Flash*, so I added an old motorcycle racing number to the end to come up with *Flash 52*.

I joined in conversation with a small group of hikers gathered on the side of the shelter. As was typical of hikers on the trail, these were mostly younger folks, somewhere in their twenties, along with a few people closer to my age. *Tiny Dancer*, a shorter woman with dark brown hair said, "I've got some pot if anyone wants to have some."

I thought for a moment. *Hmm . . . so what if I hadn't done this in over 30 years? What the heck, I'm on the Appalachian Trail.*

As *Just Dan* passed the peace pipe to me, I thought, *if I'm going to do this, I want to get enough to feel it.* It went around the circle three times, and let's just say, I definitely inhaled. It wasn't long before everything around me started to spin. *Wow! This stuff seems to have a little kick to it. I don't remember feeling this way when I was back in high school.*

I decided to play it safe and sat down on a nearby bench built into the shelter's side. I became introspective and quiet as my attention moved from one sensory input to the next. I heard the murmur of people talking and noticed the sound of the wind rustling through the leaves in the trees. Then the sunlight flickering through the branches seemed to take on special significance.

The next thing I noticed was some sort of commotion. I lifted my head from the ground—*why am I laying on the ground?*—and saw various legs and feet running towards me. I had apparently passed out and clunked over onto the hard-packed earth in front of me.

"What happened to him?"

"Are you okay?"

Then, from the back of the growing crowd, "You had a seizure!"

"Ask him what date it is." *Seizure guy taking control here…*

"Umm… March 20th?" I guessed. The girl looking at me scrunched up her face.

"No, it must be March 19th." I corrected.

"He doesn't know what day it is," the girl said.

"He doesn't know what day it is!" Seizure guy said, jumping back in. He appeared to be in his late twenties, a little on the lean side with a military-style crew cut. He was wearing a tan hiking shirt with matching pants along with a pair of trail runners. I didn't know his trail name but decided right there, lying on the ground, to name him *Commander.*

"See if he can walk!" said you-know-who.

Somebody reached out and yanked me up so hard I'd swear my feet came off the ground. *I can't walk very well on a good day, and that's when I have my hiking poles.* Despite this, I took a few wobbly steps because I felt like I'd get in trouble if I didn't.

Then *Commander* shouted out, "He can't walk! I'm calling 911!"

A few other hikers helped me over to a seat on the front

porch of the shelter, and as I sat down, I suggested, "Maybe we should wait a bit before calling."

"Nope, you sit right there! You've obviously got a concussion. I'm calling for rescue right now!" replied *Commander*. He had mentioned something about having PTSD during the commotion, and it seemed that my little fall had triggered him into battle mode.

At this point, even I was becoming concerned. I'd never had a seizure of any type and could hear *Commander* talking with another guy (who also had PTSD) who said, "Yup. That was definitely a seizure. Textbook case, no doubt about it."

I'm the type that usually isn't in a big hurry to get medical treatment, but what the heck? If I had a seizure, then I guessed I did need some help. *Commander* told everyone that rescue was going to helicopter me out due to the remote location. We were three and a half miles up the narrow trail from Dick's Creek Gap. "Oh, no! They're going to search all of us," said *Commander*. "Everyone has to get rid of all of your drugs! We don't want to end up going to jail!" This guy was really getting worked up.

It was looking like I would be taking the second helicopter rescue ride of my life. I figured it might be a good idea to give my wife a heads up so that she wouldn't be surprised by a call from the hospital or something. I tried to get a signal on my cell phone, but Verizon showed zero bars.

Hoping to get some help from someone other than *Commander*, I said not too loudly, "Could someone— anyone—please call my wife for me?"

"What's her number?" barked *Commander*.

I gave him our home number, but there was no answer. I then gave him my wife's cell, helpfully pointing out, "I think that's right, if not try the same number ending in 9025 instead of 9925."

"He can't keep his numbers straight!" exclaimed *Commander* as he made the call to my wife.

"Yes ma'am, he's had a serious fall and had a seizure. Yes, that's right, a seizure. He's got a concussion, and we've called 911. They're on the way to rescue him right now." I knew my wife and kids would be worried, and I wondered how I'd explain this little mishap to them. After all, *I was dehydrated.* I contemplated; *Maybe I wouldn't mention that part about the pot.*

"We think he was dehydrated, *and* there's another piece to it that it's not my place to get into," *Commander* said, still on the phone with my wife. "It's not my place to explain that. I'll leave that up to *him* to tell you about it or not."

Okey Dokey! I guess I will have to tell my wife the whole story here. Thanks Mr. Commander for helping me make that decision.

As I sat there on the porch, I could see other hikers arriving to join the festivities. The campfire circle where everyone was hanging out was only about twenty feet away from me, so I could hear everything they said.

"Oh, he's definitely got a concussion."

"He can't keep his numbers straight."

"He doesn't even know what day it is."

"I heard about someone else that got helicoptered out."

"So, he had a seizure?"

After an hour or so, I felt much better and suggested that perhaps I should get up and walk around a bit to see how I felt.

"You are going to stay RIGHT THERE until the medics can

evaluate you," responded *Commander*. "Then, and ONLY THEN, can you get up."

Uh, okay. Yes sir, I thought while trying to hold back a smile as I realized how hilarious this whole situation was. *If I write a book, this is most certainly going in it.*

Forty-five minutes later, headlamps began to pop out from the woods as fifteen medics from the Towns County volunteer force arrived to rescue me. They had come up a nearby forest service road on ATVs, bringing along an ambulance and a full size 4x4 truck.

John, the lead medic, was friendly and helpful. He reminded me of John Denver as he asked me various questions and had me do a few different tests like walking around and touching my finger to my nose.

"I think you're fine," he said. "I'll take you down the mountain if you insist, but I don't see any signs of a concussion, and I think you're okay." He went on to add, "I tend to be overly careful and get in trouble sometimes for taking people in who don't need our help. So, while there's no guarantee, of course, I think you're okay."

I felt fine at that point and told John that I preferred to stay at the shelter. He wished me well and let me know that since they were a volunteer department, there was no charge whatsoever for their services. I liked the sound of that and since I was hit on the head, I put "Towns County Fire Dept" into my phone so that I wouldn't forget to send them a thank you note. I thanked John profusely as well.

He must have packed up and quietly left with his comrades because five minutes later, *Commander* walked up and asked me what happened to the rescue guy.

"He said I was fine. I didn't need to go to the hospital."

He moved his face to within six inches from mine and said, "You *refused* service?"

There was more fussing from *Commander* for the rest of the evening. At one point, he came over and said, "Thanks a lot! I want you to know that you've RUINED our hike! Now we're going to have to stay up all night to keep checking on you." While *Commander* was upset with me, the other hikers were probably more curious than angry. Still, I should have apologized to everyone for the trouble I caused. I was embarrassed and kept quiet instead.

I discovered later my family was incredibly worried that night. My wife had been walking out the door to attend a special banquet with friends she hadn't seen in years but stayed home to deal with my mishap instead. She missed the event, and the lovely dress she bought for the occasion is still hanging in her closet unworn. Dealing with the ongoing pain and the challenge of hiking left me clueless about all of this. Thinking back on this, I feel bad about the hikers I inconvenienced and for the way that my antics caused so much worry and upset for my family.

The other hikers were friendly enough to squeeze me into the shelter, and they did have someone check on me during the night. The next morning, I got up early and made a quick departure, trying to make my way down the trail in the fog without attracting any more attention.

I spent the next few days recovering at the Top of Georgia Hostel. While talking with other hikers, I kept hearing, "So you're *Flash 52*? Ha ha ha ha! I've heard *all* about you!"

As I mentioned, my wife and kids were initially rattled,

but they did laugh at my experience once I filled them in on the whole story. A day later, *Commander was* sitting on the hostel's porch, and when I went to walk around him, I almost lost my balance because, well, my balance is terrible on my left side.

"Oh, so you *do* have a concussion!" he exclaimed.

"No, really, I don't."

"Are you going to tell me you always walk like that?"

"Yea, I wish I didn't, but actually, I do."

I stayed at the Top of Georgia Hostel for three days to help get my energy and confidence back up. On the third day, with rain in the forecast, the hostel was full of hikers sitting around talking about staying longer to avoid the wet weather. It was late in the afternoon when I decided to head out and asked Sam, one of the helpers, to give me a ride up to the trail.

By the time we pulled up to the trailhead, the rain had turned to drizzle. Sam said, "Everyone else is back there making excuses but here you are, heading out in the rain, injured leg and all."

I smiled, wished him well, and headed off into the mist. Because I'd waited so late to get started, it wasn't long before the trail started getting dark. I turned on my headlamp and headed north towards Plum Orchard Gap Shelter, four and a half miles up the trail.

It felt strange to hike in the dark. My headlamp lit up the area from where I stood to about twenty feet out, ending abruptly at the edge of the darkening mist. The result was that I could see well enough to know where to put my feet but couldn't see the terrain around me. I was walking in a light bubble through the forest. As I looked out into the darkness beyond the area defined by my light, I wondered what it would be like if my headlamp quit working.

I'd be marooned out here in the pitch-black forest. Just thinking about this made my heart rate go up. I had an extra set of batteries in my pack, although I doubted that I could find and replace them in complete darkness. I realized that I had my cell phone sealed up against the weather in a Ziplock bag that I could use if I needed it. Worst case, I could always put up my tent right on the trail for the night. This isn't considered good etiquette, of course, but it would be appropriate in an emergency.

I didn't get to the shelter until 9:30 PM, and everything was quiet as all the other hikers had already gone to sleep. I used the red light on my headlamp to peek around and saw a spot on the top level that was still open. Using my good leg to push me up one rung at a time, I made my way up the ladder, pulled out my pad and sleeping bag, and then crawled in falling asleep while listening to the rain hitting the roof above.

It was a little before noon the next day when another hiker caught up with me and said we were getting close to the Georgia–North Carolina state line. He said that he had hiked this section last year and was sure that the state line was just ahead.

"Oh, that's great," I responded, thinking we could hang out together. Plus, it would be great to have someone to take my picture. He went on ahead of me, and I did my best to hurry along. From what he had told me, I kept thinking that it couldn't be much further. So, I kept trudging along, trying to go a little faster. I'd come around another bend in the trail only to see more trail heading off into the distance. When I finally made it to the state line, I saw a simple wooden sign nailed to a tree that said "NC/GA." My potential new friend was already gone.

I took a few selfies, and then some hikers came by who offered to take my photo standing next to the sign. It felt great to have made it through my first of fourteen states. *That's one down and only thirteen to go.* The trail there cut across the side of the terrain, and because spring hadn't arrived yet, I could see wonderful, tall trees covering the hillsides in every direction.

It was another three miles of hiking along this beautiful path to get to my destination for the day, Muskrat Creek Shelter. While making my dinner, I met a group of hikers that I liked, all of them young, funny people. The books that I'd read about the Appalachian Trail all mentioned that one of the best parts about hiking was the friends you make along the way. I'd learned that hikers typically connect with other people who tend to move along at the same pace as they do. These are called a "tramily," or trail family, and the group typically looks out for each other, making plans to end up at the same location at the end of each day.

One of these hikers I'd met, *Hobo*, whose name meant "homeward bound" because he was from Maine, was telling jokes and feeding his dog, Cheeto. I could tell that they were close because as he ate his Mountain House dinner, Cheeto would wait for him to spoon out a big bite to glomp down right off the same spoon. Cheeto also slept in *Hobo's* hammock at night.

I tried to imagine what it would be like to have a group of fun, supportive friends like this on the hike. As much as I liked these folks, I knew that my time with them was likely fleeting. I had figured out by this point that all the younger folks hiked much faster than I did. My average speed was easy to figure out. If I went seven miles for the day, it would take me seven hours, so I clocked in at a snail's pace—one mile per hour. Most other hikers could easily do twice that or more, achieving two or three miles per hour. The next morning, they would move up the trail at their faster pace leaving me behind to connect momentarily with the next group that would be overtaking me.

What I wanted at this point more than anything, other than to heal up and be whole again, was to find someone that I could hike with. *Turtle* arrived right as it was starting to get dark, and I helped him put up his tent. I shared the story of how I'd gotten injured and how slow I was on the trail. He said, "That's not a worry, I'm quite slow myself."

Hmmmm... I thought, *Maybe I could hike with Turtle.*

The next morning as everyone was packing up and heading out, I waited for *Turtle* to leave, thinking that we could hike together. Mind you, I hadn't asked him to hike with me. I just had this idea in my head, something like *I won't have to be all alone... I won't be the slowest one on the trail. I've finally found someone to hike with.*

I left the camping area at the same time as *Turtle* did and began a conversation with him about something—I don't remember what—while trying to keep up with his pace. As I was talking to him, he kept getting further and further ahead of me. Eventually, he said, "So long, I'll see you later." And then he took off into the distance.

While it was nice to stop struggling to go faster

than I was capable, as I slowed down and caught my breath, I felt devastated. Rather than just accepting this feeling, my inner voice was scolding me. *Really? You're feeling this way about someone you just met last night?*

The real issue wasn't about someone else. The problem was I wasn't happy being disabled.

You're not disabled. You're hiking the Appalachian Trail! my inner voice shouted back.

Onward I slogged, making my way down the hill as I tried to process all these feelings swirling inside my head before slowly, ever so slowly, making my way up the next mountain.

Over the next two days, I kept my mileage down to about seven or eight miles a day, staying first at Rock Gap Shelter, and the next day I was hoping to find an open spot in the Siler Bald Shelter. It had been raining for the last two hours, so by the time I turned to take the blue-blazed trail to the shelter, I was ready to get out of the rain and change into some dry clothes. Unfortunately, when I limped up to the shelter it had already filled up.

I hung out for a while, talking with the other hikers while standing under the roof that extended out from the shelter's front. I'd heard people say, "If it's cold or raining, there's always room for one more." I was silently hoping that someone would offer to squeeze together a bit more to make room for me. I'm sure I could have negotiated this, but my foot was killing me, and I didn't have the energy to push the issue. I looked at the FarOut app and could see there was a campsite just half a mile ahead. So, I said my goodbyes and walked up the trail to find a decent looking campsite right off the side of the path.

I recalled reading about people who went out to hike the Appalachian Trail without knowing how to set up their tents. At the time I thought that was ridiculous. *I mean, who'd be dumb enough to get into a situation like that?*

Well, as it turns out, me.

I didn't mean to get into this situation, of course. Before I took the train to Georgia, I'd watched a video about how to pitch my new tent and had even picked a night when my wife was away to practice camping out in my backyard ahead of time. But on the day of the practice run, I looked out at the backyard covered with two feet of snow, and with the temperature in the teens, decided to skip it and stay inside instead.

So, there I was, trying to figure out how to put this stupid thing up in the pouring rain. I managed to get the tent up but was surprised by how small it was. When I was deciding which tent to buy, I wanted something lightweight and that packed down small. I also didn't want to spend very much because, at that point, I wasn't sure that I could pull this hike off.

I'd found a Solar Photon tent that was made in England, and from the photo on the website it looked big enough. I mean, it's a tent, right? It had to be large enough for me to sleep in. It was reasonably lightweight, and it did pack down small, but there was no room at all for anything besides me in the tent.

It became obvious that my pack wouldn't fit inside. I stood next to the tent in the rain trying to dig out my sleeping bag and other stuff I'd need for the night. I didn't want my pack to get any more soaked, so I improvised and pulled the trash bag liner out and used it to cover the top of the pack, which was sitting in a puddle of water.

The tent worked okay until I tried to sit up. As I sat up, my head hit the top of the tent, which caused water to start leaking in. Let's just say that it was a less-than-fun night. When I poked my head out in the morning, I was glad to see clear blue skies greeting me from above.

Later that afternoon, I was making progress up Standing Indian Mountain. I pulled up FarOut, a GPS app on my phone that provides maps and elevation views of the trail. It looked like quite a climb, but it went up gradually, and the path's surface wasn't too bad. The guidebook had mentioned an offshoot that went to the summit, so when I saw another trail heading off to the right, I turned onto the shortcut, went past a few campsites, and five minutes later reached the summit.

I looked around at a flat grassy area with breath-taking views towards the west. There was a perfect little stealth site, or unofficial campsite, right on top of the mountain that was just big enough for my tent. After checking to make sure the weather forecast looked okay, I decided that would be a fun place to spend the night.

I made a small fire and cooked my dinner while watching the sun drop lower in the sky. Another hiker came up to watch the sunset along with me. He pointed out Fontana Reservoir, about halfway to the horizon, which was where the trail was headed.

I attached my iPhone to my hiking pole and tried to get it to take a time-lapse video of the sun going down. I didn't have enough storage space on the phone, so it kept stopping.

I spent a few minutes trying to delete other photos and videos to open up more storage space, but realized the sun was going down fast and decided just to sit there and soak it all in.

The combination of being out on the trail, climbing to the top of a 5,499-foot mountain, and looking out at one of the most spectacular sunsets I had ever seen in my life was magnificent. Absolutely marvelous. It felt like the colors, no, the entire experience, reached out and grabbed onto part of my soul, stretching my emotions to new limits.

I understand that all of this may seem like a bit much. But things look different if you must climb to the top of a mountain to see it. Perhaps my mind enhanced the view to compensate for the constant screaming from my leg. All I can say is that it was stunning.

The next day when I woke up, I was in the clouds, and the view from the night before was a distant memory hidden somewhere out in the misty white swirls beyond the summit of Standing Indian Mountain. I made my way down the trail, which seemed to be a little steeper than the ascent from the previous day.

I took my time covering ten miles for the day to end up at Betty's Creek Camping Area. Twenty or thirty other hikers had spread out in various tents, including a Boy Scout troop and a few leaders. A couple of young scouts offered to get some firewood for us, and we took them up on their offer.

I had enough water to make dinner but needed to refill so I would have water for breakfast and the next day's hike. My foot was bothering me, and as I sat there thinking about making the trip down to get water, my leg, as if to protest the idea, started to hurt even more. I asked Josh, one of the boy scouts, if he'd be kind enough to make the half-mile traverse to get me some water. He was happy to help, and I deeply appreciated his efforts.

I sat around the fire talking with other hikers about Albert Mountain, which we would all encounter the following day. While it's less than a 500-foot climb, it's pretty darn steep. It's the first place heading north on the Appalachian Trail where you need to attach your hiking poles to your pack so you can clamber up using your hands and feet.

"You're much better off to take the blue blaze trail around it," advised *Just Dan*.

"It's not that bad, you'll be ok if you take your time," countered *Blue Beard*.

"I wouldn't want to be up there in a snowstorm," suggested another person whose name I didn't get.

I wasn't sure what to do and figured I'd decide once I got there and had a look at it.

At 11:30 AM the next day I arrived at Albert Mountain's base, and it did look rather intimidating. Yet I chose to go up the steep, white-blazed Appalachian Trail route, thinking that *if I'm going to hike this darn thing then I probably shouldn't skip any parts of it*. I did have to climb using my hands and feet in a few places and stopped every fifty yards or so to catch my breath. But before long, I made it to the top.

I took off my pack and climbed up the metal fire tower to look out at the views in all directions. It was a beautiful day, and I was glad that I didn't take the advice to skip past this first of many obstacles to come on the Appalachian Trail.

The next day I found myself walking with *Pacman* and talking about the business he ran. We came to a stream, stopped to get water, and then continued hiking together. I did my best to keep up with him. *Wow, look at you, you are moving along at a nice pace*, I said to myself just as I caught my left foot on a root and fell flat on my face. Ker-SMACK!

"Are you okay?" *Pacman* asked, as I tried to brush this off as somehow being a normal thing for me.

"Oh, I'm fine." *I always fall flat on my face like this.* Anything to avoid the real problem. I was hiking with an injured leg that didn't work so well. I wanted to be able to push myself hard and somehow make my leg heal. Working twice as hard or pushing myself had helped me accomplish an awful lot in my life so far. At this point it seemed that pushing harder or trying to go faster just wasn't in the cards for me.

I was having a hard time adjusting to the fact that I must have been the slowest one on the trail. When I heard someone coming behind me, I knew it was just a matter of time before I'd need to let them pass. Stepping aside, of course, went directly against my competitive spirit, but what was I going to do? It was impossible for me to go as fast as the other hikers I was meeting.

Many of these hikers were doing fifteen- or twenty-mile days by now, so it was unlikely that I'd ever see them again. I saw a few people multiple times either because they took a zero day, which allowed me to catch up with them, or they'd gone the same distance as me, ending up at the same shelter. The difference is that they got to the shelter at two or three in the afternoon and I struggled in around 6:00 or 7:00 PM.

Because I've always been competitive—and you might not be surprised to learn this—I still looked for any opportunity to try to go faster than other hikers despite my slow pace.

Two days later, I was moving up Wesser Bald while trying my best not to take a break until I got to the top. About a quarter mile ahead of me, I could see a woman making her way up the mountain.

As I got closer, I saw that it was *Seeker*, someone that I'd met at a shelter recently. I don't know how to say this other than to mention that she was carrying a little extra weight, and it wasn't in her pack. When I realized that I might be able to catch her, and God willing, maybe even pass her, I stepped up my gait.

I could see that I was slowly making progress as the distance between us grew smaller and smaller. "Oh, Hi *Seeker!*" I said while trying my best not to sound out of breath and pretending that I passed people every day. Inside I felt like shouting out in celebration but had the good sense to keep my mouth shut. *I'm getting stronger. I'm getting stronger*, I said to myself as I continued to push myself faster than usual the rest of the way up the mountain.

It was 6:30 PM by the time that I got to Wesser Bald Shelter, which, of course, was full of hikers. Here's the funny thing. Right in the middle, I could see someone who was already in her sleeping bag. It was *Seeker!* She must have caught back up to me and gone by while I was taking a break somewhere.

This probably doesn't sound like a big deal. But I felt deflated. I was dealing with the physical challenge of hiking with a foot that hurt only when I stepped on it, and inside my little pea brain, I felt like I was losing because I was slower than anyone else on the trail.

While some hikers were able to get up and out early, I found it hard to get moving until at least 7:00 AM or so, when

I would finally stick my legs out the side of my little tent and lace up my boots. I had gotten used to the fact that my first few steps each day were going to hurt. After putting my shoes on, using my hiking poles for support, I'd take a few careful steps to wake my injured foot up and work some of the stiffness out of it.

I then stretched the calf muscle out on my left side as it always seemed to be super tight. I looked around to see that most of the other hikers had already taken off for the day. After enjoying my two cinnamon frosted Pop-Tarts for breakfast, I carefully placed everything into position in my pack and cinched all the straps up tight.

The trail that morning was mostly smooth dirt without rocks and roots, and it made a gentle ascent up and away from the gap where I had spent the night. I expected my foot to hurt for the first few miles each day, and that day was no different. After getting the first few miles out of the way, my foot, instead of starting to feel better, began to hurt more and more every time I stepped on it. I stopped to rest for ten minutes and did some more calf stretches, hoping that would help.

My doctors kept track of how I was doing by asking me each time I went in for a visit what my pain level was. They used a pain scale of zero to ten, where zero is no pain and ten is the worst imaginable. Normally, after warming up by hiking those first few miles, my leg loosened up and the pain level dropped down to a manageable level of say a four or a five through the middle of the day. Then toward the end of the day, when my leg was getting worn out, the pain level would go back up again.

Once I was done resting and stretching, I got going again, but I was still getting shooting pain from every step. I saw another log I could sit on that wasn't too far away, and I limped over to it and sat down to give my foot another rest. I thought about my situation. There I was, taking another rest after going less than a hundred feet. I'd thought that my foot would get better each day that I hiked, but that wasn't happening.

Yet, I knew that if I could just keep going, if I could somehow make it to Mt. Katahdin in Maine, then my leg would *have* to be better. I thought about everything I'd been through so far to get to that point. Two years of relentless pain, all my preparations and hiking so far, starting with that first night where the wolf scared the heck out of me, and then all the way from Springer Mountain to here, just over a hundred miles on the Appalachian Trail.

My leg was hurting every day, and it wasn't going to get any better if I didn't do something to fix it. I figured that I could stay home and be in horrible pain with little to no chance of getting better or I could be out here hiking the trail and hopefully find a way to overcome this admittedly heavy burden. So, I got back up and started walking.

Over the next hour, as I moved along, the pain in my leg seemed to slowly accumulate until it felt like it was getting worse with every step. It worked up to a seven.

And then ever so slowly up to an eight.

And then nine.

By the time it reached a ten, tears were running down my face. With each step, my foot and leg were *screaming* at my brain. CAN'T YOU HEAR ME? *How about* THIS, *or* THIS, *or* THIS?! Once pain gets up to a nine or ten, it may as well be at two hundred. The circuits in my brain were jam-packed with neurons racing around telling me to stop walking. But I had gotten myself to a place where I couldn't do that. Sure, I could have stopped again and propped my foot up in the air. But then what? I certainly wasn't going to make another 911 call to the medics, not if I could help it.

I told myself, *I don't care if I have to walk on a bloody stump to get all the way to Maine. If that's what it takes, I'm going to keep going. I don't care how much it hurts.*

I wish that I could tell you that my stubborn persistence led to some sort of spiritual breakthrough. I did my best to make my brain ignore the pain, which, of course, I wasn't able to do. It was horrible. I felt like I had run out of options, and I didn't know what to do.

My head was so packed full of pain that the only way out, the only solution that I could see at the moment was to push harder and harder against this dragon that had taken over my life and all of my thoughts. With tears in my eyes, I put my head down and continued up the trail.

The advantage—if you can call it that—of having to deal with pain like that is that at least it couldn't get any worse. I thought about that as I walked through the vast sea of rhododendrons that were along the trail.

6

IN THE TRAUMA CENTER

Rock Bottom Became A Solid
Foundation on Which I Rebuilt My Life

"PETER! STOP SCREAMING! YOU'RE HURT-
ING MY EARS!"

The head doctor was yelling back at me after they had
carried me from the helicopter into the hospital. Hearing
my name snapped through to me and I realized that it
would be up to me to find a way to get things under control
even though I was in severe pain. I must have passed out as
my next memory was when my daughter arrived to see me.

I was propped up in a hospital gurney and heard her
talking in the hallway. I realized she was about to enter the

room I was in. I have a terrible habit of trying to make serious moments seem funny, so I went into my imitation of someone having a seizure.

"Daaad! Don't do that! Not now," she said with tears in her eyes.

"Oh. Uh . . . sorry about that."

About fifteen minutes later, my wife and son arrived. Having broken bones when I was much younger, I was thinking I'd easily heal up from this within the next three to six months. My wife understood differently. She told me that when she saw me that night, she knew our lives had been forever changed.

A doctor came in, showed us the x-rays, and explained that my hip and pelvis had shattered into twenty-three pieces and that I had dislocated my femur. Since it was my hip that was broken, that's the only part at this point that was painful. On the pain scale, I'd say that my pain was at a level of six or seven. They had checked to see if I could wiggle my toes on both sides, which I was easily able to do.

The doctor then explained that what they usually did was perform a "reduction procedure" where they would knock me out and put my femur back into the broken hip socket. He said this was to help keep the cartilage in my hip joint healthy until they could do the surgery a few days later.

I wish that we'd known enough to ask some questions rather than just blindly signing the form that was placed in front of me, thinking that it was all standard procedure. What I *really* wish we would have asked was, "How necessary is this procedure? What is the downside to *not* doing it? What are the risks? Is it possible to speed up the surgery so we can skip this procedure?"

Ideally, we would have had an outside orthopedic doctor or someone to consult. But, hey, this was the first shattered hip in our family, so we said, "Okay, go ahead."

This next part is hard to explain because it's so different from anything that I've ever experienced before (or after). The doctors put me to sleep for the procedure, but a part of me was somehow aware of being dragged down a path that I didn't want to go down. I saw a black and white circular track with sections that were clicked down in sync with a loud mechanical rhythm one after the other. I could sense that something horrible was happening to me, and it was going faster and faster, yet I was helpless to stop it.

Outside in the waiting room, my wife, daughter, and son were growing concerned. They had been told that the procedure should take fifteen or twenty minutes. After an hour passed, my wife asked what was taking so long. They said they were having trouble getting my pain under control.

When I came to, it felt like an elephant was sitting on my leg. Before the reduction procedure, I had been able to wiggle my foot and toes. Now I couldn't move anything on my left side from my hip down. My hip had been hurting before, but everything else seemed okay. Now, my entire leg was hurting like nothing I'd ever imagined. My pain went right up the one to ten scale and then kept going . . . twenty . . . fifty . . . eighty . . . a hundred!

I reached deep inside myself to tap into whatever I could find to help me through the massive, overwhelming pain. It took so much of my energy and attention that I couldn't say anything. My mind became so overwhelmed that I was no longer aware of what was going on around me. I didn't have any choice but to do my best to deal with it while hoping that if the doctors could do something for me, they would.

We didn't realize it at the time, but when the doctors shoved my femur back into my broken hip, they had just crushed the main nerve in my leg. I knew that my wife, daughter, and son were there along with a few doctors. I was too out of it to know for sure. After thirty minutes of this, I looked over at Joanna and asked, "Can't they give me a little something to help with the pain?"

I didn't realize that during the past half hour, the doctors had hit me with enough morphine to drop a horse. My wife said they were surprised they couldn't get the pain under control but were hesitant to give me any more morphine. I've told people the story of dealing with pain at this level by saying that it was "interesting" and that it helped me to "experience the full spectrum of life." While that may be one way to put a positive spin on it, the truth is that it hurt like hell. Heck, the memory of it hurts me now just sharing it with you.

The next thing I was aware of was being taken into surgery the following day. After six hours in the operating room, I came to in the recovery room.

"The surgery went well. You've got fourteen pins and four plates in your hip."

"Okay, Doc. How long will it take for me to heal back up?"

"Well, that really varies. Let's focus on getting you well enough to go home."

Why won't they tell me how long it's going to take for me to get better? My foot and lower leg were hurting me just as much as they did before the surgery.

I had a morphine pump with a button I could push to

get another dose into my IV line, but only if it had been a certain number of hours since my last dose. Much of this was a blur. As I remember, I was pushing that button all day long. The morphine helped with the pain and enabled me to think through twenty or thirty different things all at the same time. I was having déjà vu experiences.

When my business partner called to check on me and said, "my kids are playing right here in the other room," my mind wandered. A part of my consciousness walked into the other room, saw his kids playing, and said hi to them, even though they were over 2,000 miles away. Other parts of my mind were exploring many other ideas at the same time. By the time he finished his sentence, I was responding with, "Yes, I know, the kids are right here playing in the next room." It was like waking up from a vivid dream—as if it really happened, even though it was all in my mind.

Being the creative person I am, I enjoyed my new mental ability to explore all these different directions at once. From the outside, most of what I said didn't make any sense at all. I didn't realize this of course as I was busy processing all of the thoughts that were swirling around my head. I made sure to tell everyone who came into my room that I would run another marathon in two weeks' time. I even had the nurse write this down on my patient info whiteboard. I guess you could say that the morphine was making me a little crazy.

To leave the critical care unit, I'd have to be able to do three things. Number One: Get myself to the bathroom and back under my own power. Number Two: Have a bowel movement. Number Three: Get off the morphine pump.

To get to the bathroom and back, I had to learn how to get

in and out of a wheelchair. The hardest part was discovering how to do it without bumping my injured side. Within the first two days, I was able to do this on my own.

Getting number two to happen seemed to be the biggest challenge for me. Everything internally had shut down due to the surgery. Plus, the morphine relaxed everything in my body, including the muscles that move things along in the digestive track. While morphine did a wonderful job of making all the pain go away, there were a few interesting side effects. It gave me an oversized sense of self and I was a real jerk. I annoyed the nurses by asking for and expecting special treatment.

I drove my wife so crazy that after spending several nights in a nearby hotel, she packed up and made the two-hour drive back to our home in Annapolis, Maryland. In her defense, a blizzard was on the way and our son was home alone.

You can probably understand how ticked off my wife was about the whole thing. She was already quite angry at me because I had made her a promise that I wouldn't race the motorcycle. Our lives were now turned upside down because of my broken promise. So, when the morphine had me acting like the king of the world, I couldn't blame her for heading home for a bit. She told me later that she needed a break from me to cool down. She went to church the following weekend, and luckily for me, the sermon was all about forgiveness. She figured I was suffering enough from my injury and let go of the anger that she, quite understandably, felt.

I was trying to go to the bathroom and needed to get off the morphine. While I was on it, I felt no pain, but it was affecting my thinking. In a busy hospital, the nurses and other staff had to juggle all their patient's concerns and needs, with more attention given to those who were in more critical condition than I was. Yet, when the nurses ignored my various requests, I started to think that everyone in the hospital was conspiring against me. In my morphine induced fog, I became convinced that the hospital staff was doing things behind my back to keep me there.

I called Joanna that evening to explain this big conspiracy that I had discovered. I told her about my plans to break out of the hospital. I asked her (yes, I actually did this...) to contact a friend who was a former Navy Seal and ask him to sneak in and break me out of the hospital.

"What happens once you get out? Where are you going to go?"

"I've got that all figured out. I'm coming home, and I can sleep on the floor of our son's room." It was on the first floor.

"Well, if you do that, then you won't have any pain medication."

"Oh. Uh . . . I hadn't thought of that."

My wife was an angel to put up with all this nonsense. On top of dealing with my crazy requests, she was simultaneously making all the decisions required to build our house, dealing with our daughter's struggle with addiction, *and* she was running a full-time campaign for County Executive. She's an amazing woman. I'm so lucky to have her as my wife and extremely grateful that she put up with me during this time when I wasn't at my best.

By the next day, I was able to get myself to the bathroom and successfully go "number two." I'd also ordered the nurses to take me off the morphine pump. You might have guessed that they don't usually do this without first checking with the doctor. Because I was in a hurry to check off all three boxes and move out of the hospital's critical care section, I got them to take me off it.

There was only one tiny little problem.

People don't quit morphine without going on another drug. They transition over to using something fairly strong that comes in a tablet, like Oxycontin. I was in a hurry and didn't want to wait for my doctor to make his rounds, so, in my infinite wisdom, I convinced the nurses to take me off the morphine without transitioning to another pain medication.

And then I had my first lesson in pain management. Controlling your pain with medications *before* the pain becomes unbearable is much easier than what I did. Once I was off the morphine, the pain in my foot and leg started climbing and climbing until it soared sky-high. Once the pain skyrockets like that, it's almost impossible to get it under control. This is because the side effects of fighting against the pain—the stress and tension in my body—were making the pain even worse. All I can say is that this was horrible.

After six days in the Intensive Care Unit, and to the nurses' delight, I was finally transferred to a regular hospital room. My roommate was a Camden police officer who'd been run over by his own police car. It seemed that a woman managed to jump into his patrol car, take off, and nail him. I know this because the TV in the room provided "breaking news" by showing us a video of this lady stealing the patrol car and ramming into the officer. I know he was hurting, so I was surprised to see that the TV stayed on as his accident was replayed throughout the day repeatedly. I remember the TV announcer saying something like, "Wow! She really wacked him in the knees, didn't she?"

Two days later, I was moved to a different hospital room. My new roommate spoke mostly Spanish, and I could make a small connection using my limited vocabulary. It turns out that he had been stabbed. I was thinking that I was lucky to have been sent to the Camden hospital since the doctors there had plenty of experience dealing with various shootings and stabbings associated with a rough town like Camden. I felt considerably less lucky when my new roommate told the nurses, "No hay visitantes para mi" because the guys who had stabbed him had just gotten out of jail. I didn't know how likely it was for these bad guys to show up, but I didn't like the fact that my bed was closest to the door.

I took this as further motivation to get out of the hospital. Joanna found a rehab facility in Annapolis that had an open room. The problem was how to get me there. I was on a few different strong pain killers at the time. However, the ambulance that we lined up to transport me from Camden to Annapolis wasn't able to give me any pain medications.

I found out later that this was due to an insurance company policy. The vehicle looked like an ambulance, but there was nothing in the back—no medical supplies, no oxygen, nothing. It was empty except for the stretcher I was on and two guys in uniform who rode along. From what I learned later about these medical transport companies, these guys had little to no medical training and were paid something like $15 an hour.

You'd think it would be a simple matter of giving me some

pain pills right before we left the hospital, so I'd be good for the two-hour ride. Perhaps if I had been the only patient this would have happened. Instead, I was given my medication two or three hours before I was checked out and on my way in the "ambulance."

During the ride, the pain started to go up and up. Hitting bumps along the road didn't help. I ended up doing a conference call with my employees after borrowing the transport guy's cellphone to distract myself. I discovered later that my team ignored pretty much everything I had said because I wasn't making any sense.

Once I arrived at the rehab center, it was another process to get checked in. Then, we needed another doctor to sync up with the rehab center to get more of the narcotics that I needed to help manage my pain. I ended up going two or three hours past the point where I should have gotten more pain medication. Once again, the pain levels soared to a point where it was no longer possible to get them under control with a normal dose of medication.

While I was quite aware at the time of how horrible this experience was, I had no understanding of the long-term damage that was becoming established in my central nervous system each time my pain levels shot up to the moon and back. It would take me another four years to finally figure this out.

The month I spent at the rehab facility was a mixture of contrasting experiences. At times other patients were wailing and yelling out during the night. On the other hand, I remember lying there in my hospital bed looking out the window on the overcast day I'd told everyone I was going to be running a marathon. But I wasn't sad. Rather, I felt grateful. If I had been injured like this a hundred years earlier, I probably wouldn't have lasted more than a couple of weeks. I was thankful for the medical care that I had and happy to be alive.

I had to learn how to use a wheelchair, a walker, and then crutches. I was getting occupational therapy so that I could get around and take care of myself. This confused me because I was sure that I'd be completely healed within the next three to six months, *so why do I need to be taught how to get dressed and make myself lunch?*

The time between pain medication doses was the hardest part. I was taking powerful opioid pain killers that seemed to have a four-hour lifespan. However, the nurses wouldn't bring it to me until I asked for it, but they wouldn't let me ask for it until at least four hours had passed since my last dose. Right at the four-hour mark, I'd press the call button, and ten minutes later, an assistant would come into my room. I'd politely say "I need my medication. Can I get it right away?"

"I'll go check" was the typical answer. I'd wait another fifteen or twenty minutes before pressing the call button again. Another ten minutes would go by before someone else, a different person than the one who'd responded before, would come into the room.

"I really need my medication. My leg is seriously hurting now. Can I please get something right away?"

"Sure thing. The head nurse (who's the only one with the key to the narcotics) is busy with a shift change right now, but as soon as they're done, we'll get someone right in here to help you."

Meanwhile—you guessed it—my leg was going back up the pain scale. *8 . . . 9 . . . 10 . . .* and beyond.

I discovered much later that my central nervous system was becoming over-sensitized by the constant barrage of pain signals. My brain was learning to create an endless pain loop that some people claim you cannot ever escape.

But I'm getting ahead of myself.

One of the things I remember most clearly from my time at the rehab center was a morning ritual that I had created for myself. When you're in a situation like I was where you have extraordinarily little control over anything, it's interesting how something small can make a big difference. My wife was nice enough to bring in my coffee machine which I put on the table within reach of my hospital bed. I'd get up at 5:30 in the morning, make coffee, and then shave using a small pan of hot water the nurse would bring me.

The act of being able to do these two things on my own (with a little bit of help) gave me a small sense of control over a life that had very suddenly gone off the rails. The other thing that I remember from this time was when my daughters came by to assist me. One of them lived nearby, and another flew in from Colorado two different times on her own dime. I couldn't shower myself but managed to strip down to a pair of shorts and sit in a chair while my daughters washed my hair for the first time in several weeks. It felt glorious. Another time, when I was dealing with pain that was going through the roof, my daughter was there with me as I babbled nonsense in an attempt to mentally move the pain around in my head. She smiled to let me know that it was okay for me to do whatever I needed to deal with it.

After a month in the rehab center, it was finally time to go home. Since I was still unable to bend my injured leg, I was loaded into the back of the car and sat sideways across the seat. I guess I made that ride without a seatbelt. Once we arrived home, I used my wheelchair to travel up the sidewalk to the front door. At the front door, I had to get out of the wheelchair and use my crutches to get up the four-inch-high step from the sidewalk into the house.

With two people holding onto me, I managed to stand up but then wavered in the doorway, feeling like I was about to topple over. Joanna and the rehab facility person grabbed on to keep me from falling over. This was strange to me. Here I was, an accomplished athlete who couldn't even make it over a minimal threshold.

Since the house we usually lived in was being rebuilt from the ground up, we were renting a four-story townhouse. Joanna had rented a hospital bed that was set up on the second level in the living room right next to the kitchen. To get to the bathroom, I would have to make it up the stairs to the third level.

By this point, I was starting to get around decently using my crutches. I held my left foot off the ground a foot or so in front of me as I hobbled along. But I still hadn't figured out how to go up and down stairs with my injured leg. I couldn't lift my foot out of the way. My sister Debbie gets credit for coming up with a solution. She suggested I go up the stairs backwards using the handrail on one side and a crutch on the other. This allowed me to hold my foot out in front of me while making my way up backwards.

Now that I was home, Joanna oversaw dishing out my

medications. Our concern was that if I managed the pill bottles myself, I could easily take too much or get addicted to the powerful opioid medications. The first few nights, she got up every three or four hours to dole out all the pills. The following evening she put out seven or eight little dishes containing my medications with the time written on post-it notes indicating when I should take each of them.

She said, "I'm not getting any sleep, so I'm going to trust you to manage this on your own."

I downloaded a timer app for my iPad that woke me every four hours and I did fine on my own. It was wonderful to be able to take the pills that I needed without having to wait for the nurses to bring them to me. We hired a part time driver to take me to my various doctor appointments. Before we left, she'd have to put my shoes on for me as I couldn't bend down far enough to reach my feet. During this time, I ended up getting a blood clot in my injured leg, probably due to the decreased circulation. The doctor put me on a blood thinner, which meant that my assistant had to help me make another trip to the doctors each week to have my blood tested.

I also started wearing compression leggings to help with circulation, and they seemed to make my leg feel a little better. Because I couldn't bend over far enough to reach my foot, I'd have to find my wife and ask her to help me stretch them on. My wife didn't enjoy doing this and I didn't like asking her, so both of us ended up feeling kind of crappy. All in all, this wasn't the easiest time we've had in our relationship, but I'm glad that she stuck with me through all of it.

The doctor also gave me a list of things to watch out for. The risk was that the blood clot could move up into my heart and cause a heart attack. There were several cautionary items on the list, but a memorable one was excessive sweating. I remember this because one night I got all hot and sweaty. So much so that my shirt was wet, and I went upstairs to change it.

Joanna heard me and asked what I was doing. "Oh, I'm just changing my shirt because I'm all hot and sweaty."

"That's a sign of a heart attack. We're going to the hospital."

We had a drawn-out conversation where I did my best to convince her I was fine. Then she said, "Either you get in the car so I can take you, or I'm calling an ambulance. You decide."

I realized that I wasn't going to change her mind, so I agreed to go in the car. When I walked into the emergency room and filled out the intake form, there was a spot that said, "Reason you are here." It felt crazy to write down "possible heart attack." *How did my life ever get like this?*

As it turns out, I was fine. Although in my wife's defense, while I kept fussing about being dragged down there in the middle of the night, one of the nurses looked at me and said, "You don't look very good to me. Why don't you sit down and be quiet?" All I can say is I'm glad that I was okay.

By this time, I was seeing three professionals regularly: my surgeon, primary doctor, and my pain management doctor. All these doctors prescribed a variety of powerful medications, most of them being pain killers. They aimed to manage the pain while hopefully preventing me from getting addicted.

Before long, I was on a ton of different prescriptions. To give you an idea of how bad it was, when I went to the pharmacy with a new deductible at the beginning of the year, my cost for one month's worth of medications was over $1,000. While each of them seemed to help me, they all had their own set of side effects. When I complained to the doctor about the side effects, I was prescribed more medications to treat the side effects. Then those additional medications had other side effects.

Some of what happened was downright crazy. At one point I discovered upon waking up in the morning that my fingers were killing me. They were locked into a clenched fist. Hard as I tried, I couldn't open my fingers up. If I pried them apart, they hurt even worse. When asked about this, all my doctors had the same response:

"I don't know what might cause that. I don't think it's because of any of the medications I've prescribed for you."

The only thing that made sense to me was that either one of the medications, or a combination of several medications, was causing my hands to spasm during the night. Since none of my doctors were able to figure out which medication was causing this, I had to figure this out on my own.

I decided to fashion a makeshift splint to hold my hands still while I slept. I tried a set of swim paddles that I had used when I was training for triathlons. They looked like an oversized flat hand made of plastic with rubber straps to hold your hand in place. They were pretty uncomfortable and didn't stay on. By morning, my hand had fallen out, and my fingers were, once again, clenched up and killing me.

The next idea came from the sport that all three of my brothers and I played while growing up—ice hockey. At the local sporting goods store, I picked up a set of hockey gloves that were on sale. Then I used silicone sealer to glue a tennis ball into the palm of each glove to hold my hands in a slightly curved position where my fingers couldn't clasp into a fist.

By this time, we'd returned the hospital bed, and I was back in our bed with a big foam wedge at the foot to prop my leg up at night. I remember the first night I lay down wearing my latest invention.

Joanna asked, "Why in the world are you wearing hockey gloves to bed?"

I told her it was an experiment to keep my hands from hurting so much in the morning. I woke up the next day pleasantly surprised to find that my hands were no longer in pain. I ended up wearing those hockey gloves to bed every night for the next several months.

This wasn't the last time I ended up in embarrassing situations. One day, I was using my crutches at the mall by Whole Foods and decided to go up the outdoor escalator. There must have been an elevator nearby, but for some reason I thought that I could go up the escalator. *How hard can it be?*

BAM!

Down I went, falling headfirst into the rising escalator. When I fell forward, it gave me a good smack physically, but mentally I felt trashed. Embarrassed. Incapable. I couldn't even make it up a stupid escalator without falling down. Honestly, this sums up how I was feeling during this period.

I remember late one night when I called Joanna from the rehab center about two weeks after I had been injured. It was during one of those multi-hour waits to get my pain killers. The pain had reached a crescendo where I maxed out my mental abilities to fight it. I picked up the phone and called Joanna saying, "I can't take it anymore. I want them to cut my leg off."

She replied, "Well Peter, that sounds a bit extreme to me. You may want to wait before you rush into anything." She told me later that it was pretty heartbreaking to get that call. I also found out that after she hung up, she called to speak with the nurse to see if they could get me more pain medication.

I'm glad she talked me out of rushing into such a drastic decision. I searched Google and it turns out that it's possible to have your leg cut off and still have phantom pain—meaning my leg might still hurt even if it wasn't there. I doubt the doctors would have complied, but it would be incredibly devastating to lose my leg and still be dealing with the pain. I'm incredibly thankful that Joanna was able to help me navigate making crazy decisions like this.

Six months after my injury, I was taking the opioid medications that my pain management doctor had prescribed for me. But I was still in a lot of pain. I wasn't thinking clearly because of all the medications I was on. After months of listening to me complain, my wife was worn out, and I can't blame her for that. She was amazingly supportive, but your support person can only listen to so much griping before they've had enough.

The one place that gave me a glimmer of hope was the first physical therapist that I went to. They were generally cheerful and would ask about my pain and listen to my complaints. Once a month, they'd review my progress by asking me to move my foot and then, I kid you not, poke my foot with the end of a piece of fishing line and asking me if I could feel anything.

"No. All I feel is pain in my foot and my leg. I can't feel anything different at all down there."

After two or three of these monthly checkups, they announced that "because I wasn't getting any better," I would have to leave after a few more sessions. I was so upset, angry, confused, scared, and sad that I didn't say anything. Sure, I should have asked some questions like "Can I go someplace else?" but I didn't know how to say that without blowing my top.

It was right during this time that my pain got worse. You see, chronic pain isn't always linear. You can go from getting better to experiencing worse pain for a while before it starts to get better again. Every evening I'd look forward to going to bed because when I was asleep, my leg didn't hurt anymore. Joanna's friend, Tom, who had suffered from chronic pain had told me that when he had a rough day, he could fall asleep comforted by the fact that he would be able to restart the next morning. I can understand that.

When I was dreaming, everything was normal. My foot didn't hurt which meant my mind wasn't tied up in knots thinking about it. I was able to walk and run (as well as occasionally fly) because I was back to normal in my dreams. But even when I *wasn't* dreaming, my mind got a rest from the pain. Sleep was so much better than being awake.

But the moment I woke up, I was hit with this searing, burning pain in my leg and foot. *Not another day of this*, I'd whisper to myself.

It's not that big of a leap from "I'd rather be asleep" to "I'd rather not be alive."

The neurons that bridged that gap did it by starting off with the idea of *I don't want to live my life this way*. The first few neurons fired are like a trickle of water running down a hill, cutting a path that can become a stream over time. Once the stream is there, it becomes easier to think about how you might do it. I've never admitted this out loud but let's just say that I live about two miles from the Chesapeake Bay Bridge.

Before I had been unwillingly thrust into this painful journey that has revealed the full flavor and experience of life, I couldn't understand why anyone would ever want to take their own life. As long as I had hope, as long as I could see a way out, I was willing to fight, and fight hard, to get better, to feel better. But without any hope those thoughts began to wear away, carving a path through my brain. Each morning, I was hit again and again with pain that appeared to be never-ending, or perhaps even getting worse. I began to justify taking my own life, thinking *I'm such a burden. My wife and kids will be fine without me.*

Fortunately, I still had a few brain cells that kicked into self-preservation mode and made me say something. It was at the Basmati Indian Restaurant when I was having dinner with my wife and one of my daughters. I was on one side of the booth with my leg propped up beside me.

"I, um…. don't want to live anymore."

My daughter burst into tears. Joanna said, "We're going to get you some help right away."

She hopped on her phone right there and called someone she knew who referred us to the very best psychiatrist around. The next morning, she took me to see this guy who at $200 an hour was worth every penny of it. He added some more medications into my regime and helped me find a way to process this difficult part of my life by talking things through with me. Surprisingly, I was back on track and feeling better the very next day but continued to see him for another eight months.

At the time I was clueless about how all of this affected my daughter, wife, and the rest of my family. I did know somewhere deep down the importance of saying it out loud to somebody who loved me. My ongoing battle with pain had pulled me down into a dark well where I lost my capability to be empathetic or even aware of anything beyond the end of my leg. Looking back on this time I feel horrible about putting my daughter, wife, and the rest of my family through all of this.

When I initially realized that I wasn't going to heal up within a few months, I set my target to be healed up completely at six months after my injury, which was the date of my daughter's wedding. I was bound and determined to walk my daughter down the aisle without using that ugly cane that made me feel like an old man.

Now, you need to understand that this daughter of mine has always had a great sense of humor. When she was ten years old, she would joke with her sister about what her dad might say at her wedding. "Wait for me, I can't walk," she said as she imitated an old man trying to move along. It was pretty amusing at the time and had become a treasured inside family joke over the years. But once I realized it would actually happen, it wasn't so funny.

At the wedding rehearsal I grimaced and stumbled along beside my daughter until my lovely wife came up and quietly suggested that I should just accept using the cane instead of continuing to struggle trying to walk without it. I took her advice and used the stupid cane. Because I wasn't healed up in six months, I then moved my target out to one year. I told myself, *"Certainly, I'll be healed up by then."*

Author's Note: If you or someone you know is struggling with thoughts of suicide, please take it seriously and find help. Here's one resource that is available 24/7 to call or text: 1-800-273-8255.

7

I CAN'T DO THIS YET

THERE IS NO TELLING HOW MANY
MILES YOU WILL HAVE TO ~~RUN~~ **WALK**
WHILE CHASING A DREAM

ow back to the trail. As you may recall, my leg and foot had been bothering me more and more each day that I hiked. Since I felt confident that suicide wasn't an issue for me any longer, I decided to experiment and see how I would feel if I stopped taking one of my medications for a few days. At that point I was no longer taking the opioid pain killer Oxycontin but was still taking a slew of other pills to reduce pain prescribed by a variety of different doctors. I was even taking pills to treat the side effects of other pills. Despite everything I was on, I was still in horrible pain. My leg was still killing me. It was hurting worse than ever. On top of this I had the hassle of counting pills and getting refills sent to me on the trail.

I don't recommend doing anything like this before checking with your doctor. But I picked one of my medications and quit taking it for three or four days. The result? After a few days, my leg was still killing me. I figured that if my foot and leg were going to hurt whether I took the drug or not, then I really didn't need it. After a few days, I stopped taking another one of my medications and did the same "test."

The result? Yup, my foot still hurt like the dickens, so I dropped that one too. I continued this process over the next few weeks and, one by one, I quit taking all my prescribed medications. I was still taking Advil four or five times a day, mind you, but I'd managed to get off everything else.

It was somewhere during this stretch that I'd stopped to sit down and rest on a log when a hiker walked by with a large white trash bag thrown over his shoulder. Inside the bag I could see what appeared to be camping gear.

"That's a nice lightweight pack you have there," I said.

"Yeah, that's the whole idea," he responded without breaking stride, promptly disappearing into the woods. The next day, I realized that I was almost to Fontana Dam, the last stop before Great Smoky Mountains National Park. I started to see glimpses of Fontana Lake several hours before I got there. As the trail wound its way back and forth across the mountainside, I could see more and more of the lake and was thinking that I'd surely be there any minute. The trail continued to wind its way down in elevation until I finally came out of the woods to a rest stop along the road with a picnic table, restrooms with flush toilets, and running water.

There was a phone on the outside wall of the restrooms, which I used to call Fontana Lodge to come and pick me up. Perhaps this was to offset the fact that there was no cell phone coverage there for myself or any other hikers.

I enjoyed my night at the lodge, having dinner with other hikers who all had stories about their time on the trail. I went online, paid twenty dollars, and printed out the permit required to hike through Great Smoky Mountains National Park. I moved to a nearby hostel the next day because that's where I had asked Joanna to send my resupply box, and I wanted to take a zero before heading into the Smokies.

Once I arrived at the hostel, I opened the resupply box along with the bounce box I'd sent from Neel Gap and dumped it all out on the bed. I sorted through everything, breaking down individual servings into snack-sized bags and then putting each day's food into its own gallon Ziplock bag. I put all the extra white medical tape, Ziplock bags of various sizes, extra bottles of Advil, and a bunch of other stuff back into my bounce box and addressed it to Standing Bear Farm Hostel which was on the trail just north of the Smoky Mountains.

Ben, who owned and ran the hostel with his wife, was nice enough to help me install a new foot brace on my boot. He drilled holes through the leather and installed special eyelets to connect lines to a brace that Velcroed around my ankle to help hold my foot up and keep me from tripping on my injured side.

The following day, I climbed into Ben's SUV along

with *Marigold, Side Step*, and *Stick Walker* to get a ride back down to Fontana Dam. While we drove along, Ben gave us a little pep talk.

"Make sure you stay at the shelters since they'll give you a ticket for stealth camping in the park. Keep your pack with you all the time because if you put your pack down, a bear will come and take it away from you. And another thing, do *not* night hike! There are wild boars in the park, and they are nocturnal hunters. You do not want to run into one of those; they are mean, and they *will* hurt you. Any questions?"

"Uh, no, sir."

It was four years later when I heard that Ben had passed away at the age of eighty-two. He was a fine example of the incredible people you'll meet while hiking the Appalachian Trail. I found that most people who run hostels and other businesses supporting hikers seem to do it more out of a passion for helping out hikers than any financial incentive.

It was a beautiful sunny morning, and I stopped into the gift shop near the dam and bought a Gatorade and some peanut M&Ms. I then followed the trail across the top of Fontana Dam, looking out over the water on one side and the 480-foot drop to the bottom of the valley on the other side. Down there, you could see where the Little Tennessee River has been dammed up since 1944.

I'd never done a video blog before but thought I'd give it a shot. Not knowing how to do it or what to say, I felt a little uncomfortable. I told myself, *how hard can it be? Just do it.* I put my iPhone on a selfie holder towards the end of my hiking pole, and while holding the video camera out in front of me, I tried my best to walk evenly using just one hiking pole for support. The result was a lurching gait with an equally unsteady video shot.

"Hi. This is Flash 52, and I'm hiking the Appalachian–" BAM! *Ouch.* I'd been concentrating so much on looking right at the camera while walking that I didn't see a big metal sign that was sticking out over the walkway. I'd smashed my head right into it.

As I walked along looking for the entrance to Great Smoky Mountains National Park, I was somewhat apprehensive. The Appalachian Trail stretches seventy-one miles through the park, and the only road crossing is US 441 at Newfound Gap. I'd heard stories about rugged terrain and hikers getting stuck in snowstorms, and I was worried about running out of food.

I thought of the Smoky Mountains as a challenging, yet potentially dangerous section. I had expected to hand my hiking permit over to a Park Ranger standing in a booth of some sort, so I was surprised when I came to a small brown box mounted on a pole that said "AT Thru-Hikers Deposit Permits Here." I tore the receipt off the bottom of my permit, stuffed it in the box and then signed the trail register with my trail name and date. I thought for a moment and then added 10:42 AM.

It felt weird to be leaving a note for people that might come looking for me someday. If a bear—or God forbid, one of those wild boars—got me, then they'd be looking at this notebook saying, "Well, he was right here at 10:42 in the morning." Joanna asked me how long she should wait without hearing anything from me to "send in the troops." With cell coverage that's pretty spotty along the trail, that's a tricky question. I found that I could get texts to go out in places where I wasn't able to make a phone call. I told her to wait three days before starting to worry about me.

The trail heading up into the park was primarily smooth dirt, although it was a steady climb up as I gained elevation. I met a park ranger coming down the hill who asked about my hike and wanted to see my permit. For some reason, I felt better about paying the twenty-dollar fee after the ranger checked my permit.

It was a seven-mile day to get to the Birch Spring Gap camping area. This was the only place in the park without a shelter, so camping was allowed. I set up my tent and made dinner while chatting with other hikers around the fire when someone said "Bear!" With no leaves on the trees, we were able to look across a small valley to see a large black bear lumbering across the hillside. It was nice to observe this large creature with a quarter mile of distance between us.

The following day, it took me seven hours to hike another seven miles, reaching Russell Field Shelter just after 4:00 PM. While my leg was bothering me a fair amount, this was offset by the ongoing picture-book vista along the trail. Towering trees surrounded by rocks, branches and fallen logs covered with thick carpets of vibrant green moss stretched out on both sides of the trail as far as I could see.

Although the shelter was already full, everyone squeezed together and made room for me because it was raining out. I went out looking for the privy only to discover that in Tennessee, the shelters don't have privies. They have a shovel instead. The setup is that no one is supposed to dig a cat hole on the side of the mountain that slopes down to the water source. That made sense to me.

I followed the signs that directed me across the trail to the other side of the mountain. I then followed a short trail down to find a minefield with cat holes located every few feet, where prior residents of the shelter had done their business. As you can imagine, this was not a pleasing site. You're supposed to dig a hole at least six inches deep and ideally cover the location with a good-sized rock or log to keep animals from disturbing the, uh, deposits left behind.

The various places flagged with white toilet paper streamers coming up out of the ground, combined with plenty of water from the rain, gave this area a starkly different look and aroma compared to the pristine forest I'd been walking through all day long. I did a one-eighty to go back out to the trail and headed south a few hundred yards to find an appropriate and less popular spot. I decided that while in Tennessee, I'd find a way to go during the day somewhere along the trail instead of contributing to this problem which appeared to result from the increased number of hikers who were now hiking the AT.

By the time "hiker midnight" arrived, between all of us on the sleeping platform and others who squeezed in on the dirt floor, I counted a total of twenty-four people and one service dog in the shelter. The shelter had been designed to sleep fourteen comfortably. Hiker midnight can be anywhere between 7:00-9:00 PM depending on the time of year. It's basically whenever it gets dark out, and everyone goes to sleep.

There are two places on the Appalachian Trail where dogs are not allowed—here in Smoky Mountains National Park and in Baxter State Park at the northern end of the trail. Service dogs are the exception to this, and I spent the night on my side sandwiched between a well-behaved dog in front of me and another hiker behind me.

The next morning, my foot was hurting more than usual, so I took my time doing various stretches and ankle rotations to try and loosen things up. It was still raining out, and I wasn't in any hurry to get going. Everyone had left except for me and two other hikers, *Wild Turkey* and *Tag Along*. *Wild Turkey* pulled out a big honking bottle of—you guessed it— Wild Turkey and explained that because it was his birthday, he was going to get sloshed. He asked both of us if we wanted to join him. *Tag Along* took a swig or two but I told him I'd pass. I wondered if perhaps every day was *Wild Turkey's* birthday.

Later that day, I arrived at the Derrick Knob Shelter to find that not only was the shelter full, but there was a sea of tents everywhere. I scouted around to find a flat spot to claim for my little tent and settled on a narrow strip of land down the hill past a bunch of other tents. There were probably fifteen or twenty of us stationed around one campfire, and I counted three other campfire circles of a similar size. I guessed that there were between sixty and seventy hikers there for the night.

While stopped for lunch the next day, I met *Burl* (named after the knobs that grow on the side of trees) and *Long Beard*, a nice-looking young couple who told me they were headed for the same place that I was—Siler Bald Shelter. When I finally made it to the shelter late in the afternoon, I was surprised and, I'll admit, somewhat elated, to have made it there before them. After claiming my spot by laying out my sleeping pad and bag, I made my macaroni and cheese dinner using my Pocket Rocket stove.

It was about an hour later when *Burl* and *Long Beard* arrived, explaining that they had taken a wrong turn and gone several miles out of their way before realizing their mistake. And get this. I was *pleased* to hear of their misfortune. I didn't admit this to them, of course, but I had gotten there faster than they did and for whatever reason, it gave me a little thrill. While I'm not super proud of this, I think it exemplified how desperate I was to find a win of any sort at this stage.

A little bit later, I asked, "Anyone want to hike up Siler Bald to go see the sunset?"

"I don't need any extra miles," said *TJ*.

"I can see the sunset any day, I don't need to walk any further," responded *Rapunzel*.

Okay, I thought, *no worries. I'll just go up there myself.*

I limped my way back to the trail and found a small sign pointing the way to Siler Bald up through a grassy meadow. Balds are mountains without trees or brush, so they give great 360-degree views. The theories on why balds exist vary. One idea was that severely cold climates drove down forests, which were then replaced by grasslands or tundra. Some people say that Native Americans kept the trees from growing back. Others believe European settlers maintained balds by grazing livestock, but the balds are known to predate European settlement. Descriptions of the balds date back to the seventeenth century, but why they exist is still a bit of a mystery.

At the top, I met two section hikers who had a tent set up. This seemed to be a cold and windy place to camp, but they appeared prepared for it. I put my iPhone into the holder on one of my hiking poles and stuck the pole into the ground.

I wanted to make another attempt at taking a time-lapse video of the sun going down. I sat down on a rock so that I could be in the video. We could see Fontana Lake off in the distance to the west as the sun got lower and the colors became more vibrant.

I tried to sit still for the time-lapse shot but ended up turning my head back and forth as I talked with the other two hikers. The sunset came out great, but when I played it back, it looked weird because my head had been moving. *Oh well. There will be other sunsets.* Looking back, I see the irony. I'd been seeking company and not wanting to be alone. Then once I had company, I was busy fussing around trying to get a nice video instead of just enjoying the sunset and the conversation.

This moment was also one of my first experiences trying to capture some of the magic that happened along the Appalachian Trail. I was enthralled with that moment on top of Siler Bald. I think it was a combination of the views in all directions, the smell of fresh air, the cool breeze, and the satisfaction of having made it through another day of hiking that created a welling up of emotion. A sense of *Wow! This is so incredible, it's a once in a lifetime view of mountains, lakes, and plains as far as I could see. So beautiful.*

Once the sun went down, I retrieved my iPhone and hiking poles, wished the two guys good luck staying warm as it would be a cold night, and started back down the hill to the shelter. On the way down, I met another hiker, *Caveman,* who as it turned out, was the same guy that I saw a few days ago hiking with the white trash bag as his pack. He told me that he couldn't find the shelter and was worried about being stuck overnight out in the cold without other people around. He had seen us up on top of the bald so came to see if we could help him.

"Sure thing. You can follow me. I'm going there now."

As I made my way down the hill at my usual slow pace, *Caveman* stayed right with me rather than walking ahead as most other hikers would. I was thinking he wanted to make sure that he got to the shelter. One thing I couldn't help but notice was that he was hiking in a pair of penny loafers.

Hard as I tried to capture that moment up on the bald, by the time I was back down in the shelter and going to sleep, the ethereal essence was already drifting away. I had lived the experience but could not hold on to it. Sure, I had the video along with a few photos to help me remember what that one moment was like. But if the experience was all 120 colors of crayons, then a photo was like showing you one crayon. Maybe the video was worth two crayons.

But once come and gone, that one moment forever lived in the past. I think this is one reason that something like an Appalachian Trail hike is so special. I knew that I would be at each of these spots along the trail one time in my life. For me, even though my foot was shouting out at me every time I stepped on it, I was content in knowing that I made it up the hill to see that sunset.

I'm sure that it was freezing for the two hikers who camped up on Siler Bald that night, as I had a hard time staying warm down in the shelter. A few different times, I woke up and did sit-ups in my sleeping bag to generate some heat.

The next morning, *Caveman* salvaged an old backpack that he'd found in a hiker box by using my sewing needle and floss to reattach one of the support straps that had ripped out. The two of us headed out together, and I was pleasantly surprised to discover that, once again, he was willing to walk along with me at my slower pace.

I stopped by an Appalachian Trail sign and asked him to take my picture. As I was handing my phone over to him, it slipped and fell on the rocks breaking the screen. *Caveman* immediately apologized and insisted that I take his phone to replace mine. I thanked him for offering but let him know that it wasn't a big deal even though I was a little upset about breaking it.

While hiking along that morning, I got to know more about *Caveman*. He was quite a character. I learned that he had started hiking the trail with only twenty dollars in his pocket and claimed that he did the first nineteen miles with no shoes on. He managed to find enough food and gear from hiker boxes at hostels or hiker motels, which was where he found the pair of penny loafers. He told me that he preferred wearing them because he could "feel the trail" when he walked. *Caveman* said he made sure to hit hiker boxes at every stop along the trail to get food along with all his gear.

Later in the day, he opened up a bit more, but I'll have to admit that not all of it seemed to make sense. He told me that his parents sent him off to college and were paying all his expenses to get a good education. He told me how he concluded that to learn about the things that truly mattered, he wanted to interact with people and that college wasn't the right place to do that. He then left college and moved to San Francisco where he decided to be homeless on purpose to "master the psychological relationships between people."

This guy was articulate and wasn't lacking in confidence. I think that in ordinary life, most of us probably tend to hang around other people who are just like ourselves. But on the Appalachian Trail, I had the chance to meet all sorts of people. Here's some of our conversation from that day.

Caveman: "At times I feel like I don't know anything at all. And then other times, I realize that I know everything there is to know."

Me: "Really? Is that so? Are you going to keep hiking all the way to Maine?"

Caveman: "I don't know, I'm going to see how it goes. If I'm having fun, I'll keep going. If not, I'll go do something else. My biggest problem with hiking is that I can't find anyone who's as interesting to talk to as I am."

I'm not sure where that leaves me.

Caveman was certainly one fascinating guy. I sometimes wonder how much further he made it on the trail and what he's doing now.

The weather forecast wasn't great for the rest of the day, so I stopped at Double Spring Gap Shelter to position myself three miles short of Clingman's Dome, which at 6,643 feet above sea level is the highest point on the Appalachian Trail. I thought I'd get up early and hike up to see the sunrise the next morning. I didn't want to wake up the other hikers in the shelter by setting an alarm. I figured that I woke up often enough that I'd be able to look at the time and pack up quietly and leave at about 4:00 AM so that I'd arrive in time for the sunrise. I woke up, and it was still dark out, but I felt like I'd been sleeping for a long time. I couldn't see what time it was because my phone had run out of power, and I didn't want to make any noise digging around to find my battery pack. So, I packed up quietly and left.

I made it most of the way up to Clingman's Dome, but it was still dark out. On top of that, the weather wasn't looking that great with a thick fog mist blowing across the landscape. I still didn't know what time it was but decided to hunker down and wait for the fog to burn off and the sun to start coming up before I hiked up to the very top.

I moved off to the side of the trail and found a moss-covered depression underneath a pine tree. I pulled out my Tyvek ground cloth, blew up my sleeping pad, and climbed into my sleeping bag so that I could stay warm. It wasn't very comfortable because I was sliding down the hill, and the mist was getting my sleeping bag all wet. I stayed there for an hour or so, thinking the whole time that it wasn't a good idea.

Once several hikers came past me headed up the trail, I packed everything up and continued up the hill. *Bookworm*, an older gentleman, caught up to me and told me that he was starving. He explained that he had accidently left his food bag behind on the bear cables at a shelter two days ago. I gave him two of my protein bars, but he refused to accept any more food saying that his wife would drive up the tourist road and meet him up on Clingman's Dome.

Once I made it to the top of Clingman's Dome, I walked up the circular ramp to the observation tower to look out into the white fog blocking my view. *No sunrise for me today.* I looked at photos on the placards mounted on the railing to give me an idea of what the view would have been on a good day, and then headed back down the circular ramp.

After eight miles of mostly downhill hiking, I came to Newfound Gap. When I stepped off the trail into the parking lot, *Toasty* offered to give me a ride into Gatlinburg, Tennessee. She was hiking the trail using two cars, driving each car north a few days from the spot where she'd previously left a car, then hiking south to get to the other car. This meant she was hiking south each day while the segments she was completing were moving northward.

I stayed at a hiker motel that had cheap rates along with décor and service to match. For example, it was 10:30 at night when I finally decided to climb into bed. I pulled the bed cover down to see the previous occupants' rumpled sheets still on the bed. Apparently, housekeeping had done a quick room cleaning that included pulling up the covers but not much else. I called the motel office, but there was no answer, so I pulled out my sleeping bag and slept on top of the bed.

Gatlinburg was a town packed full of tourist attractions, including t-shirt shops, go-kart tracks, water-slide parks, a Ripley's Believe it or Not, and a huge variety of fast food, ice cream, candy, and fudge shops. A couple of young hikers, *Go* and *Fast*, went around to every place that offered free samples of moonshine.

"Hey, it's free. Why not?"

I did my laundry at the motel and bought resupplies nearby so as to not have to walk very far on my zero day.

Two days later, I came to an unnamed camping area towards the end of the day and saw that many other hikers had already set up their tents. I found a spot to put up my little tent, inflated my air pad, and pulled out my sleeping bag, fluffing it up to be ready for the night. Someone had already started a fire, and I sat down to make dinner and talk with other hikers. *Macho Man* said he'd found some glasses up at one of the overlooks and wanted to know if anyone had been missing a pair. I looked at them as they were passed around, and they looked familiar to me. I checked the pocket inside my pack to confirm that I, indeed, was missing my glasses.

"Yes! These are mine. Thank you so much!"

Since it was April 1st, our conversation wandered into talking about good April Fool's Day jokes that we might be able to play on someone. We contemplated a few different ideas, such as telling our wives about a broken leg, making up a bear attack story, or sending a message saying we were lost in the woods. We ultimately discarded these ideas after thinking through the possible repercussions. A hiker called *Dirt* came up with an idea and decided to try it out by sending his mom a text.

Dirt:	how to treat snake bite?
Mom:	let me find out
Dirt:	ok
Mom:	suck venom out
Dirt:	ok
Mom:	no wait—don't do that
Dirt:	??
Mom:	lie down with wound below the heart
Mom:	keep calm, remain still as possible

After about ten minutes of this, *Dirt* figured he'd taken the joke far enough and let his mother know that it was an April Fool's joke. We all had a good laugh, although I'm sure this maneuver was hard on his mom. She may not have appreciated it as much as we did.

I woke up the following day, and all was well. I could hear a light rain coming down on my tent, but I was warm and cozy inside my sleeping bag. I couldn't help but notice that my foot was hurting, and I stretched out my leg to find a position that felt slightly better.

I could see from the light making its way through my tent that the sun was up, and I could hear other hikers moving about and packing up for the day. Despite sleeping for the past twelve hours, I was still feeling tired. *Just another thirty minutes*, I thought to myself.

By the time I exited my tiny tent, everyone else had already left for the day. Each time I stepped down on my left side I winced in pain. *Ow! Oocha!* This thing was really killing me. On top of that (not that I'm complaining mind you) when I stepped down on my right side, I experienced shooting pains from my overworked knee. And that was from my *good side*!

I realized that I'd obviously overworked my good leg. As my injured leg was hurting more and more each day, I had spent more time on the side that wasn't injured. Instead of half my time on each leg like normal people, I took good long steps with my right leg combined with a mini limp on my injured left leg.

To make it even worse, the Smoky Mountains, as you might imagine, have plenty of ups and downs to get up and over various hills and mountains. To help keep the trails from washing out, and make it easier to climb the steep sections, the trail maintainers (whom I do appreciate, by the way) put logs across the trail and filled in the uphill side with dirt to make steps.

These log steps can vary in height from as low as four inches up to two feet high. To protect my injured left side, I always stepped up using my stronger right leg. That added up to hundreds of steps each day. Now, the knee on my good leg was hurting so badly that I could barely put any weight on it.

I sat down to think for a bit. *I can't go any further,* was the first thought that went through my head. *Oh sure! What are you going to do? Call 911 for another rescue?* I thought about how crazy stupid I would look after my rescue three weeks ago at Deep Gap Shelter. I pulled out my phone and turned it on to see if I had any service.

Nope. No signal whatsoever. *Not that it matters. I'm not calling 911 even if I did have coverage, so let's figure out another way to handle this situation.*

Sometimes, I'd pretend that there was someone else with me to bounce ideas off. One of my beliefs is that we all discount our abilities, whether they are physical or mental. By asking my imaginary friend what they think I might be able to do, I'm able to set aside my own limiting beliefs for a moment and ask my brilliant imaginary friend what he thinks.

"Your injured leg is going to have to take over as your stronger leg."

"WHAT?" my injured leg replied.

Yup, I've overworked, overdone, chapoooched, my "good" right side. You've had it easy, so now you (my injured leg) *are going to have to step up and over every log, rock, root, and tree that we come across on the trail. That's the only way that we can give Mr. Right Leg a rest so that he can have a chance to heal up.*

"Maybe that will allow it to get better," my imaginary friend chimed in.

Okay, that's my challenge for the day, I thought. *All I have to do is find a way to use my crappy injured leg to step up every time I come to a log or rock step as I make my way through the rest of the Smokies. Once I get through the park, I can always hitch a ride somewhere and get some help if I need it.*

I heard the voice of a former business partner in my head. You know, the guy who kept telling me I couldn't do something because he knew that it would challenge me to prove him wrong?

"I don't think you can do this, Peter," he would say. "Nope, this is going to be too hard for you. I don't think that you can get that done."

Oh, yeah? I'll show you! I'll find a way no matter what to make this happen.

Once I had packed all my things up, I slowly limped northward up the trail. With each big step I encountered, I'd use my injured left side to do the work of stepping up. I'd tell myself that *this is just for the next few days so that I can rest up my good leg.* Or when I got even more tired and sore later in the afternoon, *it's just for the next few hours.* Even if I had to break it down into the lowest common denominator like *it's just one step up,* that's what I did to keep going. *How hard can that be? I don't think that you can do this. OH YEAH?? Watch me!*

Over the next few days, I continued this process. I moved along even slower than my usual snail's pace, taking my time and using my injured leg to do all the heavy lifting. I also used my technique of going backwards while going down steep hills to make it easier on my knees. After doing this for several days, my right leg appreciated the break from doing all the work and felt better. My knee stopped hurting.

It was mid-morning the next day when I came across a side trail with a sign indicating the Mt. Cammerer Lookout was a little over half a mile away. The guidebook said a unique fire lookout was built out on a rock looking across the valley. As I pondered whether I was willing to walk the extra distance, *Frostbite* came by, looked at the sign, and said, "An extra 1.2 miles? No thanks." He kept going. Most thru-hikers want credit for every step; extra steps really need to feel worth it.

I thought, *what the heck? I'm only coming by here one time; I'm going to go see it.* The trail heading over to the lookout was relatively flat, although I had difficulty climbing up the rocks to get to the building itself. I wasn't sure I could climb up to the building, but after trying for ten minutes, I finally figured a way to make it up to the lookout.

The building was an octagonal structure that was built on a rocky point beginning in 1937 by the Civilian Conservation Corps. It had a 360-degree view of the surrounding area and operated as a fire lookout until the 1960s, when modern fire detection methods replaced it. It then fell into disrepair until it was restored in 1996.

Realizing that I had cell service, I sat inside the building keeping an eye out for occasional breaks in the clouds while chatting first with one of my daughters and then my wife. Later in the afternoon, I finally arrived at the north end of Great Smoky Mountains National Park. I realized I had made it through the Smoky Mountains and thought, if I could do that, then I could surely make it to Mt. Katahdin.

I walked along I-40 looking for a white blaze to show me where the trail went. The most complicated place to follow the Appalachian Trail can be on a road walk or through a town. The white blazes aren't front and center on the side of a tree like they are in the woods. Perhaps to have a minimal impact on the area, the trail maintaining clubs don't put up a wooden post with a blaze on it as I'd seen when going over mountain balds.

The white blazes seem hidden away, almost like they were hints rather than guideposts. You must look carefully to find them on guardrail posts or maybe on a narrow stop sign pole. There's no set distance for how far apart the blazes are, so if you don't see anything, it's hard to know if you're "off the trail" or just need to go another hundred yards to get the next "hint."

I could have pulled out my phone and opened the FarOut app, but I was dead tired, and my foot was killing me. I didn't want to expend any extra effort. I don't know if it was due to walking on the road or what, but my left foot was really hurting each time I stepped on it. I just wanted to find the hostel so I could sit down and put my foot up. I was heading up a gravel road, wondering how much further it could be, when a dusty white pickup truck came to a screeching halt next to me.

A weathered and somewhat grimy looking man asked, "You'ins heading to that thar Hostel?"

"Uh, yes sir. I am."

"Hop on in back. I'll take ya thar."

I swung my poles and pack into the back of the truck and climbed up into the bed myself. The driver took off spinning the wheels and we bounced along up the bumpy road. I watched a big cloud of swirling dust that followed us for a few minutes. Soon, we pulled up in front of the hostel and I did my best to gracefully climb out. I then met *Grumpy*, who oversaw running Standing Bear Farm Hostel.

He was barefoot, wearing a dirty white shirt, a pair of overalls, and (I'm not making this up) chewing on a piece of hay that was sticking out of his mouth. The driver asked him if he needed any more moonshine and *Grumpy* pulled out a bottle, took a swig, and assured the driver that he was doing fine.

"Hi there! My name is *Flash 52*, and I'd like a bunk or bed for the night."

"Uh-huh. I'll bet you do with all that thar rain headed this-a way. I gotta spot in a queen bay-ahd. Run ya twenty bucks."

"Ok, sounds great. I'll take it," I said.

"Alllllll riiiiight. We're pretty full so I might put another hiker on the otha side of the bay-ahd."

"Oh really? Let me get you another twenty dollars. I'd like to buy both sides of the bed."

"Nope. No can do. Gotta leave room for someone else to get out of the rain."

Okey dokee then.

Outside the door to the bunkhouse were twenty pairs of hiking boots lined up with flowers planted in them. There was a creek that ran right down the middle of Standing Bear Farm. The footbridge handrail was made of an old chain welded into the shape of, well, more flowers. The courtyard was filled with a huge half-finished tile mosaic with, you guessed it, flowers.

The "laundry" was an old washboard in a sink and an electric dryer that was still working away at drying my trail clothes after over two hours. The whole place had sort of a hippy style Gilligan's Island-type feel to it. The kitchen area was outdoors with an overhanging roof and was built out of, from what I could tell, leftover building supplies.

An old explosives shed had been converted into a resupply room with a hundred times the variety of any other place I'd seen along the trail. They provided you with a small tally sheet to add up the food and supplies you took so that you could settle up when you left. I liked this system. The only problems was, except for some frozen pizzas, everything in there was years past the expiration date.

Don't get me wrong. It was all well-organized and marked with prices. It just looked like generic house label stuff bought from a remnants store after it had gone out of business. I grabbed a few supplies I needed and a frozen pizza. The "kitchen" didn't have an oven, but it did have a small pizza oven designed to cook one at a time.

I stuck my pepperoni pizza in and turned the knob to high. I sat down to chat with some other hikers while looking at my guidebook pages to plan out how far I might hike over the next few days. To save weight, I had torn out eight or ten pages of the guidebook and sent the rest of the book up the trail in my bounce box. After thirty minutes, I checked on my pizza. It was warmed up a little but still had a way to go before it would be done.

One of the other hikers there was *Matchu*. She was maybe twenty-three years old and wearing a matching lime green and blue hiking outfit. After talking with her for a bit, I mentioned that I was a real estate investor. She glared at me and said, "Oh, so you're someone who CHEATS people who are in foreclosure out of their homes."

"No, that's not how it works," I replied. I was surprised to hear a comment that was not only negative but attacked my character as well. Every other hiker I had talked with so far was, for the most part, positive and supportive of the other hikers around them. Having made my living both investing and teaching others how to invest in real estate, I took this as a bit of a personal attack, but I kept my mouth shut.

Since it was raining, the little sitting area in the kitchen was the only place to stay dry while waiting for my pizza to heat up. *Matchu* went on to make various negative comments about any other topic I brought up while chatting with the other hikers, and I did my best to ignore her.

I checked my pizza every half hour or so, and after two hours, I finally pulled it out because I was getting rather hungry. The cheese mostly melted, but the inside, while not frozen anymore, hadn't really heated up. I think the trick to enjoying moments like that was to think about how that was the only time in my life, my only opportunity, to experience a place as wacky as that while hiking the Appalachian Trail. I felt like I was in a separate reality as I sat there eating my hardly warmed pizza for dinner.

The next morning, I came back into the cabin after eating my usual trail breakfast of two cinnamon-frosted Pop-Tarts. Lucky for me, no one else was assigned to the other side of my queen bed. There were a few other hikers in my cabin and one of them was *Matchu*.

I noticed that she had left her pack ready to go except

142

for the top, which was left open like a lunch bag waiting for an apple. A terrible idea went through my head. I laughed to myself and contemplated.

I stepped outside, looked around. I didn't see her. I'm sure I had a strange smirk on my face as I grabbed a soda can-sized rock. Actually, it was more like the size of a bag of coffee, a big bag of coffee. I carried it over to her pack, dug down a ways, and hid it carefully towards the bottom. Let me say that I'm definitely not proud of that. Not proud at all. But you're along for the ride with me on this adventure, and that's what I did. And while I didn't see *Matchu* on the trail again, I'm sure that when she discovered the rock in her pack, she knew who put it there.

Two days later, I arrived at Max Patch, my favorite part of the trail thus far. A big grassy bald located 4,629 feet in elevation, it's not the highest summit in the immediate vicinity. Still, with a 360-degree view of blue and purple mountains off in the distance, it's gorgeous. *Frostbite, Sandman*, and *Freeloader* had their tent set up and were cooking something for lunch.

They were running forward, doing handsprings, and landing on their feet again. I tried doing this, but since I can't actually run, I hobbled along and ended up doing a headstand with my legs sticking up at odd angles. They were nice enough to take some photos for me which, due to an intense-looking cloud cover, came out looking amazing when you turn the photo upside down.

It was another couple of miles to reach Roaring Fork Shelter, where I would be the only occupant for the night. The logbook mentioned a nearby kennel that I could verify due to the sound of dogs barking all night long. Another night on the trail, another unforgettable experience.

In the morning, I left by 7:00 AM so that I could make it to Lemon Gap to catch a 10:30 shuttle to Asheville Airport to fly down to Florida and see my son compete in the Collegiate Paintball National Championships. He didn't know that I was coming. I thought I'd surprise him.

He was the president of his paintball team at Clemson University and had done a great job promoting and expanding the paintball club. When he took over the position, the team was barely getting by with $1,500 a year in funding. He managed to grow the team, so they had several lines of players, multiple sponsors and eventually received $30,000 a year in funding from the college.

Once I arrived in Florida, I rented a van, bought a bunch of orange and purple removable paint, and plastered the side of the van with "Go Tigers!" and other phrases to rally the team. I got to the event early to get a good parking spot and positioned the van where he and his team would see it when they drove in. My son told me later that when he arrived with his teammates and saw the van, he said, "Hey guys, we've got fans!"

I got up at 4:30 AM the following day to catch an early flight back to Asheville, then had the same shuttle driver drive me back to Lemon Gap to continue my journey northward on the Appalachian Trail. As I started back hiking, my foot and leg were hurting more than usual. You'd think that after a few days off, my leg would be feeling better, but for some reason, it wasn't.

That was a long day. I had to make it over fourteen miles to get to Hot Springs where I planned to sit in a hot tub and rest up for a few days. I was tired, frustrated, and mentally worn out from dealing with the constant pain in my leg. It was late in the afternoon, and I still had miles to go. With each step I took, it was pain, pain, pain.

Somehow everything piled up inside my head and I started crying. Well, actually, I was bawling my eyes out. I figured I was all alone out on the Appalachian Trail, *so why not?* As I write this, I realize it wasn't long after I had stopped taking all of the meds from my psychiatrist and that might have something to do with the surge of emotions. Perhaps inserting myself back into civilization and seeing my son also had me feeling a bit nostalgic for a normal, non-hiking life.

As I walked down the trail crying like a baby, I worked my way through all the frustration, all the anger… *Why is my leg hurting so much?* and *Why do I have to deal with this? Why is this trail so long and why am I feeling so sad?*

I opened up and let it all out.

"Waaaaaahh!"

After about an hour of sobbing my way along the trail, things started to stabilize. Maybe this was an outlet for the continuous pain I'd been experiencing; somehow a place for it all to go. My crying had helped to alleviate (or at least acknowledge) the pain just a bit, for that moment at least. So, I stopped, wiped away my tears, and kept walking. It was well past sunset when I finally got to the edge of Hot Springs.

If I'd known better, I would have stayed at a hostel just off the trail, but I'd made reservations to stay at the Hot Springs Lodge, figuring that was the place to be if I wanted to make sure that I could go for a dip in the hot springs. I limped my way across town, feeling every step on the hard concrete sidewalk.

When I arrived at the lodge, there wasn't a sign indicating where to check-in. I called the phone number, left a message, and then checked the doors, which were both locked. Drats! And I'd pre-paid for both that night and the next. I saw a small picnic shelter over on the lawn about ten or fifteen feet in diameter. I put my air mattress and sleeping bag under the picnic table and sat down, cooked my dinner, and went to sleep under the table.

The next day, I finally found the registration office. It was down the street in another building. They kindly refunded the previous night's fee and gave me the key to my room. I signed up for a hot tub in a little cabana right by the river. They filled it up with water from the hot springs—lovely, except that it would have been much nicer if I had some other people to hang out with. The hot water felt incredible as I stretched my calf muscles out on my injured side.

I went to the outfitter to pick up a few boxes of things I had ordered from Amazon. I made sure to buy some of my supplies there since they were nice enough to allow me to ship my packages there. I had lunch, went back to the lodge, and sorted out my food by putting each day's supply in its own gallon Ziplock bag. When it got dark, I went to dinner, hoping to meet some other hikers but ended up eating by myself.

I realized I should have stayed at the hostel; I could have saved some money, and I'd have had other hikers to talk with while not feeling so isolated and alone. I hadn't yet learned the importance of deliberately looking for little things that I could control, like seeking out companionship. This could be a helpful distraction, someone to share my story with, someone to help me hold the pain rather than having to do it all by myself.

As I fueled up at the breakfast place the next day, I realized it had been seven weeks since I started hiking the trail. With all the rest days I'd taken along with going to see my son, I estimated that I had accomplished a total of four weeks of actual hiking days so far. Considering what I'd been through lately, I felt good about the progress I'd made, yet also realized that I might have to get by with less rest days if I was going to make it to Mt. Katahdin in time.

I followed the white blazes marking the Appalachian Trail right down Main Street and over the French River, making the mistake of hiking past the turn that was just past the bridge. I went another hundred yards before realizing I hadn't seen a blaze in a while and turned back to find the trail along the west side of the river.

The river was flowing briskly with the water level high enough that the trail almost touched the river's edge in a few places. I stopped to talk with hikers who were camped right by the river. Most of them were going to the jazz festival in town the coming weekend. The trail turned uphill, and switch backed steeply up to the top of the ridge. I walked by Lover's Leap, where legend has it a Cherokee girl named Mist-on-the-Mountain jumped to the river in the hope of being reunited with her recently deceased lover.

I found a little campsite along the trail, decided to stop for the night, and put up my tent. I walked a short way back down the trail, found some firewood, brought it back to the campsite, and made a nice campfire. As I sat by the fire eating my dinner, I thought about my experience so far. I was content to be there on the ridge, making progress on the trail and, hopefully, healing my leg.

Two days later, I worked my way north after spending the night at Spring Mountain Shelter with four other thru-hikers. It was a lovely morning, and the birds were singing, but I found myself dragging along, something that I didn't usually feel until the end of the day when I was worn out. I called a friend of mine, Nate from North Carolina, thinking that maybe he'd want to come hike with me.

"Wow! I can't believe you're hiking the trail," he said. "Maggie and I have been knocking out portions of the trail hiking with Warren Doyle's group, and I hope to finish the rest of the trail as soon as I can get caught up on my work around here."

I knew that he was an active outdoor person, but I wasn't aware that he'd been hiking the AT. He wished me good luck and promised to follow up when he had more time to go hiking again.

When I reached Allen Gap, I saw a flyer announcing the Greeneville Hiking and Cycling Club's annual trail magic event.

"Food, drink, pastries, burgers, grilled chicken and more, only six miles north of here!"

Just what I needed as a pick-me-up. Maybe this would help give me a boost to counter the drab feelings I'd been experiencing lately. My previous experiences with "trail magic ahead" had usually ended with my arriving just after the food was put away and the trail angels had left. The flyer said the Hiking Club would be there for the entire weekend, but I picked up my pace and did my best to move along so I could get there before the food was gone.

After a steady climb up 2,500 ft in elevation, I finally arrived at Camp Creek Bald. I found a massive, long tent built out of blue tarps that enclosed a vast buffet line with all kinds of fresh fruit, home-baked bread muffins, nuts, bagels, homemade jams and jellies, sodas, three different types of fruit juice, and much more. Outside, a couple of guys wearing chef's hats were cooking up a selection of meats on a giant grill. They had put down a significant section of indoor/outdoor carpeting, covered it with a canopy to keep the sun off, and had tables and chairs for us to sit down while we were eating.

I started off with a bunch of fresh fruit followed by a few BBQ chicken pieces, a couple of cans of Coke, along with some home-baked bread and chocolate chip cookies. I sat around enjoying this goldmine of great tasting food and the company of club members and other hikers who stopped by. I figured I'd stick around for breakfast the next day, so I flattened some weeds in the field on the other side of the parking lot to make a place to put up my tent. Then I joined the club members as we sat around a nice campfire, and I had three or four S'mores before finally retiring in my tent for the night.

Breakfast was scrumptious as well: eggs, bacon, sausage, pancakes, French toast, more baked goods, orange juice, and plenty of coffee. A special thanks goes out to the Greeneville Hiking and Cycling Club. I reluctantly picked up my pack, slung it over my shoulder, and bid these wonderful trail angels goodbye.

After another seven miles of hiking, I ended the day camping out on top of Big Butt Mountain. My thinking was that a stellar view might give me a big dose of encouragement or motivation. To see the view, I had to climb up on a big rock, which was where I watched the sun go down. Sounds nice, but there wasn't any place for me to sit down, so the whole time I was standing up there I was thinking about how my stupid foot was bothering me instead of enjoying the experience.

I felt conflicted. I was trying to have a good time while realizing that I wasn't. Because my tent wasn't setup in an actual campsite, I made a campfire in the middle of an old dirt road that ran through the area and cooked my dinner. I sat there looking at the flames while thinking about my hike. There I was, sitting on a dirt road all by myself, alone yet again, feeling lonely and worn out.

The following day I trudged along, unable to escape the black cloud of despair that had been hanging over my head lately. I was tired and didn't have my usual "I'm doing this anyway" pep in my step anymore. On top of this, of course, my foot was hurting like the dickens.

I came down through a meadow to where the trail crossed a paved country road, and I pulled out the pages I had torn out of the guidebook to see what might be nearby. There was a listing for a hostel seven-tenths of a mile down the road. I sat down, fantasizing about how nice it would be to shower, get cleaned up, and resupply. But my foot was hurting so much that I'd struggled just to keep going down the trail. The thought of walking over a mile to get to the hostel and back just did not compute for me. There was no way that I was going to walk there.

I got up, took a deep breath, and swung my pack onto my back. I headed across the road and started climbing over the stile, which had been built for hikers to get over the barbed wire fence. A flyer for the hostel had been posted on the top of the stile. It said, "Need a ride? Give us a call."

Bingo. Ten minutes later, I was in a Jeep with the wind whistling through my hair as Jeff, the hostel owner, drove me down the road. The hostel was made up of a tiny store housing the resupplies, along with a one-car garage that had been converted into a bunk room. The garage's front had a window screen across the front of it, making it look like a chicken coop. Instead of grass, bushes, or trees, the entire area was covered with gravel. The idea of trying to rest up with cars whizzing by twenty-five feet away didn't appeal to me.

I went into the store, plugged my phone and battery pack in to charge, and paid to use the shower. Since I was feeling so low, I knew that staying in that crappy garage wasn't going to cheer me up but figured I'd at least take a shower and get cleaned up. The shower stall was teeny tiny with water that barely trickled out. I could stand up but didn't have room to reach down and wash my legs without opening up the door first. At least the water was warm.

One of the sayings on the trail is: "You have to embrace the suck." When it gets really bad, like if it's been raining for days, you have to find a way to laugh at how miserable it is, knowing that it's all just part of the journey.

I hadn't learned that yet, and I wasn't laughing.

I dried off, put my dirty hiking clothes back on, and walked around to see what my resupply options were. My breakfast of two frosted cinnamon Pop-Tarts gave me 420 calories and the mental boost that comes from one of the best parts of hiking: you can eat whatever you want without worrying about gaining weight.

Cinnamon frosted Pop-Tarts hold a special place in my heart as one of my favorite childhood foods. Coming from a family with seven kids, we didn't get many extras, so Pop-Tarts were just for special occasions. My affection for them was cemented one day when my two brothers and I were in trouble for one thing or another. The three of us had been sent to our room, where we were to stay until we cleaned it up.

As I recall, one of us said, "This is going to take forever… are you going to STARVE us, or can we have something to eat?"

"Once your room is cleaned up, then you can have your supper."

There was some further conversation about slave labor and child abuse, and one of us cried, "But Mom, you have to feed us!" In hindsight, I don't know why we didn't just clean the room and get it over with. I'm guessing that we were intimidated because our room was an absolute disaster zone.

So then, one of us (I can't remember who, but it may have been me) snuck downstairs and got a box of frosted cinnamon Pop-Tarts to feed the "prisoners." We had a great time eating the Pop-Tarts before finally doing a quick clean of our room. In case you're not familiar, a quick clean is where you push everything that's on the floor under a bed or into the closet. It's brotherly teamwork at its finest.

I sure did enjoy having my share of those frosted cinnamon Pop-Tarts, and to this day, I still hold them as dear to my heart. Back to the hostel, I browsed through Jeff's little store where everything was cheap off-brand stuff. Instead of Kellogg's Pop-Tarts, it was X Brand toaster pastries. They look kind of like Pop-Tarts but don't taste nearly as good.

Since that was my only choice, I bought the fake Pop-

Tarts, paid eight dollars for the shower, and asked Jeff to take me back to the trailhead. I really needed to take a break and recharge, but here I was, being picky about where I would stay. I was so worn down that I had started looking for what was wrong rather than staying positive. I was upset about the stupid Pop-Tarts. I was frustrated that I couldn't get to know other hikers because I couldn't hike fast enough to keep up with them for more than a few minutes.

I was lonely, tired, and worn out.

More than anything else, the constant fight against the pain was slowly but surely wearing me down. It seemed like each day, my foot was hurting more and more. This was slowly eroding the determination that had taken me this far. I needed all the willpower I could get if I was going to make it to Mt. Katahdin in Maine. Jeff gave me a ride in his Jeep back up to the trail where I stepped out, climbed over the stile, and slowly limped through the grassy meadow into the woods.

I managed to hike another three or four miles before deciding I'd had it for the day. I began looking for a place to spend the night. I came across two other hikers who had squeezed into a little flat spot along the trail, but there wasn't room for me to put my tent up.

Despite this, because I was so tired and wanted someone to talk with, I decided to squeeze my tent onto the far edge of the trail, even though there really wasn't room. And then, for good measure, I accidentally broke the main tent pole that holds everything up. It seemed like everything around me was coming undone.

I noticed as I talked with the other hikers that night about our reasons for hiking the Appalachian Trail that I didn't seem to have as much conviction as I've had in the past. I'd started my hike almost two months ago with a massive supply of hope and optimism. I had been determined to make it to Maine no matter what. But my foot hurting every time I stepped on it combined with the isolation and loneliness I was experiencing had punctured a leak in my giant balloon full of "get up and go."

The next day my leg and foot were hurting so much that all I could think about was getting to the next place where I could stop and rest. The only way I can describe it is if you imagine trying to walk with a broken foot—that's what it was like. I didn't notice that springtime had arrived, bringing with it warmer weather, birdsong, and greenery along the trail. My focus was on the pain in my leg and the insanity of what I was trying to accomplish.

Somehow it never occurred to me that the overwhelming pain could be related to the fact that I had stopped taking all my pain meds just ten days before. Looking back, I'm surprised that I didn't consider taking anything stronger than Advil at this point. I'm not sure why I didn't think of this other than I had already tried that route. I was sick of being on all those medications and just wanted to leave it behind. I wasn't any more likely to start back using strong pain killers than I'd turn around and walk southward back to Georgia.

I tried pushing myself along with more pep-talks.

"You can do it!"

"You've got this!"

"Just keep going!"

All I could think of was getting off the trail. At 10:30 AM, I sat down on a log, pulled out my guidebook pages, and looked for someplace that I could take a break. It was another twenty-five miles to Erwin, Tennessee, which is where I had planned on taking a zero and resupplying my food again.

Then I realized I could get a shuttle into Erwin from Sam's Gap, which was less than a mile ahead. I called and spoke to Tom, who arranged to have his wife pick me up an hour later. I felt relieved as I walked the rest of the way downhill and then underneath Highway 26 to a small, paved parking area where Mary picked me up in her Subaru.

Fifteen minutes later, I was dropped off at the Super 8 Hotel, which I chose because it was inexpensive and close to both restaurants and downtown Erwin. I checked in and flopped down on the bed, where I dozed on and off throughout the day until I noticed that it was getting dark outside.

I ordered a pizza and had it delivered because I didn't want to have to walk anywhere. I wasn't feeling any better the following day, so I ate the leftover pizza for breakfast and laid back down on the bed. I was so worn out that I hadn't even opened up the covers. I slept through the day, occasionally waking up to nibble on a couple of protein bars. I finally forced myself to get up and walk a quarter-mile to the Huddle House next to the Shell gas station for dinner.

The next day I tried out the Super 8 breakfast, which was rather basic, but I was glad that I didn't have to walk anywhere with my foot hurting as much as it was. My energy supply was utterly depleted, and I knew that I had to feel better before going back to the trail. I figured that if I laid there long enough, I'd eventually get my strength and ambition back.

I kept my walking to a minimum by eating some trail mix I found in the hiker's box for lunch and ordering another pizza for dinner. Based on my non-existent energy level, I thought I might be sick, but I didn't have any other symptoms, so I didn't go to urgent care or to see a doctor. I continued to lay on the bed, wondering when I'd start to feel better so that I could continue my hike.

The next day, I still felt terrible, so I got by with another Super 8 breakfast and then used my camp stove to cook some pasta from the hiker box for lunch. I headed out to walk to a restaurant for dinner, but I couldn't get there because a train had stopped on the tracks. It would move back and forth every now and then. I guessed they were adding cars on further down the line. I was tempted to jump through to the other side but didn't want to take a chance; my leg made any such antics so much more difficult for me.

I thought about calling a shuttle, but I figured that the train had to be moving again soon. After an hour and a half of this, I gave up, went back to the motel, ate a protein bar, and then went to sleep. On the morning of my fifth day in Erwin, I felt exactly the same. If I had felt even a little bit better, I might have been able to motivate myself by doubling down on my inner encouragement.

"You CAN do this!"

"You're hiking the Appalachian Trail!"

"You can do anything you want!"

After five days of lying flat on my back without seeing any improvement, I had lost hope. I didn't know if or when I'd be feeling any better. I knew that I couldn't average fourteen miles per day with my foot hurting more and more each day. It would be next to impossible to make it to Maine before Mt. Katahdin was closed for the winter.

It was time to go home.

I picked up the phone and called my wife to let her know. She sounded surprised and did her best to encourage me to keep going.

"Are you sure, honey?" she asked.

"Yup. I've had it. I'm coming home."

I had pushed and pushed myself to keep going for so long that once I let go of the idea that I absolutely must make it to Maine, it was like a rubber band snapping back into place. I called the shuttle service, and Mary told me that Tom would be over to pick me up. He drove me up to Tri-Cities Airport and wished me well as he dropped me off at the curb.

During the plane ride home that night, I thought about my hike, especially about my decision to quit. When I was lying there in the Super 8, it seemed like this decision was made in mere seconds. The truth was that by pushing myself so hard to continue, I had slowly eroded away all my reserve capacity.

The person I thought I knew, the one who was able to tackle any challenge put in front of him, was gone. He was worn out, exhausted, and spent—physically, mentally, and emotionally.

8

SUMMER—GETTING ENERGY BACK

THE REST OF YOUR LIFE SHOULD
BE THE BEST OF YOUR LIFE

As I sat in our family room looking out at the Chesapeake Bay over the next few weeks, I tried to think about my adventure in a positive light rather than thinking of it as a loss. While I had failed to make it from Georgia to Maine, I knew that I wasn't the same person I was before starting my adventure. Before leaving to hike the Appalachian Trail, I was paralyzed with pain, waiting for someone else to fix my leg.

All I wanted was a doctor or procedure that would make the pain go away. The only thing I could see was a lifetime of chronic pain. By attempting a thru-hike of the Appalachian Trail, I felt that I had accepted the responsibility to heal myself, no matter how long the journey. When people told me, "Well, that's not bad at all. You did over 300 miles," I accepted the compliment while knowing inside that my leg and foot still had a long way to go.

I had started riding my bike outside to continue building strength in my injured leg. I didn't want to lose whatever strength I'd gained from hiking. One of my favorite rides was to go to my favorite coffee shop at the Bay Dale Shopping Center. I brought my laptop along in my backpack and sat down to write in my journal.

Here's a question that I asked myself, along with the answers I wrote down:

What was right about your hike?

- I did it.
- Now I know how to backpack and hike.
- I made it 318 miles along the Appalachian Trail.
- I got to enjoy my time in the wild.
- I quit all my pain medications.
- I took charge of my situation and took action.

I had proved that I could hike. I could sleep out in the woods with the bears. I could go up and over mountains, one step at a time. I also discovered that trying to force my injured body to hike fourteen or fifteen miles a day was beyond my capabilities. Oh, sure, I could push myself to go that far, but then the next day, I would start out feeling depleted and struggle to make it even ten miles.

At this point, I figured I was done with the Appalachian Trail. I had a new appreciation for the beauty I saw and all the wonder I felt while out in the wild. I wanted to experience more of it. Having lived with everything I need on my back; I was interested in living a simpler yet satisfying life. When I sat down in the coffee shop and wrote down my thoughts about the journey, I didn't realize that my adventure wasn't over yet.

It was well into July, three months later, when I finally got my energy levels back. I had been sitting around at home waiting to get back to normal when Joanna finally suggested I go to see my doctor. I don't know why men can't think of that on their own. It probably has something to do with the same reason we don't ever ask for directions. Anyway, once I saw my doctor, I began to feel better. Part of this was because I stopped taking my thyroid supplement at the same time I quit all my pain medications. It turns out that you're not supposed to quit that one without talking to your doctor first. Where have I heard that before?

In August, we took a trip to Europe with all our kids and our first granddaughter. I used my cane to walk while doing my best to keep up with the other family members, my leg was of course hurting with every step along the way. While staying in a villa on the Italian Riviera, I walked in the pool and discovered that this simple physical therapy method still had the power to help my leg feel better.

Once we were back home from Europe, I added bike riding to my healing routine. I rode about twenty miles a day, either heading down into Annapolis or up the Baltimore and

Annapolis Trail to the therapy pool, where I walked each day. I got in the habit of wearing my Bose headphones and listening to podcasts or music while riding my bike. Safety-wise this was a super bad idea, but I like audio for places without cars, like when I'm on the bike path.

Knowing I needed a helmet but wanting to retain the ability to hear audio, I searched around to see what my options were. I decided on a white snowboarding helmet with Bluetooth speakers in it. It was easy to turn the audio on and off while on the bike path. I knew this wasn't a hundred percent safe, but wow, if I had known where this would ultimately end up, I don't think I would have gotten that helmet.

When I arrived at the therapy pool, I locked up my bike and walked in with my fifteen-visit punch card. Pretty simple, you come in, they punch one of the fifteen spots on your card, and you head into the locker room. Except that lately, the main pool lady seemed to have stopped punching my card.

Whenever I gave it to her, she would give me some reason, like, "We're closing in an hour, so don't worry about it today." That's cool once or twice, but then she took the card and pretended to punch it by hitting an already punched circle so that the same number of visits remained.

To be clear, I liked this pool, and I *wanted* to pay. The free passes were starting to make me uncomfortable. Besides, I don't know what (if anything) the pool lady expected in return. Maybe she had a thing for me? I don't put out that type of vibe, but that's the only thing that seemed reasonable to me.

I mentioned this to my wife one night, thinking it wouldn't hurt to let her know how popular I was. It took a moment for her to process this before she doubled over, laughing.

"What's so funny?"

"She thinks you're disabled!"

"You mean, because I walk funny?"

"No, it's—ha ha ha ha ha ha ha! No, it's the—ha ha ha ha—HELMET!"

Ohhhhhhh. Okey Dokey.

Now I got it.

I walk in wearing my jeans, a small backpack, and the white helmet. I didn't have a typical biking helmet or any other biker gear to make me look like a bike rider, so I could see how it looked as if I was wearing a helmet like those that kids wear to prevent additional brain damage if they're prone to having seizures or something.

I really should have been able to figure all this out on my own.

I continued walking in the therapy pool when we got back from Europe and walked a few miles each day, along with doing one-leg jumps on a mini-trampoline to help build the strength in my injured leg. Somewhere in the back of my mind, I thought I might continue hiking the Appalachian Trail at some point. After resting up for the summer, I had my energy back, but my leg was still hurting every day. I hadn't let go of the idea that if I could hike the entire trail, then my leg would have to be better.

I also started taking the helmet off as soon as I dismounted my bike.

9

FALL—TINY STEPS FORWARD

You Are Bigger Than Your Problems.
You Are Stronger Than Your Pain.

At the beginning of October, I was working on strengthening my leg by swimming twice a week in a master's program, using an elliptical machine at the gym every other day, and walking the college stadium steps three times a week.

I thought I would test out hiking shorter distances on the Appalachian Trail near my home to see how my leg might handle doing shorter sections at a time. It took some effort to gather all my hiking gear together because I had flung it in various areas around the house when I got off the trail in

May. I planned to take it easy by hiking about ten miles a day for just two days to start off and then come back home to rest my leg up and see how I felt.

After making the hour and a half drive from my home in Annapolis, I left my car parked right by the Appalachian Trail Conservancy office in Harper's Ferry. I hired a shuttle driver to take me down to the AT trailhead in Purcellville, Virginia, which would leave me with about twenty miles of hiking to get back to the car. The seventy-five-dollar ride seemed expensive to me, but I didn't know anyone else that could take me for free, so I paid the man. I was determined to find a way to hike without pushing myself beyond the limits of what my body and injured leg could handle. It seemed like a decent way to test out doing smaller parts of the trail at one time.

The weather was great, and I enjoyed taking my time instead of pushing hard to try and get more miles in. It took me about seven hours to hike the eleven miles to David Lesser Memorial Shelter, where I spent the night with three other guys who were out for the weekend. I didn't set any records. It worked out to only a mile and a half an hour, which was just a little faster than I had been hiking earlier in the year.

It was great to finish the next day with a shorter hike of only eight miles that took me right back to my car. As I hiked along, I knew that all I had to do was make it back to my car, and I liked that. My goal at this point was to make sure that I didn't overdo it. I was curious to see if I could hike for a few days and then rest for a week or so without causing my leg and foot to flare up with nerve pain.

Driving home, I decided that I would hike a few more sections of the AT by going out for three to five days at a time. I would continue to hire a shuttle service to get down to my starting point while leaving the car at my endpoint. It provided me with a good challenge and would hopefully help me figure out if I would be able to go back out and finish up hiking the AT or not.

I also made an admission to myself. I was overweight. I wished that I could dress that up and make it sound better, but that was the truth. When I started hiking the Appalachian Trail last year, I didn't have time to lose weight before leaving on my hike. I had gained a significant amount of extra weight during the first two years after I was injured, sitting around watching Netflix on pain meds. I ended up losing ten pounds hiking from Georgia to Erwin, Tennessee, but at this point, I had gained that same ten pounds back and was up to 198 pounds.

I checked my Body Mass Index, and as a 5'8" male at 198 pounds, here's what the chart told me:

Your BMI is considered obese. People with obesity are at increased risk for many diseases and health conditions, including cardiovascular disease, high blood pressure (Hypertension), Type 2 diabetes, breathing problems, and more.

If I was going to have a chance at hiking the whole AT, then I'd need to lose some weight. If I could lose twenty pounds and get my pack weight down to twenty pounds, that would be like hiking without any pack weight at all.

When I needed to lose weight earlier in my life, I ran a bunch or worked out super hard. Now, with my injured leg, I could walk, but I couldn't run. If I pushed too hard doing physical therapy or other workouts, the pain in my leg would flare up and leave me sitting on the sofa for four or five days recovering. I had to find a way to lose weight without exercising much.

I knew I'd need every advantage that I could get to make it to Katahdin. Losing the extra body weight would help me when I was hiking, and it would also be great for my overall health. I bought a food journal, started eating healthy stuff, and tracking how much I ate each day.

I used to travel around the country, giving seminars to three or four hundred people at a time. I discovered that only five to ten percent of people in any given group were serious enough to take the next step by hiring me as a consultant. At times this percentage might be only four percent. Other times, it got as high as eleven or twelve percent, but generally, it ran at five to ten percent. I always wondered why this was.

Over twenty years, I taught hundreds of workshops. But these numbers never changed. I found the same thing was true for everyone who bought a course, only five to ten percent of that group succeeded. The best reason I've been able to figure out was that most people like the idea of taking on a challenge that could improve their life, but very few are willing to put in the work and effort to make it happen. When they reach an obstacle, most people will tell themselves, "I knew that I couldn't do this, so I may as well give up now."

The same thing happens on the Appalachian Trail every year. I met hundreds of people who told me, "Yes, I'd like to hike the Appalachian Trail someday." Out of this group, I guessed that five to ten percent would make the time available and put forth the effort to start on a thru-hike. This past year, there were 3,863 registered thru-hike attempts.

Out of those, twenty percent dropped out by the time they

reached Mountain Crossings after the first thirty miles. They discovered by trying it that it was too hard, too boring, or it wasn't what they had expected. Another twenty-five percent dropped out by the time they reached Harpers Ferry, which was almost to the halfway point. Surprisingly, about twenty to twenty-five percent end up making it to Mt. Katahdin in Maine. This was a larger percentage than what I saw from the real estate investors I'd worked with, which tells us something about the determination and mindset of thru-hikers.

The factor that's often left out is that many of those "failed" hikers still ended up getting something of value from the experience. I learned that hiking the whole Appalachian Trail within one calendar year wasn't possible for me to do with my injury. But maybe I could do it within eighteen months. I believed that everyone who tries doing something new and challenging ends up expanding their confidence and ability to take on more significant (or simply more interesting) life goals.

Over the next month, I made several return-trips to the trail while making sure to take it easy by only hiking two or three days at a time, followed by at least a week of rest back at home. For my next trip out, I hiked for three days from Manassas Gap to Snickers Gap, which was about twenty-six miles. I used the same formula of leaving my car at the north end and hiring a shuttle to take me to the south end of this section.

On the second night out, I stayed at a shelter with *Optimistic Dreamer*, a South Bounder. He had recently lost some family members and then a son to an accident. He told me that after losing his son, he was either going to kill himself or he was going to hike the Appalachian Trail. Since he lived in Maine, he gathered up some rudimentary supplies and then started walking southbound from Mt. Katahdin three days later. His sleeping bag and gear looked like he had gotten it at a thrift store, and he was also unique as the only hiker I'd met who carried a full-size pillow.

He told me that people kept giving him stuff so he hadn't had to buy anything yet. While we were sitting around the campfire, he went into a discourse about how unfair it was for Smoky Mountains National Park to charge thru-hikers twenty dollars for a permit. I thought about giving him a twenty-dollar bill for a minute but hesitated because something just didn't feel quite right. A short time later, a couple arrived at the shelter and set up their tent about fifty yards away from us.

Optimistic Dreamer went down to talk with them and came back ten minutes later holding up a Mountain House dinner. "Look what they gave me," he said, "God provides!" I wasn't sure if God was responsible, or if he was a master manipulator. In any case, he was another remarkable person that I'd met on the AT. Even though he was hiking southbound, this wouldn't be the last time I saw him.

On the last day out, I made my way through the roller coaster section, which has about ten significant climbs ranging from 250 to 450 feet in elevation. It was quite rocky in a few areas where I had to pick my way through slowly because of my foot. Mid-day seemed to be the most challenging part for me. I thought about stopping to camp a few times, but it was only 1:30, so I kept going. While going through these rocky areas, I wondered if I'd ever make it through the rocks of Pennsylvania. If I were going to hike the entire Appalachian Trail, that state would be quite a challenge.

While I was back home resting up in between these section hikes, I continued walking in the pool and riding my bike. One of my favorite places to ride to was City Dock Coffee shop, which was four miles from my house.

Here's what I wrote in my journal while sitting at the coffee shop one day:

- I can heal myself.

- I am healing each and every day.

- I can hike the entire Appalachian Trail.

I liked the way that sounded. As I did these local section hikes, I started thinking about hiking the entire Appalachian Trail again. I didn't know if I could do that, but, wow, If I could, then maybe I could completely heal my leg and foot in the process. If you've been reading along with me this far, you might be able to guess that I started the process by asking a few introspective questions. Here's what I wrote that day:

If there were a way for me to hike the rest of the Appalachian Trail and make it fun and easy, what would that look like?

How can I protect or nurture my injured leg to keep me from overdoing it, which causes the pain to spiral out of control?

I realized I could bring my car along with me, just like I had on my recent section hikes. I could park it a few days ahead of me at a trailhead and then get a shuttle down to where I left off from the previous section. I could keep a bunch of non-perishable food in the car so that I wouldn't have to worry about shipping resupply boxes or getting stuck eating fake Pop-Tarts again. Heck, I could drive to a steakhouse if I wanted and have a nice meal. It would beat the heck out of standing by the side of a road trying to hitch a ride into town.

If I had my car with me, I could also drive to an outfitter to get parts and supplies and go do laundry, get more food, or whatever. I could even keep my extra gear in the car so that if the weather looked like it would turn cold for a week, I could trade my summer bag for my warmer (and heavier) winter sleeping bag.

I could also find a place to get a massage on my legs, and while I was at it, why not find a therapy pool that I could walk in for an hour or so? For some reason, this seems to help my leg. After I walk in a pool for an hour, my leg feels so much better for two or three days afterward.

Yay! This sounds like fun!

And yes, I realized that it was also kind of cheating. I wouldn't be an official "thru-hiker" because that's a label reserved for someone who completes the entire trail in one calendar year. That was my goal when I first started hiking down in Georgia but after my crash and burn in Erwin, TN, I had a much better idea of my capabilities. If I could find a way to complete the rest of the trail this coming year, then I would be thrilled. My leg would be so much stronger, and who knows, maybe it would even heal completely.

A quick note about the thru-hiker label:

All the Appalachian Trail designations, including the speed records, are done on an honor system. I've seen thru-hikers who "yellow-blaze" ahead by getting a ride in a car so they can catch up with their hiking friends. I've seen other thru-hikers who took blue-blazed shortcut trails or even skipped entire sections of the trail for one reason or another. I've also seen hikers who insisted on walking every inch of the white-blazed trail, and they refuse to slackpack as well. The mantra you'll hear on the trail is "Hike your hike." It's up to each hiker as to how they want to do it.

At the rate I was going, I wasn't going to be a thru-hiker because it would take me longer than a year to complete the trail. That was fine. The curious thing about this is if I meet someone who's only thirty miles into a planned thru-hike, then they are called a thru-hiker, at least until they give up.

If you're thinking that I'm fussing about this just because I failed in my bid to be a real thru-hiker, then you're absolutely right.

For my next trip out on the Appalachian Trail, I decided to go for four days, starting this time in Shenandoah National Park at Elkwallow Wayside, and hiking northward to finish at Manassas Gap, where I had left off about a week earlier. I followed the same routine, parking my car at the north end and paying a shuttle driver to take me down into the park. I took my time and did fine walking eight to twelve miles a day.

Several weeks later, I went back out for another three days of hiking in Shenandoah National Park. I planned on getting an early start so that I'd have time to get some hiking in, but it was almost 3:00 PM by the time I pulled into the Ivy Creek Overlook. I planned to leave my car there and catch a ride down to the south end of the park at Rockfish Gap. I talked with a few people and started to figure out who I would hit up for a ride when I noticed that something was happening at the far end of the parking lot.

A mother black bear with two cubs was right on the trail about a hundred feet from the parking lot. The people I had been talking with went to that end of the parking lot, and a few of them even went up the trail to take pictures. I know enough about bears to respect them and give them plenty of room. In my opinion, this was the bears' territory, and we were just guests. I know that bears who get used to being around people can end up associating people with food. Once that happens, the bear can end up on the losing end of a ranger's gun. I stayed right where I was. Even though I was a hundred yards away, I could see enough for me to enjoy the experience with my glasses on.

Meanwhile, one fellow had his camera out and was now about twenty feet away from the cubs, who climbed trees. I didn't want to go over there, but everyone else was now over there, so I didn't have anyone to ask for a ride down to Rockfish Gap. The bears finally headed off further into the woods, and I walked over to try and get a ride. After pretending to be interested in the photos he took, I ended up getting a lift from the guy who was way too close to the bears. Since he was nice enough to give me a ride, I figured I probably shouldn't chastise him.

By the time we made our way down Shenandoah parkway with its twenty-five-mile-per-hour speed limit to Rockfish Gap, it was 4:30 PM. I began hiking. By six o'clock, it was getting dark, and I turned on the trusty headlamp that I had sewn onto the front of my wool cap during the initial train ride down to Georgia. The trail surface wasn't too rocky, which was typical here in the Shenandoahs, so I made decent time, but I still had a way to go to reach Calf Mountain Shelter, which was my goal for the day.

By 9:00 PM, it was pitch dark out and my headlamp

illuminated just the pathway right ahead of me. I was tooling along through a meadow filled with various bushes when I wondered what it would look like without my light. *Maybe I could see all the stars*, I thought. I turned my headlamp off, and was transported from the well-lit, friendly Appalachian Trail in Shenandoah to complete and utter blackness. I felt a rush of fear course through my body as I realized I was out in the middle of nowhere surrounded by darkness.

It was crazy because one moment I was fine and the next I was terrified. I quickly turned my headlamp back on. I felt fine again, so I turned the light back off—more scary darkness with animals and other "things" out there. I turned the light back on. I thought it was interesting—scary interesting—that I was standing in the same place, either with the light on or off. I wasn't in any more danger (unless something actually was sneaking up on me), but I felt fine with the light on, and without it, I was afraid.

The stars did look amazing, at least for the five or ten seconds that I managed to keep my light off. About an hour later, as I was walking near a fence, I noticed two green dots shining back at me. *It must be a set of reflectors on a fence post*, I thought. Then I saw more of them! They turned out to be deer eyes reflecting the light back at me like a set of nickel-sized bike reflectors.

A little further along the trail, I saw a similar reflection coming from a single point on the ground. After a little investigating, I discovered that a spider's eyes also reflected light in this same way. *Wow!* I was surprised by how many spiders I could see.

It was 10:30 PM by the time I turned onto the side trail

to the Calf Mountain Shelter. I switched my headlamp to the red light setting and was careful to be relatively quiet as I came in. The red light allows you to see while preventing you from blasting hikers trying to sleep with the bright white spotlight. I made sure to make at least some noise so that I didn't surprise someone. I did want anyone who might be there to know that I was a hiker and not a bear.

I heard a soft voice from within the shelter, "Hey, come on in. My name's *Postman*. It's just me here tonight." We talked for a bit before going to sleep. The following day, we compared notes, and I realized that we were both going to be hiking similar distances the next few days. I, once again, started thinking, *hey, maybe we could hike together.* But within five minutes of leaving at the same time, *Postman* said, "I'll see you up the trail," and he was off ahead of me.

At the end of the day, I caught up with *Postman* at Blackrock Hut, and we sat around the campfire, sharing stories with three engineers who were out section hiking for a few days. I mentioned to *Postman* that I had my car at the Ivy Creek Overlook, and he asked if I'd be able to give him a ride into town at the end of the day. I told him, "Sure, no problem. I'll meet you at the car," when I really should have said, "Sure, but you're going to have to wait a long time for me to get there."

You see, during the day, I was worried about keeping him waiting for me, so I pushed myself along much faster than I usually hike. I ended up twisting my ankle (my injured side, of course) on some rocks hidden underneath the leaves covering the trail. Then it was even more challenging for me to try to go faster because my dang foot and ankle were hurting so much.

After making it back to the car, I gave *Postman* a ride down into Elkton and then drove back home. I took a few weeks off from hiking to give my ankle some time to heal.

Once I recovered, I drove back to Shenandoah National Park, left my car at the Bearfence Parking Area, and caught a ride down to Ivy Creek Overlook to resume my hike. Over the next few days, I'd met a few people in the shelters at night, but hadn't seen anyone on the trail during the daytime. I was thinking about how nice it was to be out in the beautiful fall weather when I looked up and saw another hiker coming down a slightly rocky section. Something didn't look quite right. It took me a few seconds for my brain to figure it out. *That guy doesn't have any clothes on!* He was outfitted with a pair of hiking boots, socks and had a small day pack on his back.

I'd heard of the Summer Solstice "Naked Hiker" day in June on the Appalachian Trail, but we were well into fall and probably much closer to the winter solstice. I tried to piece together the words to say something witty like "Looks like the summer solstice came late this year," but I was so surprised that I couldn't seem to get any words out of my mouth. A moment later, as he walked right by me, I managed to say, "Uh . . . uh, hello." He said, "Hi," and kept on walking. He was definitely "hiking his own hike."

By breaking my hike up into sections, I got to see the Shenandoah's while all the trees were dressed in their fall glory. I stopped at three different vistas, and the colors were amazing. I really enjoyed hiking here which is why I'd suggest that if you want to put together a family trip or try out some of the Appalachian Trail by yourself, you'll want to consider Shenandoah National Park. Stretching more than a hundred miles along the Blue Ridge Mountains of western Virginia, Shenandoah National Park offers a patchwork quilt of wilderness and pastoral landscapes with more than 300 years of history.

Inspired by Yellowstone and other parks in the West, a national reserve in the Blue Ridge Mountains was first proposed in 1901. When the campaign stalled, Virginians took it upon themselves to make the park a reality. Using eminent domain, the commonwealth acquired the property from some 5,000 landholders and donated the parcels to the federal government. The Park was established the day after Christmas, 1935.

If you aren't up to hiking a portion of the Appalachian Trail in the park, you can drive down Skyline Drive, constructed in the 1930s by the Civilian Conservation Corps. Skyline Drive includes 105 miles of scenic overlooks, trailheads, picnic areas, and campgrounds between Front Royal in the north and Rockfish Gap in the south. When you drive on Skyline Drive through the Park, you're following the old Appalachian Trail path. The road replaced the old path, and the trail was moved off to the side.

The Park is a great place to get an introduction to the Appalachian Trail for three reasons. The trail surface is primarily friendly, with much of the AT following old forest roads or Jeep paths. This means there aren't many rocks, making for a reasonably level hiking surface. The second thing is that for most of the 100-plus miles of Appalachian Trail in the park, you're not far at all from the road. In a few sections, the trail may swing around the other side of a mountain, but even then, you're only a mile or two from the road. This makes hiking less intimidating for someone worried about being out in the middle of nowhere. If you had a problem, you could either hike out yourself, or a rescue team could get to you fairly quickly.

Lastly, while hiking in the park, you're going to be going right by toilet facilities at various picnic areas, and you'll be walking by food! Between the camp stores, waysides, and lodges, there are six different places you can buy food, warm up, get a blackberry milkshake or find someone to give you a ride back to your car. You don't have to carry very much food in your pack, so you can enjoy having a lighter load.

10

JANUARY—I'M PERFECTLY FINE

SOMETIMES IN LIFE YOU CHOOSE
YOUR CHALLENGES, OTHER TIMES
THE CHALLENGES CHOOSE YOU.

—TRAVIS ROY

After taking almost a month off to avoid a stretch of cold weather that came through, I decided to head out for a few more days. I left my car near Smithsburg, MD and had my father, who lives nearby in Frederick, pick me up and give me a ride over to Harpers Ferry. As we got near town, we could see a bridge where trains went across the Potomac River. Dad told me how he and a friend had gone across a bridge like that when they were growing up. He explained how they put their ears down on the train track to listen for any trains before running across the bridge. But if a train *did* come by, they would have to either jump in the river or get hit by the train.

What he didn't know was that when I was fourteen, my friend Calvin and I each told our parents we were going camping on a group trip in Harper's Ferry. The two of us then hitchhiked from Washington, DC to the Harper's Ferry area, and we did a similar—yup, you guessed it—"run across the train bridge" maneuver at the very same train bridge we were looking at.

I didn't have the courage to tell him this right then, but I did share it with Dad and Mom later. I was concerned that they might be upset, but I guess there's a statute of limitations on things like this because they didn't seem to mind and brushed it off, saying, "Oh, yes, you were quite a handful at times, Peter."

I spent another night in the same Rocky Run Shelter where I had the "wolf" encounter just over ten months ago. I was joined by a large boy scout troop this time around, and didn't hear any animals that night. The next day I crossed over the I-70 overpass and arrived at the Pine Knob Shelter, an older four-person shelter with a dirty metal floor and notes indicating where the roof leaked.

I collected some wood and made a decent fire even though everything was still wet from the rain and fog. I enjoyed sitting there by myself, my foot felt better, and I was starting to feel more confident about another attempt at hiking the entire Appalachian Trail. By this point, I'd lost eighteen pounds, so I was feeling good about that, and I was happy to have settled into a nice hiking routine. If I kept my mileage down and didn't try to hurry, I'd be able to keep from wearing myself out. I sat there enjoying the moment, cooking lentils (my new favorite dinner) and watched it get dark. It was all cloudy except off to the west, where some pink colors were peeking through.

I went back home, took another break, and thought about how I could add in some knee strengthening for my *right* knee so that it wouldn't bother me so much.

Two weeks later, I spent the night at Open Arms Hostel in Luray, Virginia. I used it as my base that week to see if I could finish hiking the rest of the trail in Shenandoah National Park. My sister Lisa had left me a message letting me know she was concerned about some cold weather and a storm coming into the area. I was planning to drop my car at the Elk Wallow Wayside and then catch a shuttle to Black Mountain. I'd hike for three days, spending two nights out at shelters before getting back to my car.

Sunday night's weather didn't look bad for Luray, which was only eight miles west of the trail. It was showing a high of thirty-two and an overnight low of eighteen. But when I pulled up the shelter weather forecast using atweather.org, it predicted a low of one degree Fahrenheit, with winds of twelve to fifteen miles-per-hour and occasional gusts of twenty-eight to thirty. *Brrrrr!* Monday, the prediction was a high of eight degrees with winds of fifteen to twenty miles-per-hour. Pretty cold.

So, despite my earlier conviction of being able to hike in January no matter what my sister said, I shortened my three-day hike to one. Then I made the (not too wise) decision to leave most of my gear, such as my sleeping bag, tent, etc., in my car so that I wouldn't have to carry the extra weight. I figured that since I was just hiking for the day, I didn't need it with me.

I've done this before, but it was always in warmer weather. My full pack had gotten lighter as I'd gotten rid of more things over time, about twenty pounds without food and water, so after leaving everything behind except my lunch, down coat, raincoat, rain pants, hat, gloves, and mitten-type glove covers with me for the day, I probably had ten pounds left to carry.

I moved my target from ten miles to the next shelter up to thirteen miles, ending up at Timber Hollow Overlook, one of the many overlooks along Shenandoah Drive. I figured that I'd get in a few more miles while I had the advantage of carrying less weight. When I first started hiking the AT, one of the biggest worries my family and friends had was, "What if something happens to you or you get hurt?"

Since I was hiking all by myself, this was a valid concern except for the fact that I'd typically see anywhere from three or four to as many as twenty or thirty other hikers in a day on the trail. If I did slip and fall or have something incapacitate me in some way, I'd be able to ask a passing hiker to get me some help. I might even be able to make it out myself to a road crossing if it wasn't too far away.

The other worry for both my family and me was the threat of frostbite or hypothermia. The hikers who get in trouble from getting too cold typically go out unprepared for the conditions. Their downfall usually includes some version of getting themselves, or their gear, wet so they can't retain their body heat. Another common cause of fatalities is when someone planned to be out for the day but ended up in a situation where they had to spend the night outdoors.

The well-prepared hiker manages this risk by bringing enough cold weather gear for the conditions, ensuring that everything stays as dry as possible, and ideally, doing whatever possible to avoid getting stuck somewhere in cold, wet weather without adequate shelter. Generally, my safety net included carrying my tent in addition to my sleeping bag with me even though I hiked from shelter to shelter. With fewer hikers on the trail in the fall and winter, I was usually assured a spot in the shelter even when arriving towards the end of daylight.

Still, bringing my tent with me allowed me to have a safe, warm place to hole up in case of bad weather. It also served as an emergency shelter in the unlikely (but possible) event that I was injured or couldn't continue hiking for some reason. The weather was predicted to include snow flurries from 9:00 AM to 3:00 PM with half an inch accumulation. I checked my watch as the first flakes came down. 9:03 AM. *How in the heck can they predict that so closely?*

I decided that it was a good day just to walk and think. It's wonderful to be able to enjoy the quiet in the mountains. We are surrounded by sound everywhere we go, so much so that we don't even realize it. Almost every restaurant, coffee shop, and store has at least one music or TV source, along with all the noise from people using their cell phones and talking.

So, I hiked along, enjoying the extra quietness that the falling snow provided. I stopped to remove my rain pants so that I wouldn't sweat inside of them. Then I pulled out my mitten-type glove covers since my Merino wool gloves seemed to be getting wet. This combo usually kept my hands warm, but that day I had to wiggle my fingers to keep them from freezing.

Finally, I stopped to put on my raincoat and wool cap. This helped block the wind, kept the snow from melting on my wool pullover, and kept me nice and warm in the twenty-five to thirty-degree temperatures. I met another hiker named *Short Step,* who told me she'd slipped in a few places where there was ice under the snow. She also mentioned a rocky section where the snow-covered boulders made it hard to walk without falling. A few hours later, I stopped to eat a protein bar and thought I'd stretch my calf out while I was standing there. I heard a few hikers coming up behind me and decided to keep stretching my foot and calf while they hiked past.

It turns out this was a larger, spread-out group of hikers. I got antsy waiting for all of them to amble by, so when there was an opening, I decided to continue walking for a while and then moved over to the side to let the rest of the group pass me.

As the last two people in the group came up behind me, they noticed my limping gait and one of them said, "Are you okay?" I'd heard this so many times before. This used to make me angry, but I didn't know why. I originally thought I was mad at the person for asking the question, but eventually realized I was angry at myself for being dumb enough to race a motorcycle in my 50s.

I was angry because every single day, my hip, leg, and foot would hurt. Sometimes it was aching or searing pain. Other times, my foot would feel cold or numb. I often experienced tingling sensations caused by the damaged nerves in my leg and foot. The feeling is similar to what you feel when your foot falls asleep and you try to get up and walk on it. Except it doesn't go away.

So, it used to be when someone would ask me, "Are you okay?" I'd respond with, "YES! I AM PERFECTLY FINE!" (While thinking inside my head, *No, I'm not fine, I'm totally screwed up!*) Well, I finally figured out that this wasn't a healthy way for me to respond. I decided that I should develop a better way to handle this so that I wasn't spewing my anger out at other hikers who were only trying to be nice.

"Thanks *so* much for asking," was my new response, which was supposed to come out in a kind, caring voice, the way your grandmother might sound after you've asked her how her arthritis is doing. But when the last two hikers came by and noticed me limping, one of them asked how I was doing. My response sounded more like a sarcastic snap from a wounded dog than the grandmotherly voice I had planned on. Then I added, "I was injured three years ago, and every day that goes by, I get just a little bit better."

"But are-you-okay?" he asked, drawing out the words as he said them, perhaps to make sure that I could understand.

"Well, three years ago, I was living in a hospital bed. Now I'm hiking the Appalachian Trail."

"Oh, okay. I see," he responded.

I made a mental note to practice answering the "Are you okay?" question so that I could answer it without getting worked up and sounding like such a jerk. In an attempt to focus on the positive, I thought back on all the progress I'd made since I was injured.

One of my biggest challenges before hiking was getting off the heavy-duty opioid pain medications that I was on. I told you about what happened when I was in the hospital, the ambulance transfer ride, and the rehab center when I needed painkillers but didn't get them in time. My pain levels shot up to the moon, and it was impossible to get the pain back under control once it had skyrocketed like that.

The Oxycontin medication that I was on is powerful stuff. It's designed for short-term use, usually three months or less. There's no question that I needed something that strong in the beginning. Two things caused the problem I had getting off opioids. My experience in rehab was that if I took Oxycontin, I still felt pain, but it was at a manageable level. When I went several hours past the time I was supposed to get another dose, my pain levels passed excruciating.

It's hard to explain what it's like to get hit with a massive dose of pain like this. I hope that you never have to find out. Imagine a tornado or hurricane blasting its way through your nervous system. In my opinion, it left devastation in its wake and changed my internal wiring.

Here's the formula imprinted on my brain: No Oxy = Massive Pain. So much so that many months later, if I were due for a pill at 12:30, I'd look at the clock, see that it was 12:40, and suddenly my foot would start hurting. I'd take a dose of Oxycontin, and within five minutes, I could feel the effect. The interesting thing is that the medication doesn't work that fast. It takes twenty to thirty minutes to get into your bloodstream. I was physiologically addicted to opioid medications.

The other challenge was due to the pain management

center that was handling my prescriptions. At every monthly appointment, I'd ask if there was any way that I could get off the pills. Each time the doctor would say, "Some people are able to taper off, some stay on it for two or three years, other people stay on it for life. How's it going for you?"

My answer, keeping in mind the physiological addiction I've just described to you, was, "It's going okay."

At this point, the doctor would say, "Then let's keep your prescriptions the same for now."

What I didn't know at the time was this doctor was getting over $100,000 a year in kickbacks from the company that sold Oxycontin. Unlike many patients, I didn't end up taking larger and larger doses. I was able to slightly taper down the amount I was using. This doctor had a plan to get me on it, but he didn't have a plan to get me off it. Joanna pushed me to quit, but I was worried that my pain levels would skyrocket without it.

After eighteen months of this, my short-term memory had turned to mush. It got so bad that Joanna would ask me a basic question at dinnertime, such as, "What did so and so tell you when you talked with them this afternoon?" I wouldn't be able to remember the conversation, so I'd change the subject to keep Joanna from realizing this. I knew I needed to be off this stuff but was afraid of what might happen when I quit. There were conversations about sending me to various treatment centers that claimed they could help me get off opioids. I didn't believe they could pull this off, and, as I just mentioned, I was terrified of getting hit with another massive dose of pain.

Meanwhile, I got an appointment at John Hopkins

University with a pain specialist, and he recommended surgery to put in a spinal implant. This is an electronic device that gets implanted in your *nalgas* (that's Spanish for buttocks). It has a lead placed along the spinal cord, which generates electrical impulses to interrupt pain signals from reaching the brain. I was uncomfortable with the idea of having surgery for something to manage pain levels that Oxycontin was obscuring.

I realized there was no way to gauge how much pain I was dealing with until I got off the opioids. A few days later, with my mind getting even hazier, I finally said, "That's it, I've had it."

I quit opioids cold turkey.

I knew it wouldn't be easy, but the withdrawal symptoms would only last for four or five days. I was extremely uncomfortable. I had jittery "restless leg" type symptoms over my entire body. I felt queasy, so much so that I was constantly right on the precipice of throwing up.

I called the pain management doctor (the one who was taking kickbacks to keep me on opioids) and left a message saying I'd quit cold turkey—call me ASAP. I got a call three days later from an assistant who said, "I wish I'd known that you went cold turkey. I can give you something to make yourself more comfortable." He prescribed something to help with the nausea and an arm patch that helped lower my blood pressure to reduce the withdrawal symptoms.

Four days after quitting, my withdrawal symptoms finally began to diminish. And get this. My pain levels actually *went down* after I got off Oxycontin. It's called "opioid-induced hyperalgesia," and *none* of the specialists that I'd been to over the past eighteen months had mentioned that this might be a possibility.

I had a drawer full of left-over pills because I'd been taking slightly less than the prescribed amounts for the past year yet had continued to refill the usual amounts. I'm not sure why I did this. Maybe I was hoarding this supply in case my doctors cut me off at some point. In any case, I figured that since I was quitting, it wasn't a good idea to have a bunch of opioids sitting around. I packed them all up into a gallon Ziplock bag and returned them to the pain management doctor's office. They made me wait while they counted every last pill and then had me sign something.

As you're probably aware from reading my story, I wasn't out of the woods yet. I was still taking many other medications. But I had escaped the tendrils of these potent yet problematic opioids. Compared to overcoming the challenge of getting off opioids, I felt *so much better* at this point that it's not even funny.

Later in the afternoon, I came to a place where the trail traversed a hillside, and water flowing across the trail had frozen. *Short Step* had warned me about this, but the snow had covered the ice so that I couldn't see it. I slipped and fell. This seemed more than a little treacherous to me, so I slowed down in an attempt to keep from falling again.

Despite being extra careful, I slipped and fell a few more times on icy spots like this, with the last fall almost putting me over the edge of a cliff. I started thinking maybe it wasn't a good decision to be out there, hiking without my tent in the cold and snow. With the cold, snowy weather, there were fewer hikers out on the trail, and if I were to slip and break a leg or something, then I'd likely need to spend the night waiting to be rescued. To make things even worse, I realized that I hadn't had a cell signal for most of the day.

Because of this, I went slower than usual for the rest of the day. That included going through a hundred-yard-long snow-covered rockslide. On a positive note, Skyline Drive wasn't very far from the trail in that section. But if I were hurt or lost, I could have ended up spending the night out on the trail. I thought carefully about that for the rest of the day and was relieved and delighted to finally make it back to my car.

There was a notice on my car letting me know that Skyline Drive had been closed due to the snow. It provided a phone number to call so that the park rangers could come and open the gate for me to get out of the park. I gave them a call and was told to drive to the gate, then call the rangers back.

With three or four inches of snow on the road, it took me forty-five minutes to drive ten miles to the gate. The road was closed off by two long metal gates that appeared to be locked in the center of the road, so I obviously couldn't get out. I tried calling the park rangers back but didn't have a cell signal. I slowly drove back up the hill to see if reception would improve. After driving fifteen minutes without finding a signal, I turned back around and carefully drove back down on the snow-covered road until I came back to the closed gates.

I knew there was a payphone at the park entrance about a half-mile away. It looked like I had to walk over to the payphone. I grumbled to myself as I got out of the car. I was tired, and my foot hurt. I just wanted to get home. I noticed a metal box covering the lock on the gate, and I lifted the cover in a last-ditch effort to avoid walking another mile to get to the phone and back.

Bingo!

The gate was latched but didn't have a lock on it. I opened the gate, moved my car through, and closed the gate behind me. I was so tired that I decided to stay another night at the hostel instead of driving home in the dark.

After this experience, I decided to make sure that I always had my tent and sleeping bag with me when hiking in cold weather or anytime the nighttime temperature would be in the fifties or below. It would obviously be safer for me to walk with someone else, but I hadn't met anyone yet who hiked as slowly as I did.

Another way to manage the risk of being injured or lost is to carry an emergency locator.

Personal locator beacons are satellite-synced devices that send an SOS signal to rescue agencies, along with your location. Satellite messengers are similar to personal locator beacons in that they also allow you to send SOS distress signals from remote areas where cell phone coverage is sketchy or nonexistent. Satellite messengers also include the ability to exchange texts from home and provide GPS navigation, including a webpage where your family and friends can track your progress.

I must admit that I didn't carry an emergency locator device. I used the FarOut app to show my GPS location in relation to the trail and, in fact, I used FarOut to get back on the trail a few times when I wandered off. I figured that if I stayed on the trail and was injured, another hiker would come by sooner or later. I know that's not ideal, but that's what I did.

11

FEBRUARY—BACK ON THE TRAIL

A MAN CAN FALL MANY TIMES,
BUT HE'S ONLY A FAILURE WHEN
HE REFUSES TO GET UP

—EVEL KNIEVEL

After losing twenty-five pounds, building up my leg strength, and proving I could hike shorter distances without the nerve pain in my leg flaring up, I decided to return to the point where I quit the previous year and continue my hike of the Appalachian Trail.

I had been on a website that showed the snow depths near Erwin, Tennessee, where I ended my hike last year. As soon as the snow melted, I planned on restarting my hike at Sam's Gap. Of course by taking longer than one calendar year to hike the entire trail, I certainly wouldn't qualify as an official thru-hiker. That was fine with me. I wasn't doing this for bragging rights. The quest to heal my leg and get my life back was what counted.

While section hiking in Maryland and Northern Virginia that winter, I discovered how much nicer it was to have my car waiting for me when I was ready for a break. While paying for shuttles could get a little expensive, this allowed me to keep my options open. If the pain in my leg flared up or I felt worn out, either emotionally or physically, then I could hop in my car and drive myself to get whatever I needed. I was confident that this would allow me to take better care of myself and hopefully avoid running myself into the ground as I did the previous year.

Was I "cheating"? If you asked a purist thru-hiker they would tell you yes. But a big part of my journey was to find a way to hike the entire trail with my physical limitations. I'm slower than other hikers, so I didn't have a tramily to walk with. I found that the ability to drive to an Airbnb or get anything else I might need did wonders for my outlook on this adventure. Rather than feeling isolated, alone, and stuck with limited resupply options, I'd be able to provide top-notch support, and I could do it all by myself.

I stocked up the car with *real* Pop-Tarts, plenty of lentils, and other non-perishable food. After hiking for three or four days, I'd get to the car where I could resupply and keep hiking, go get a steak dinner (if I needed it), move the car up the trail, see a movie, visit the local outfitters, buy more food, or whatever I might need to help keep me in shape. I also kept extra supplies and alternate gear in the car so that I could swap items out as the weather changed. No more hassling with mailing bounce boxes ahead of me.

I realized that this wasn't the most environmentally friendly hiking method, and that bothered me some. However, to make the AT experience work for me and to make it easier with my injured leg, that was how I decided to do it. After driving eight hours from Maryland, I arrived in Erwin at 10:00 PM. I stayed at Uncle Johnny's Hostel, which was right on the trail where I expected my hike to take me over the next three days.

The following morning, I shuttled over to Sam's Gap, which was the spot where I had stopped hiking the previous year. I was obviously pretty excited to get "back on the trail," but I was amazed at how much more energy I had compared to when I quit the previous year. I was pretty worn down mentally and physically back then. I did a few things differently this time to avoid falling into that same trap.

One big thing is that I'd had another ten months for the nerve damage to continue healing. I had completed a four-month-long weight loss and training program. I used the elliptical at the gym for an hour each day, swam twice a week, did thirty minutes of daily physical therapy exercise, and, of course, ate super healthy. Over the previous four months, I'd lost twenty-five pounds. That's more than my pack weighed! All of this helped. I didn't get out of breath as quickly, and my leg didn't bother me as much.

I took my time and arrived on top of Big Bald without running into any snow. The views were so incredible that I considered tenting on top of the bald for the night, but the gusting cold winds encouraged me to keep walking until I made my way down to Bald Mountain Shelter. At the shelter, I met *Slipknot*, a North Bounder (or NOBO) who started January 8th at Springer Mountain. We made a fire and shared stories while we dried our socks and warmed our feet. It turns out we both liked outdoor activities and had kids about the same ages.

That was the coldest night I had been out on the trail. The weather forecast said it would get down to twelve degrees. *Slipknot* taught me a few things about how to stay warm. He used a pair of Gooseneck Gear down slippers to keep his feet warm at night. He talked about the challenge of dealing with three things—wet, cold, and hunger. His theory was that you could handle any one of these at a time, but you'd want to avoid dealing with two or more at once.

My water bottles were frozen solid in the morning, and I moved pretty fast once I was out of my sleeping bag. My leg muscles were sore despite my pre-hike training program. I looked forward to getting in even better shape by actually hiking. I wore every bit of my gear that morning, including my raincoat, rain pants, hat, neck warmer, gloves, and a light pair of over-mittens. I had a pair of lobster mittens in the car I decided to add to my arsenal when I got to Erwin.

I listened to an audiobook called "What about the Boy," a story about a family who worked hard to assist in their son's physical and mental development. He had suffered some brain damage at birth. It motivated me to listen to other stories of hardships overcome as I limped my way along the trail.

Later that day I arrived at No Business Knob Shelter and

found *Slipknot* sitting on the picnic table eating his Mountain House meal for dinner. I cooked some lentils and then mixed in some instant mashed potatoes. We took turns trying to start a fire, but the wood was too wet, so we gave up and decided to hit the sack early. I heated some water and made a hot water bottle to put in the foot of my sleeping bag for the night. Once I settled in, I remembered my father's advice to appreciate the stars at night. I got back up, dug my glasses out of my pack, and gazed at the stars until the cold chased me back into my sleeping bag.

The next day was a beautiful day with an easy hike of about six miles, so I took my time and tried to soak up the experience. I tried to remind myself this was the only time I was likely to pass this way, so I needed to appreciate and enjoy everything I saw and all the people I would meet. I stopped to enjoy the lovely views of the Nolichucky River from up on the ridge right before the trail headed downhill for the last mile into Erwin.

A big storm was coming in, so *Slipknot* and I split a room at the Super 8. We checked the various weather sites to see when and how much snow was coming our way. The following day, we had a nice breakfast at McDonald's, where *Slipknot* announced he had found a shuttle to take him north past Roan Mountain the next day. He wanted to bypass the deep snow and move to a point on the trail that was 3,000 feet or lower in elevation. He'd already skipped the Smoky Mountains just south of there but planned to hike both sections later in the year.

I decided to wait out the storm but needed to get out of the Super 8. It's not a particularly bad hotel, but this was the same hotel where I crashed last May and had laid on the bed for days before finally heading home. Not the best memories.

I looked on Airbnb and found the Poplar Creek Farm and Hostel near Indian Grave Gap. This was the next road crossing on the trail, so it would be the perfect place to leave my car and hike back to it. As I drove east up into the mountains, I discovered that the storm had already dumped six inches of snow at the higher elevations. My Honda Accord struggled to find traction going up the last hill, and I couldn't get it to go any further. Fortunately, Mike, the owner of the hostel, came looking for me and diplomatically said, "Let me give it a try. I don't know if I can do any better than you, but maybe I can." I was happy to see that he was able drive my car up the hill to the hostel.

So, with Mike's help, I made it there. It was *so nice*. I was the only one there, so I had the run of the place. There was a big living room with a wood stove, an outfitted kitchen, and my own room with a snug-looking queen bed.

The snow piled up outside while I waited out the storm at the hostel. I had plenty of time to think about all the challenges I'd face if I were going to hike the entire Appalachian Trail. My biggest issue was still my frigging leg. I'd have to make sure to take it easy enough so that I didn't wear myself out again like I had the year before.

A few days later, I finally got back to hiking the AT, now in freshly fallen snow. As I headed north from Uncle Johnny's Hostel, it was easier than expected to stay on the trail. The white blazes weren't too far apart, and the trail had been hiked for so many years that in most cases, I could see an indentation of six to twelve inches indicating where the path went.

While the pain wasn't as intense as it was the year before, my foot and lower leg still hurt most of the time. But hiking helped strengthen my leg (and my shaky foot) while giving me something else to focus on besides how much my foot was bothering me. I noticed the soft sound of the quiet forest blanketed in snow, and the beauty of the wilderness, while wondering all afternoon how far it might be to the next shelter where I could stop to take a break. All of this was *way* better than sitting at home watching Netflix with my leg propped up on a heating pad.

I tried out two different devices designed to provide better traction in the snow. The first set was made by Kahtoola and had ten carbide tips that looked like they might work better on ice than on snow. I also tried using a set of Stabilicers that I had REI ship overnight to me at the hostel after *Slipknot* recommended them. They look like a thin hiking boot sole with big plastic cleats on the bottom with ice screws in each cleat.

They seem to work best for deep uphill snow by keeping your foot from sliding back while going uphill. After trying both, I kept the Kahtoola's in my pack to use in icy conditions and left the Stabilicers in my car. The Stabilicers grip so well that they made my foot hurt more than it usually did. In the deep snow, they worked great, but in areas with only four to six inches of snow, they grip the edges of partially covered rocks on one side while the other side clunks down suddenly without warning, twisting my ankle from the unexpected movement.

Besides making the first set of tracks, the best part of the day was the outstanding quietness of hiking through the snow, which absorbed any existing sound. *Nice.* I had left my car at the end of the day's hike so that I'd have more options available with the cold weather expected to be coming through the area. I went back to stay another night at the Poplar Creek Farm and Hostel. I really enjoyed staying there.

With the weather forecast getting even colder that weekend, I decided to take the overnight bus home to Maryland so Joanna and I could celebrate our twenty-second wedding anniversary. It didn't seem like we'd been married for that long. It's been a wonderful and amazing time.

During my hike from Georgia to Tennessee last year, my decision on where to stay when I stopped to recover was based on what was closest to the AT or who perhaps offered a free shuttle to and from the trail. Most of the time, I stayed in either a hostel or a hiker motel.

While I was packing up this morning at Poplar Creek Farm and Hostel, I came up with the idea of renting a room in one central location, perhaps in a house, where I could keep my extra supplies and return to over the next month or so. This would remove the uncertainty of where I would stay and help ensure that I had a clean and quiet place to rest up on my days off. Of course, this would mean I might spend more time driving, but my primary goal at this point was to make sure I supported and nurtured myself.

While stopped for lunch on my way to Johnson City to catch a bus home, I was sending emails out to possible owners of houses with rooms for rent when I realized it might be hard to find someone who'd agree to a thirty-day lease. I found one owner who initially agreed to my proposal but then sent me a text while I was on my way to see the place, letting me know they had changed their mind. I finally found someone willing to rent me a furnished basement room in a house on Holston Lake for $400 a month.

This room was near the trail at mile 450, halfway between Erwin, Tennessee and Damascus, Virginia. This would allow me to drive to my "home base" within an hour or so when I was ready to take a zero. Hiking purists might scoff at this idea, but hey, at this point, I was definitely "hiking my own hike."

The snow started coming down as I drove over to check out the house. I didn't want to get stuck, so I left my car up on the road and walked down the winding snow-covered driveway. I met with the owner, who lived on the immaculately-kept main floor of the house. He seemed a little unsure about taking an unknown hiker into his house, but after we got to know each other, he warmed up and agreed to provide a place for me. I wrote him a check and let him know that I'd be back Wednesday night after taking the bus to Washington DC for our anniversary.

I walked back up to my car and was about to leave when I realized that I could store my hiking gear and the piano keyboard I'd brought with me in my new basement room. This was better than leaving it exposed to theft in my car while it was parked at the Johnson City bus station. Yes, I did bring a full-sized keyboard along on my hike. I started playing piano fifteen years earlier, and I figured I'd be able to get some practice in during my days off.

I took my hiking gear out of my pack to use it as a travel bag on the bus. I grabbed the Hefty bag full of all my pack contents in one arm and hoisted the rather heavy full-sized piano keyboard under the other arm. I made my way down the now darkened driveway taking tiny steps due to the steep hill, the slippery snow, my wacky injured leg, and the amount of weight I was carrying. I had stopped to put things down to rest for the fourth or fifth time when my sleeping bag, which was in its compression sack, jumped out of the Hefty bag and started rolling down the driveway.

It did a decent job of finding its way down the slope until the driveway made a sharp turn, and it went off the side. It appeared to go over the edge of a steep embankment that went down to the lake. As I slowly made my way down the driveway, I could see that a small tuft of grass had saved my trusty sleeping bag from a cold certain death in the dark waters below.

After retrieving the sleeping bag, I noticed that there was only one set of footprints coming down the driveway. Somehow, I'd made a wrong turn down the wrong driveway. The keyboard was getting heavier as I shuffled my way back up the hill. The hilarity of the situation had me laughing at, rather than berating, myself.

Here I was, carrying all my hiking gear along with a fifty-pound keyboard up a slippery driveway in the dark, and because it's part of "hiking the Appalachian Trail," I was enjoying it. I didn't understand it, but hiking the AT allowed me to change my outlook on life. I finally made it back to the correct house, left my stuff there, and drove down to Johnson City to catch the bus that would take me home for our anniversary.

I arrived at the Greyhound terminal in Washington,

DC after riding all night on the bus. There were some odd characters at the station and on the bus, so I had a good time people-watching. One of my favorites was the driver, an ex-marine, who acted like we were at Boot Camp. He yelled all of his instructions. "When we get there, you have FIFTEEN MINUTES… DO YOU HEAR ME? FIFTEEN MINUTES to get something to eat and take a bathroom break. And one other thing! NO SMOKING by the gas pumps!"

We finally arrived at Union Station. It was great to see my beautiful wife, who was waiting to pick me up. We drove home, I cleaned up, then took a nap before some old friends from Colorado stopped by for dinner.

I enjoyed the next few days at home as we celebrated our anniversary and Valentine's day. I spent an hour walking in a nearby water therapy pool, which felt great. The buoyancy of the water means I weighed twenty percent of my normal weight, so I was able to practice walking more normally—balanced between each leg—rather than my usual limping shuffle. The water also allowed me to use and exercise all the tiny muscles in my foot that needed further strengthening. Even though it had been almost three years since my accident, I walked in the pool practically every day during the final six months leading up to the restart of my hike.

The last day I was home, I met with Wendi Winters, a reporter from the Annapolis Capital newspaper, who wanted to write an article about my hike. Joanna listened in from the next room as I shared my enthusiasm for hiking and explained my belief that hiking more than 2,000 miles was sure to heal my leg. I told her that I was going back down to Erwin, Tennessee, to restart my hike from Georgia to Maine. Wendi said, "All the way from Tennessee to Maine? How long are you going to be out hiking?"

Now before I tell you my answer, let me explain that Joanna's expectation at this point was that I'd continue to hike the trail just like I had when I section-hiked Shenandoah National Park and portions of Maryland during the winter. She thought I'd be gone for intervals of four or five days at a time and then return home for a week or two before going back out. I had told her I would restart my "thru-hike," which meant going from Tennessee to Maine, but she didn't understand the connotation.

So, when Wendi asked, "How long are you going to be out hiking?" I responded, "About eight or nine months." In the next room, Joanna said her knees buckled, and she almost fell on the floor. She couldn't imagine being alone for that long and was shocked, frightened, and angry. Of course, I didn't realize this at the time and continued sharing my story with the reporter.

When she told me later how upset she was, the main thing I heard her say was, "But I also want to support your journey." I assured her that I'd stop by once I hiked through Virginia and probably a few other times as well, but that didn't seem to make her feel any better. If there's a way to frame this in a way that puts me in a better light, I can't think of it. I was determined to do whatever it took to heal my leg, and for me, this meant hiking the entire Appalachian Trail. I told Joanna that I was so sorry to leave her on her own and I hoped our love for each other was strong enough to make it through.

Tragically, Wendi Winters was killed by a gunman along

ONLY WHEN I STEP ON IT

with other Capital staff members a little over two years later. She was an amazing person with incredible spunk, writing articles about various topics including "Off Limits" where she would tour various closed government facilities and let her readers know what she found. When faced with the shooter, Wendy grabbed a recycling can and attacked him, creating a distraction that was credited with saving the lives of several other people.

After spending several days with Joanna (and assuring her that I really do love her), I took another bus trip back down to Tennessee. I spent the night at the place I'd rented on Holston Lake and got up incredibly early to head back to the trail. The sun was just coming up as I pulled into Carvers Gap, elevation 5,512 ft.

I planned to leave the car there and shuttle south to start hiking again at Indian Grave Gap, where I'd left off before my trip back home. After waiting an hour for Tom's shuttle service to arrive, I retreated down the mountain road in my car to see if I could get cell service. As I drove around a bend in the road and picked up coverage, my phone dinged with a text from Tom letting me know that he'd run off the road and hit a tree on Hughes Gap.

So, I drove down to the Mountain Harbor Hostel on Route 19 to see if they could shuttle me. They said they could but that I'd have to wait an hour or so. I asked *Einstein*, a younger NOBO, about the trail conditions up on Roan Mountain. He said higher elevations were still covered with two or three feet of snow in places.

He had a hard time finding the trail due to thick fog and that he didn't have any snow cleats but was able to make his way. He mentioned another NOBO, *Bear Whisperer*, who was so concerned about getting lost that he turned around to head back south on the trail. I decided to head out anyway because, well, I didn't know any better. I was hiking all alone, with a grand total of one day's experience in the snow. *What could go wrong?*

I grabbed two more days of food from my car, which I had decided to leave further up the trail right at Mountain Harbor Hostel. It was 10:00 AM by the time the shuttle dropped me off at Indian Grave Gap, and I began following the white blazes north on the trail. The snow increased as I climbed in elevation but never got more than a foot deep. I followed the tracks from two other hikers until midafternoon, when the wind and snow falling from trees erased the prints I was following.

I managed to find enough white blazes to stay on the trail, and Cherry Gap Shelter came into view just before sundown. Looking down the hill, the shelter looked beautiful, half-hidden and blanketed with a foot of snow. There was a lovely, piped spring close behind the shelter, and I cooked some lentils for dinner. I had picked up a new digital thermometer which showed thirty-four degrees. This device records the high and low temperatures for the previous twenty-four hours, and I figured I could better dial in my cold-weather gear if I knew the actual low temperature each night.

I watched an Amazon Prime movie I had downloaded on my iPhone, a stark contrast of modern convenience in the cold, snowy wilderness.

I awoke in the morning and gazed out of the shelter at the winter wonderland spread out before me. It got down to twenty-eight degrees the previous night, but I managed to stay warm by zipping my sleeping bag up tight around everything except my nose. When I was out hiking in the wind, I had everything on, including my raincoat and down jacket to stay warm. When the trail advanced into the mountain's leeward side or went up a steep hill, I was shedding layers only to put them back on again once I reached the top.

The trail was primarily snow-covered with sections where two to three-foot-high drifts made for slow going. The circulation was not very good on my injured side, and the pain would get worse when my left foot got cold, so I put a couple of foot warmer inserts into my left boot each day to help with this. I was still following the two sets of tracks made by hikers ahead of me except for the places where the wind had covered them with snow.

At 1:30 PM, I stopped to sit down on a log and rest. I was worn out from working my way uphill through the treacherous snowdrifts. I had to either step into previously made holes, or attempt to stay atop the drifts, where the snow had hardened some. I never knew if the snow was going to support my weight or if I was going to drop down a foot or two. This is called "post-holing." The combination of the steady wind blowing and not knowing if or when I'd break through the snow was unsettling.

What the heck am I doing out here in the snow? I asked myself. *Maybe I should wait until this weather gets better.*

My original plan had been to wait for the snow to melt before restarting in Erwin, Tennessee. That's what I did, resuming at Sam's Gap on February 5th. Then another storm came through. I had sat out the storm and the week of cold weather that followed it, yet I still found myself hiking in snow once I started again. My feet were wet and cold, and I wasn't looking forward to another night out in a shelter followed by a strenuous climb up Roan Mountain the next day.

I pulled out the guidebook to see what options I might have. The Greasy Creek Friendly hostel was just three miles ahead. I decided to get out of the cold for the night and take a zero the next day to boost my energy and lift my spirits.

The hostel had plenty of character as it was basically an unheated bunkhouse combined with sharing a kitchen and living room in a small house with Connie, the owner, and her boyfriend. There seemed to be rules for everything, including about seven different places to reuse, recycle, or compost trash and leftovers depending on the item in question. I met another NOBO there, *Santiago*, who said at one point, "I want to throw this out, but I don't want to get in trouble."

Santiago also introduced me to Gore-Tex waterproof socks. He said, "You can stand in a puddle, and your feet will still be dry." I ordered a pair to be delivered to my room at the house on Holston Lake. Connie, the hostel owner, was kind enough to drive down to a restaurant to bring us back dinner. It was nice to be warm inside and connect with some new friends.

I was glad that I decided to stop there and take care of myself rather than pushing on. I needed to pace myself even though I felt like I was making such slow progress. I called my wife to let her know about my change of plans, and in her typical supportive fashion she reminded me that I was doing much better than I was a year before, when I had gone just three miles the first day of my hike.

After my zero at Greasy Creek Friendly, I put together a leisurely day by slackpacking five and a half miles in the rain to Hughes Gap. The only things I took were my rain gear, lunch, and a couple of protein bars. I didn't mind the rain at all since every bit of it that fell was helping to melt the snowdrifts on Roan Mountain, which I'd be climbing the next day. Connie picked me up at Hughes Gap and would run me back over there the next morning.

I had been reading journals of some of the hikers starting in Georgia. Many of them were doing fifteen to seventeen miles a day already. I felt a little—uh—slow and lame doing five to ten miles a day. I mentioned this to one of my daughters, and she said that if I were doing fifteen-mile days, I'd want to be doing twenty, which was probably true. *Slipknot* reminded me in an email that it wasn't a race. I had a great day despite all the rain.

The next day I headed back out and after climbing all morning, ended up in a spruce forest near the top of 6,285 ft. Roan Mountain. The snow wasn't too deep while coming up the mountain, but at the top, the snow was packed down and had turned to ice. I stopped to put on my carbide snow grippers, which were a lifesaver for me. The last thing I wanted to do was fall on the ice and break or injure something else.

I explored a side trail that led to the site of the 166-room Cloudland Hotel, a three-story resort built in 1884 for "pleasure-seekers and hay fever sufferers" where "100 mountain top peaks could be viewed without leaving the porches of the hotel." Folks back then traveled to the Cloudland by first taking the narrow-gauge railroad to Roan Mountain Station, Tennessee, where an inn provided an overnight stay. Guests then rode by carriage for twelve dusty miles on the newly constructed Carvers Gap Road.

The hotel sat on the North Carolina–Tennessee state line and had a white line drawn down the middle of the dining room floor. Alcohol was legally served on the Tennessee side, but not in North Carolina. The Cloudland got its name because most of the time, clouds enshrouded the mountain, as they were indeed while I was up there. There wasn't much left of the Cloudland Hotel; the only clue of its former glory was an old stone chimney off in a field. The hotel was shut down in 1904 and dismantled ten years later.

A bit further up Roan Mountain, pretty much at the top, I stopped to see the highest shelter on the AT, the Roan High Knob Shelter. It was the first shelter I'd seen that had a door on it. Heading down the other side of the mountain, the Kahoona ice grippers I was wearing kept me from slipping on the ice-covered pathway. Melting snow created small water streams that followed along the trail, eating away at the ice and creating small ice bridges where at times the ice would crack as I walked over a weaker spot.

I grew up in a family with seven kids, and I was lucky to have two younger brothers near my age to play with. When I was twelve, the three of us would go down to the creek behind our house in the wintertime to entertain ourselves. We'd walk along the ice until we found a deeper spot, usually a few feet of water covered by an inch or so of ice.

We invented the game to step, run, or slide across the ice, one at a time, without breaking through into the water. Eventually, the ice would start to weaken and crack, which increased the excitement and anticipation of the game. Finally, one of us would break through so that he was standing in about two feet of frigid water.

The game rules, which we modified on the fly, required you to "glug" once you were in the water. Glugging was the sound made by the water as it replaced the air inside the fur-lined boots that we wore. You had to wait until your boots were full of water while the two other brothers hooted and hollered.

That's what I thought about as I walked down the north side of Roan Mountain in my wet socks and boots. By the time I descended to a lower elevation and crossed Carver's Gap, the ice and most of the snow were behind me for the day.

It was dark by the time I arrived at the Red Barn Overmountain Shelter. The fog was rolling in so thick that I could see better with my headlamp off than I could with it on. I climbed the stairs to join four NOBOs for the night, who had arrived ahead of me. Once I settled into my sleeping bag, I enjoyed the sound of the rain coming down hard and heavy on the roof of the barn. During the night, a mouse ran right over my head, and for some reason, it didn't bother me. I must be getting used to life on the trail.

I spent the next morning climbing Little Hump Mountain and Hump Mountain, which are part of the Appalachian balds. These mountains don't have any trees on them, making for incredible views on a clear day. I could only see about a hundred feet ahead due to the thick fog, which persisted throughout the first half of the day. This provided an interesting perspective: I could see the trail ahead of me going straight uphill before evaporating into the fog, like a stairway to Heaven. The cold and persistent wind off my right shoulder seemed to wear at me as the day went on.

The afternoon included various terrain, including rocks, roots, and six-inch-deep mud in places where the rain washed soil down onto lower parts of the trail. It was late in the day when I reached US 19, and I ambled down the side of the paved road to get back to my car. My foot complained about the hard pavement surface. Or perhaps it was reacting to hiking bonus miles.

It felt great to change out of my hiker clothes into jeans when I arrived back at the car. I hit the Lone Star Steakhouse for dinner on the way back to my room at the house on Holston Lake. I was going to take the next two days off to give my foot a rest and stay off the trail during the impending snowstorm.

When I returned to the house, I had two packages waiting for me—a pair of Rocky's Gore-Tex Waterproof socks and a new Elevate Foot Brace, which kept me from tripping on my injured foot. I had used this type of brace from Footscientific. com for the past year while hiking. The old one was getting worn out, so I emailed the company a few weeks prior, telling them about my adventure, and asked if they would sponsor me by providing a replacement brace for free.

They said yes! I had my first official sponsor.

I made a video explaining how well the brace worked for hiking and sent it to them. Overall, my leg and foot were doing much better compared to when I had first started hiking the Appalachian Trail. To a certain extent, the searing nerve pain had transitioned at times into numbness, feeling cold, and a pins and needles sensation similar to walking after your leg falls asleep.

When it got annoying, I took some Advil and reminded myself that it wasn't as bad as it was the previous year. Back then, I had been doing three things to make the pain worse. I had spent most of my time thinking about how much my leg was hurting and lamenting over things like, *why did this ever happen to me?* When the pain was bothering me, I would hold my breath or only take in small gasps of air. And I was tensing up nearby muscles to compensate, causing my upper calf and hip muscles to ache at the end of the day in addition to my foot and ankle.

I now did a few things differently. One of the simplest was to repeat *breathe* or *relax* in my mind as I hiked along. In the past week, I took this a step further by creating some positive, uplifting thoughts to listen to as I walked. I recorded these on my iPhone in a slow, gentle, reassuring voice so that I could play them back while hiking. This probably sounds crazy, but it actually helps.

Here's what I recorded:

As you're walking along

Listening to all the sounds around you

And the sounds of my voice...

Taking in a deep breath ... Now...

Letting out any stress

Or busy thoughts

Breathing in again... Now...

Drawing in pure—fresh—oxygen

And breathing out...

Letting go of anything that's been bothering you...

As you're walking along...
Your entire body is letting go
Moving along the trail
Completely loose and relaxed
Right—now -
You're taking in all the beauty around you
This day, this hour, this minute, in the wild, on the trail
As a special—celebration—of this very moment in your life
Your entire body is healing...
Completely and effortlessly...
Building strength with each and every step
It's wonderful to be living this life
Hiking the Appalachian trail
While enjoying any pleasant, enjoyable thoughts
That may be coming to you ... Now...
You're living a vibrant, healthy life
Enjoying the healing in all parts of your body
As you're becoming more and more comfortable
Relaxed, and content... right now...
You'll find that these thoughts will carry through
The rest of your day and night...
Leaving you content, relaxed, and enjoying every moment of this
Very special day.

I did feel more content over the course of the next few days and enjoyed "the moment" more than I used to. *Maybe it's because I've been listening to this audio script.*

I've found during my life that our thoughts can affect the way we respond to the world around us. Rather than just accepting the negative thoughts that pop into our minds,

I think it makes more sense to choose the thoughts we want to hear.

The next day it was snowing and cold, so I decided to take another zero. I drove up to Damascus to get a new set of Superfeet boot inserts from the outfitters. I'd put over five hundred miles on the pair I had, and the arch on my right foot (on my good leg) had begun hurting. Perhaps a new pair of inserts would help with that. Once I got back to the house, I divided most of my food up into Ziplock bags ahead of time to make it easier to resupply from the car. I sat down to watch TV with the house owner and ended up glued to the screen until I went to bed. *So much for making time to play my keyboard.*

The next morning, I was driving back to the trail and saw a hiker walking along the road in the cold, so I stopped to give him a ride. It turned out that "Terry" wasn't hiking. He was homeless. I asked him if he was able to stay warm in the cold weather, and he told me he did okay, except it was harder to keep warm at night.

He rode with me up to Mountain Harbor Hostel, where I parked the car. I gave him some protein bars and a few Pop-Tarts. He turned down an extra set of gloves I offered him and walked away bare-handed as the snowflakes were falling. Which reminds me, how do you tell the difference between a thru-hiker and a homeless person?

The homeless person smells better.

I headed north on the trail. The snow multiplied from one to three or four inches as I increased in elevation. It was nice to be out in the winter wonderland, and I found that the snow wasn't difficult to walk through. The Rocky's Gore-Tex waterproof socks were worth every cent of the $85 I paid to keep my feet dry for the first time all week.

That afternoon, I followed a single set of tracks in the snow until I came to the Jones Falls turnoff. The hiker in front of me went straight rather than turning off to see the waterfall. Incredible beauty, just a tenth of a mile off the trail? It amazed me that some people were in such a hurry to get up the trail that they missed some of the best parts.

At the end of the hiking day, just before getting to the Mountaineer Shelter, the trail went right by another stunning waterfall, Mountain Falls. With no other hikers to join me, I was alone in the shelter enjoying my lentils and polenta for dinner. That day felt good. I reached the four-hundred-mile point and stomped out "400" in the snow, taking a selfie to celebrate.

My new Super Feet inserts did make a difference. It was hard for me to see how a shoe insert can wear out, but the arch on my (good) foot wasn't hurting anymore. It was all part of the process of keeping my body as whole as possible so that I had a chance of making it to Mt. Katahdin.

The next morning, I left Mountaineer Shelter and had to find my way around ten different trees that had fallen across the trail. These are called "blow downs." In most cases, I could step over the tree trunk or through the branches. Several situations required hiking out around the tree, something that was hard to do if the trail was cutting across a steep hillside.

At the top of the day's big hill, I stopped to rest on a bench by the side of the trail. There was a great view looking back south at Big Hump Mountain and Little Hump Mountain.

It filled me with pride to look out at the mountain vista and know that I had hiked across that entire landscape.

That afternoon I had difficulty finding the turnoff to the Vango Abby Memorial Hostel because the snow was covering everything. The Appalachian Trail Conservancy doesn't want the trail to be commercialized, so they don't allow signs to nearby businesses (including hostels). After hiking up and down a small valley several times, I finally found some surveyors tape on a tree branch that marked the turnoff, and I made my way over to the hostel.

One reason I stopped there was to play the porch piano that the guidebook had mentioned. Scottie, the owner, removed the blue tarp that covered the piano and let me play a few songs. He then asked to play a few tunes and proceeded to play one song after another for the next hour until the sun was going down and it got pretty darn cold. I would have preferred to have a little more playing time myself, but I figured that Scottie was probably more than a little lonely living out there all by himself. He probably didn't get too many visitors in the wintertime.

I noticed a makeshift apparatus in front of a commercial video game on the porch. There was a metal grid on the floor wired up to one side of a 110-volt extension cord. The other side of the power cord was wired up to the video game console. When I asked him about it, Scottie replied, "Yeah, I had a problem with a neighbor's dog that used to pee on that every day. Once I zapped him, I haven't seen him around."

It's incredible some of the crazy stuff that you can find on the Appalachian Trail.

After spending the night alone in the freezing cold

bunkroom at the Vango Abby Memorial Hostel, I hiked twelve miles and arrived at Kincora Hostel by 4:30 PM. But couldn't find anyone. The hostel was open, so I went in, picked a bunk to drop my pack on, and started to figure out how to light the wood stove to warm the place up. Before long, I was joined by *Tin Man* and *Ice Breaker*, a couple of young NOBOs hiking together.

The owner, Bob Peoples, eventually arrived and came in to get to know us. Bob is a legend on the trail. He's helped run Kincora, maintained the AT, and hiked worldwide. Bob told us he's had 22,000 hikers come by over the years. The walls and ceiling are covered with Katahdin victory photos. Bob loves talking with and helping hikers. He's a super nice guy and I really enjoyed hearing his stories and sharing my own.

Bob was giving us an early ride back to the trail, so I made some dinner and got my pack ready to go so that all I had to do was grab it in the morning. I figured I'd wear my hiking clothes and sleep in the bunk using the provided wool blankets. The four of us ended up having a great time playing Trivial Pursuit, and we were up much later than my usual sundown bedtime. When I finally made my way back to the bunkroom, I was so tired that I was having trouble keeping my eyes open. I took my boots off, climbed into the bunk, and pulled the blanket up. That's when I smelled it. Cat urine. This wasn't just a whiff. It was powerful.

I lay there for a minute, thinking about getting up and opening my pack to get out my sleeping bag to use for warmth instead of the questionable wool blanket. You'd think this would be an easy decision, but because I was wiped out from hiking all day, this simple operation seemed like a monumental task. On top of this, I thought I'd have to repack everything in the morning. While this isn't usually a big deal, I struggled to find the energy to get up and deal with the situation in my overly tired state. After a minute or so of cloudy thinking, I decided that it's all in my mind anyway, and I pulled the blanket back up. I closed my eyes and thought to myself, *Ahh! The smell of cat urine. Now I'm really a thru-hiker.* Within a few more seconds, I fell fast asleep.

The next morning, Bob Peoples dropped me off at the trailhead and I continued my hike northward. It was a gorgeous day with no snow at all on the trail. Several miles in, I stopped to admire Laurel Falls. The guidebook mentioned a dangerous whirlpool at the base of the falls, and a small sign on a tree mentioned the death of a father and son there in 2012. Bob told me later that he was part of the rescue that sad day, and that eight or ten people had died there over the past ten years.

Later, Bob helped me to hike without carrying all my gear by shuttling me from my endpoint back to where my car was parked on US 19 at the Mountain Harbor Hostel. I changed out of my hiking clothes (that felt so good!) and drove back out to my room at the house on Holston Lake for the night.

12

MARCH—A NEW TENT

STRENGTH DOESN'T COME FROM
WHAT YOU CAN DO. STRENGTH COMES
FROM OVERCOMING THE THINGS YOU
ONCE THOUGHT YOU COULDN'T.

I rested up by taking a zero the next day and then the following day I drove up to Damascus, Virginia to visit the outfitter and leave my car at Woodchuck's Hostel. I shuttled back down to Lake Watauga and headed north on the trail from the spot I had reached a few days earlier.

It was three years ago as of this date, March 3rd, when I was injured riding my motorcycle in a hare scrambles race in New Jersey. I smashed my hip, dislocated my femur, and damaged the nerve in my leg. Life as I knew it changed in an instant. I was doing triathlons and running marathons. I was set to run my third marathon in another two weeks. Well, as they say, life happens.

It's taken three years for me to begin to accept that I may never heal completely from my injury. I decided while hiking that I probably won't be able to run again—ever. And I'm okay with that. I decided that I'd rather focus on what I CAN do rather than focus on what I CAN'T do. If I weren't injured, it's likely that I'd never have decided to hike the trail. It's not what happens to you. It's what you do about it. With all that said, this was a day to celebrate.

By the end of the day, I was at Vandeventer Shelter with two other NOBOs, *Tyler* and *Ox,* who talked about doing a whopping thirty-two miles the next day into Damascus. It would take me four days to go the same distance at my pace of six to nine miles a day. The snow was blowing into the shelter, but I was warm inside my sleeping bag with just my nose peeking out into the fresh nighttime air.

As I headed out the next morning, the snow and ice that covered the trees broke off as it melted, falling to the ground in hundreds of little thunks. This had the effect of covering the trail in snow-covered candy canes that crunched underfoot as I walked along the path. I was trying to process the three-year anniversary of my injury that I had reached the day before. The fact that I was so slow on the trail bothered me. I was comparing the 6.8 miles that I'd hike that day to the 32 miles that *Tyler* and *Ox* set out to reach, starting at 5:00 AM that morning, and it left me with a "less than" feeling. I was a slowpoke out there.

The following day I arrived at Double Spring shelter at 2:15 PM and sat down to ponder the idea of hiking eight more miles to the next shelter. *Let's see. At my 1.25 miles-per-hour pace, that would get me in at 8:00 PM. I'd have to use my headlamp,* I thought. Then I remembered telling my father before I left on this five-day stretch that my next goal was to get to Damascus, but my main goal was to keep from getting worn out physically or mentally. I decided to be content with my seven-plus miles for the day.

I gathered up some wood, looking for the more combustible smaller sticks because of the dampness caused by the recently melted snow. I was able to occupy several hours by nurturing a small smoky campfire along.

Two day hikers stopped by to say hi and (I hate this) stuck their hands out to shake mine. Because of the risk of getting something like Norovirus, most thru-hikers will either skip the handshake entirely or use the more hygienic fist bump method. My natural response has always been to shake hands when someone sticks their hand out. (This all happened before Covid, of course.)

After they left, I washed my hands and thought about how I could avoid shaking hands with someone on the trail without offending them. I decided to respond by putting my hands together in front of me, accompanied by a slight bowing motion. I could even say "Namaste." I checked my thermometer and noticed that it was warmer than it had been lately—forty-one degrees, and it had just started to snow. I was sure glad I wasn't still out on the trail trying to make the next shelter. I was feeling better, and I was doing okay on the five day stretch thus far.

A few more days of excellent hiking brought me to the Tennessee/Virginia State line. This was an emotional experience for me as I thought back to my start the year before in Georgia. I remembered how wonderful it felt to reach the Georgia/North Carolina border at mile seventy-six. I thought about how I pushed and pushed myself until I finally crashed, utterly wiped out and exhausted, in Erwin, Tennessee before going home. At that point, I thought I was done. Now there I was with three states down and only eleven more to go!

After hiking another few miles, I reached Damascus, Virginia, which is known as Trail Town, USA. In addition to the Appalachian Trail and the Virginia Creeper Trail, there are five other nationally known trails in Damascus. I rested for a day at Woodchuck's Hostel and enjoyed talking with other hikers while I was there.

Since the Appalachian Trail goes right down the main street of Damascus, the next day I stopped into a deli to get a Rueben sandwich on the way through town. I saved half of it for a second lunch out on the trail. I spent that night in a shelter with a couple of day hikers planning on hiking the AT the following year. It was fun to be the one answering questions instead of the newbie hiker that I used to be.

Towards the end of the next day, I went through an open pasture and then up the hill to find a nice camping spot in the woods. Because I was ahead of the hiker bubble this year, there were plenty of dry branches, all within fifty feet of the fire pit. I was used to the wood being mostly wet, so I was a bit surprised when the fire grew quickly. The wind shifted towards me, pushing the flames right at me. I immediately jumped up and over the big log I had been sitting on, forgetting for the moment that my leg didn't remember how to jump.

I enjoyed another dinner of lentils and polenta as I looked out at the surrounding beautiful pine forest. There's something special about sitting by a campfire. I sat there feeling the warmth, remembering camping with Dad, and thinking about the connection to many generations past who stayed close to the fire for warmth, protection, and food preparation.

The following day, after hiking for a few hours, I stepped on a wet rock and my feet went right out from under me. I fell off the trail with my leg caught between a few rocks. Thankfully, I was okay. After dislodging my leg, I was able to roll over onto my back with my pack behind me. *I hope no one sees me,* I thought and then realized how funny that was.

If anything, I needed someone to come help me up. So, I pulled out my iPhone, grabbed my nearby hiking pole with a selfie phone holder on it, and made a video about falling. I got back up and felt energized by being able to take a mistake like that and turn it into something amusing.

In the afternoon, I came down the last step into the parking lot at Elk Garden and my right knee—on my *GOOD* leg—gave out and went backward in the wrong direction. I cried out in painful surprise, but within a minute or so after walking across the parking lot, it felt fine. I realized I needed to get a serious knee brace so that this body of mine could have a chance of making it to Maine.

Later that day, I climbed up the rocky, rooted trail to Thompson Knob Shelter. I enjoyed sitting out on the rocks behind the shelter, eating my dinner and enjoying the spectacular view. I was alone in the shelter until some younger section hikers who had camped nearby joined me in the middle of the night. They were having trouble staying dry in the rain and decided to move inside.

The next day I saw a bunch of wild ponies! I wasn't sure I would see any of them until I met a section hiker from Canada who gave me some carrots to feed them. I found out later that you're not supposed to feed them anything.

The U.S. Forest Service released the ponies into the area surrounding Mount Rogers National Recreation Area and Grayson Highlands State Park in 1975. The balds here maintained a clear-cut appearance through the first half of the 20th century due to cattle ranching, but after the government transformed the area into a state park in 1965, there were no more cows to keep the brush eaten down. That's why the ponies were introduced to the area.

The Appalachian Trail routes through hundreds of unique geologic formations, with the feature of the day being Fat Man's Cave. Inside there was ice on the floor, and it was fun to go through. About a half-mile past the cave, I stopped to make a video to celebrate reaching five hundred miles on the trail. I was so excited that I was screaming when I made it. Five minutes later, I ran into a day hiker who asked, "Are you the five-hundred-mile guy?"

"Oh, did you see me when I made that video?" I asked.

"No, but I heard you making it."

I heard my first grouse of the year. They beat their wings in the air while standing on a log, making an interesting thumping sound. Partway through the Grayson Highlands, I stopped and looked around. The area was grassland with sparse small trees and brush. The colors were more western United States looking, with coppers and browns that are rare in the East. I was awed by the ability to look 360 degrees around at wilderness as far as the eye could see. I just stood there and soaked it up, knowing that this was the only time I'd be in that beautiful spot on the trail.

The following day the trail had seemed to become much more manageable—smoother and far fewer rocks and roots than the Grayson Highlands. It was mostly ordinary woods until I was surprised by a waterfall down in the valley, not on the AT. I could see it and hear it, but it looked like a long hike to get down to see it up close, so I just kept going.

Over the last few days, I tested out adding Crystal Light flavor packets to my water to help me drink more water. I figured that if it tasted good, then I'd probably drink more water. Unfortunately, my Sawyer Filter began clogging up, even with regular backflushing.

I decided to switch to MSR tablets—little white pills that take forty minutes to treat the water. This meant I wouldn't be able to "camel up" or drink right at a water source, but I'd avoid carrying the extra ounces that the filter weighed, and I could add flavoring without worrying about clogging up the filter. Once I did this, I noticed that I was drinking about twice as much water as I had before adding flavoring, so I finally got the hydration that I needed.

I rested for the next two days because, well, I was tired. They were also the last two days of my months' rent at the house on Holston Lake. After pulling my various boxes of food and supplies out of the car, I inventoried and sorted everything on the dining room table. I made a big stack of all the Cinnamon Frosted Pop-Tarts and took a photo. I had enough food to make it for the next month and a half.

It'd been great to hang out in the house. Using the place for zero days meant more driving but ended up costing less than hotels and hostels. On top of that, it'd been good to know I had a nice place to stay rather than some of the questionable places along the trail. I was surprised by how quickly my zero days passed. Between sleeping in, running errands, and getting some good meals, there wasn't a ton of extra time. I had brought my piano keyboard with me but never played it because I was tired when I wasn't hiking. My experiment of having a home base to drive to worked out well enough for the month, but I planned to stay in either hostels or Airbnb places over the next month or two.

The next day I left my car near Atkins, got a shuttle to Dickey Gap, and had a short walk in to start my four-day run. While hiking that day, I saw the first signs of spring. The yellow flowers on bushes by the shelter had started to bloom, and the farmers' fields in the valley seemed to turn bright green overnight. I was enjoying the solitude both on the trail and in the shelters at night.

I used to feel upset and lonely when I couldn't find anyone who would hike slow enough to stay with me, but I had come to discover the beauty of the quietness, the stillness, the realness that happens when all of the everyday distractions disappear. No one else was at the Trimpi Shelter, which was nicely built of stone and had a privy and a fireplace inside.

After a long day of hiking the next day, I was excited to get to the Partnership Shelter to find out if it was true that you could have pizza delivered right to the shelter. When I got there, I met two younger NOBO hikers called *The 60s*, so named because their packs both weighed sixty-plus pounds when they started at Springer Mountain in Georgia. They explained that, yes, the rumors were true, but there was a thirty-dollar-minimum to order. I wasn't sure about getting two large pizzas for myself. So I sat down to rest a bit and enjoyed hearing *The 60s*' stories about hiking through the Smoky Mountains in the deep snow.

I finally succumbed and was about to walk over to the Mt. Rogers Visitors center to place my pizza order when one of *The 60s* offered to let me have the last two slices from his box. "Are you sure?" I asked, making a concerted effort to not grab the pizza too quickly. *Two slices are about all I need,* I thought as I stuffed them down.

One of them talked about how he needed to get from the Relax Inn in Atkins to the actual town three miles down the road to get his resupply box from the post office. I surprised him by saying, "That's where my car is. Go ahead and use it." I asked him to leave the key for me in the super-secret location on top of the front tire.

Each shelter along the Appalachian Trail has a hiker journal where you can sign in, leave notes for other hikers behind you, or share something about your day. There was a NOBO named *Dr. John* who'd been writing rather extreme political statements in the journals. He blew by me in the Grayson Highlands, saying something about how far he was behind schedule as he walked right past me without breaking his stride. At the Trimpi Shelter the night before, I noticed that he had written something that started with, "The reason the Republicans are such morons is . . ."

I decided to have some fun, so using the same pen and mimicking *Dr. John's* shaky lettering, I added "Trump Supporter" right after his name. *The 60s* had obviously stopped in to sign the Trimpi shelter journal since they brought his name up along with his inconsistent entry.

"Really, he wrote that?" I asked, testing to see if my forgery had passed muster.

"Yes! I looked carefully at it, and it was in the same handwriting."

I decided to let them in on my little joke.

In the Partnership Shelter journal, *Dr. John* had written another note, finishing with, "I write interesting things. At least I don't write, 'Last night, I had pizza.'"

So, *The 60s* made the following entry:

"Last night, I had pizza."

I really enjoyed my conversations with *The 60s*. It was nice to have someone to talk to for a change. One of *The 60s* was into listening to music while he hiked. I told him I had tried using Pandora a few times but had given up because it was hard to get a cell signal while on the trail. He suggested using Spotify. He told me that he liked Spotify because you could download as many songs as you wanted to your phone and then play them back when you didn't have cell coverage.

I dropped my subscription to Pandora and switched to Spotify. Over time, I ended up with a good selection of songs that I liked due to the algorithm's recommendations. Most of these were from new artists that I had never heard of before.

The download to your phone feature works great for hikers, although I discovered that you need to go online at least once every thirty days to keep listening to the songs you've downloaded. One significant advantage of having so much time while hiking is that you can do things like really listen to music. It was exciting to discover new songs that I absolutely loved. For the last thirty years, I'd been stuck with just the songs and artists I'd listened to back when I was a teenager.

When I started getting tired in the afternoon, I found that I could turn on the playlist of all the new songs that I'd discovered in Spotify and just soak them up while I walked along. Before long, I'd have gone another two or three miles with the music helping me down the trail. I gained a new appreciation for music and have made listening to my song list a regular part of my hiking (and normal) life.

I also joined Audible and tried listening to audiobooks. I'd done this in the past, but my choices were usually limited to either business or history books. I found that for hiking, I preferred listening to John Grisham-type stories. I also listened to *When Breath Becomes Air* by Paul Kalanithi.

Audible provides a daily audio version of the New York Times included with membership. I had to have a cell signal to download each new day, which wasn't much of a problem as I would usually have a signal at some point during the day. Even if I listened a day later, I could stay updated on the world while out on the trail. One nice feature with Audible is that you can "return" any audiobooks within the first year after purchase. This allowed me to try out various books that I wouldn't usually purchase.

That evening I began hearing insects in the forest and wondered if this coincided with the arrival of spring. I had started to sleep really well at night. It seemed that somewhere along the line, I had settled into hiking. I no longer felt out of my element.

The following morning, I woke up while it was still dark at about 5:00 AM. I stayed in my sleeping bag, turning from side to side and massaging the sore muscles in each of my hips. I had picked up a knee brace with metal hinges at a drug store to keep the knee on my good leg from hyperextending, as it did a few days ago. It must be helping as my knee didn't hurt last night.

After an hour or so of massaging my sore muscles while staying warm in my sleeping bag, I got up and made hot chocolate to accompany my Frosted Cinnamon Pop-Tarts for breakfast. I had planned to take two days to get to Atkins but decided I felt well enough to make it in one day. It was only twelve miles, and the trail elevation looked relatively easy.

I stopped at the Settlers Museum and checked out an old one-room schoolhouse open for hikers to visit. The local church had left several boxes of trail magic. There were foot warmers, hats, mittens, gloves, and some handmade scarves. I didn't need anything, but it felt nice to know that people are looking out for you.

It was late in the afternoon when I made it to Atkins and walked across the road to the Relax Inn where *The 60s* had returned my car. I found the key on top of the front tire. *It's so nice to be able to trust other hikers. I lent my car to someone without even knowing his real name!*

I wondered if the Relax Inn owner was going to charge me for parking in his (completely empty) parking lot or for holding the two boxes I'd shipped there from Amazon.

Sometimes places will do that if you don't stay there. I had no intention of staying because the Relax Inn looked like it was about to fall over and had (I'm not kidding) a half-star rating. When I limped into the parking lot, the owner came out from vacuuming a room, asking if I was okay.

"I'm fine. Old injury," I said and then asked him how his day was going. After I mentioned the boxes, he went into the office and brought them out to me.

"Here you go. No charge," he said, smiling at me.

"Wow. Thanks."

I realized then that I hadn't gotten angry about him asking if I was okay. I felt as if I'd turned the corner and was finally walking on hope rather than dragging along resentment over my injury.

The Appalachian Trail was slowly healing me.

That evening, I drove down to Bristol, Virginia where I had booked a massage therapist to work on my leg the next day. I stayed in a $25 Airbnb, which I'd describe as adequate for my needs, but I didn't think that my wife would consider staying there. It was nice to take a day and relax, allowing my leg and muscles to catch up with all the hiking I'd been doing.

I drove halfway back to Atkins and stayed at the Woodchuck Hostel again in Damascus. There were several people I enjoyed talking to while I was there. One, named *1046,* was a writer. He took notes and recorded me as I shared my story of hiking the trail with my injured leg. I also met *Bandit,* a thru-hiker, who recounted getting shot in the head while serving our country in Iraq. He was doing fine, and had a remarkable story. One of the best things about staying at hostels was getting to know other people who also have an adventurous spirit.

I moved my car up the trail the next day and then shuttled back down to Atkins. Over the next few days, I enjoyed the decent weather and relatively friendly trail surface. In the afternoon on the third day, after climbing up a long grassy meadow, I met *Salty*, *Waffles*, and *Cosmo* at the Knot Maul Branch Shelter. They were all young, energetic people and fun to talk with, although I still struggled with the fact that all the hikers I'd met so far were moving up the trail much faster than I was.

The next evening, I was by myself at the Chestnut Knob Shelter, which is on a ridge with no trees. The wind was really howling. Luckily, the shelter had four walls and a door, and metal cables that go through the walls to hold the roof on and keep it from blowing off.

The following two days were great hiking. The temperature was in the mid-sixties, and with the trail following along ridgelines, the pathway was smooth and level. Off to my left was Burke's Garden, a valley surrounded on all four sides by mountains. This was also called God's Thumbprint. To my right was another valley with more ridges lined up beyond it on the other side that look like a big blue ocean. Gorgeous.

The next day I moved my car up to Woods Hole Hostel, where I had dinner and stayed overnight in the bunkhouse. The owners, Michael and Neville, put on a good show, including getting most of the hikers to help make dinner along with a special ceremony of holding hands and going around the circle to share something for which we were thankful. We have a similar tradition every Thanksgiving at home. We go around the table once, all sharing one thing we're grateful for, and then go around again to share something we're hopeful for in the coming year.

In the morning I shuttled from Woods Hole back down to Bland, Virginia, where I had left off hiking a few days earlier. I passed the six-hundred-mile point and could hardly believe it. It felt great to be out on the trail, and my mental and physical health seemed to be doing well, although my injured leg bothered me towards the end of the day.

A day later, after following an easy trail with just one hill, I hit the road crossing where Trent's Grocery was a half-mile away. I debated getting a hamburger. The guidebook said they offered shuttles, so I called to see if I could pay them to drive me the one mile to get there and back. The driver wasn't in, so I kept hiking. With my leg hurting and so many more miles to Maine, I didn't want to walk any further than I had to.

The rest of the day was pretty smooth hiking along Dismal Creek surrounded by rhododendrons. I reached the camping spot I had selected ahead of time by 3:00 PM, but I decided to continue walking since I was still feeling good, and the trail was so nice. Before long, it was only a few more miles to get to the shelter. It was easy to keep going for my longest day of fourteen and a half miles!

The next day I had just seven miles to get to Woods Hole Hostel, where I had left my car. It was only noon when I reached the road above the hostel, which was a half-mile down the hill. This was a half-mile that was *not* on the AT—the kind of miles I tried to avoid. Luckily for me, there was a guy in a red pickup truck right there with the motor idling. He was waiting for the rest of his crew to install a new cell phone tower, which sat on the back of a nearby tractor-trailer.

"Any chance I can get a ride down the hill?" I asked.

"Sure thing! Hop in," he responded.

I had a package waiting for me at the hostel. It was my new Zpacks Duplex Tent! I had made it that far using a tiny little tent that didn't have room for anything other than my pad, sleeping bag, and myself. I couldn't sit up without hitting my head on the roof, which causes the water to come in if it was raining. At twenty-two ounces, the new tent was lightweight, had room to move around, and now I could finally bring my pack in out of the rain to unpack and repack all my gear.

I spent another night in the bunkhouse at the hostel and woke up to enjoy a savory breakfast of French toast, juice, and hot coffee. After breakfast, I did some planning for the pieces of the trail that were coming up, deciding how far I would go each day and where I would stop at night. I finally headed up the hill towards the trail at noon and was soon on my way hiking along on a beautiful day.

I saw three or four NOBOs on the trail. One of them, *TP*, was kind enough to walk slower with me for a while and chat. I stopped to camp at a site on the cliffs overlooking Pearisburg, which has beautiful views. I unpacked my new tent and managed to put it up after watching a few YouTube videos. I started a fire to warm me up a bit while I made dinner. It was supposed to drop into the low thirties at night, which would be a good test to see if my spring bag, which is what I had with me, would be warm enough.

The wind picked up and blew the flames from the fire four or five feet sideways. I watched the sparks fly off into the forest while thinking how stupid I'd feel if I caught the Appalachian Trail on fire. I should have thought of that before making a campfire on the top of the ridge. I spread the wood around and used the rest of my water to get the fire down to smoldering.

The next day I made my way down the steep trail into Pearisburg and hiked back up the other side, where I stopped to look out across the valley at Pearis Mountain where I had been the previous night. Even the uphill climb was enjoyable. At 5:30 PM, I came to the Rice Field Shelter and decided to keep going for a few reasons. First off, no one else was there. Secondly, my legs still felt good, and the third reason was that I didn't have much water as I'd skipped my chance to fill up at a stream while coming up the mountain.

So, I made it another couple of miles north to get to a water source but didn't see a decent spot to camp for the night. The problem was that the wind had really begun to blow—strong enough that I didn't know if my tent was going to make it through the night. As I wandered around trying to find a flat spot for my tent on the lee side of the ridge, I wished I'd stayed put at the shelter where I could have been out of the wind.

In the morning it felt good to get started hiking after such a long windy night. I guessed that the gusts were thirty-five or forty miles-per-hour from the sound of them. I needed to learn how to stake out my new tent properly as the top was flapping in and out in the breeze, keeping me awake for a good part of the night. It didn't help me sleep any better when a tree fell at 2:30 in the morning, about a hundred feet from my tent.

ONLY WHEN I STEP ON IT

In the afternoon, I ran into two NOBOs that I had met before, *Nice Guy* and *TP*. They were willing to hike along with me for an hour, and I pushed myself to move faster as I enjoyed the conversation with them. They eventually pushed on ahead of me. I was surprised when I caught back up to them at a shelter where they had stopped for a break.

"Want to go to The Captain's with us?" they asked as I walked up.

"Sure, why not?" I responded, thinking that I might like to sit down and rest instead. I again pushed myself to hike faster than I usually did so that I wouldn't slow my companions down too much. Before long, we came to a zip line used to cross over the river to get to The Captain's place. The Captain met us at the zipline and admitted that he got his name because he looked a bit like Captain Kangaroo.

He showed us around his yard, which he made available for hikers to pitch their tents. I noticed a well-made fire pit with benches around it that could seat fifteen or twenty hikers. The Captain gave us sodas and declined any type of donation, simply saying, "Just pass it on." I had a root beer and then "zipped back" across the river to hike another mile to meet a shuttle from another hostel that I was going to be staying at. I was taking a well-deserved rest day after six days on the trail.

13

APRIL—MAGIC SPOTS

YOU NEVER KNOW HOW STRONG
YOU ARE UNTIL BEING STRONG IS
THE ONLY CHOICE YOU HAVE.

—BOB MARLEY

I enjoyed the sound of the rain pouring down on the bunkhouse roof at the hostel while staying warm and dry. I'd realized that the perfect hike has it raining only when you're inside a shelter, bunkhouse, or motel. I'd had pretty good luck with this lately, and didn't know how long my luck would last, but I was enjoying it for the moment.

I wanted to do something for April Fool's day, ideally tricking my kids somehow. The only idea I could think of was telling them a made-up story about how I broke my leg. The other hikers at breakfast that morning said that wasn't a particularly good idea, so I decided to skip it.

It might be better if I don't mention the name of this hostel because I have a few stories to share about my experience there. It seems that at many of these hostels, the owners not only have to work all hours, but depending on the setup, they also must handle being surrounded by hikers without having much personal space.

We talked about this at dinner that night, where the hostel owner was telling us how it drove him crazy that so many hikers ask the same stupid questions. "What's that you're growing there?" he mimicked as he talked about hikers questioning him about his garden. He probably didn't realize that I had asked him that exact same question earlier that day.

Then, there's the way he showed me around the place on the first day I arrived.

"Here's the bunkhouse. This building has a shower room, and here's the indoor privies. Please don't use the bathroom in the house as that's for our bed and breakfast guests only." No problem, I can follow directions.

In the privy room, there was also a urinal. It was a little lower down than most other installations I'd seen. There was an upper part made of porcelain with a number of ceramic rocks piled up on the floor underneath it. I thought it was a little funky but not out of place compared to numerous other hostels along the trail where I'd seen stuff cobbled together out of spare parts. So, what else would I do? I used this "urinal" the day I arrived, spent the night, and shuttled six days south.

When I hiked back to the hostel and spent another two nights there, I could have walked out in the woods to pee, but I did the civilized thing and used the urinal. Then I moved my car four or five days up the trail and shuttled back to spend another night. Why not? It's a nice place to stay. Oh, and yes, I did use the urinal—probably five or six times. It's not like I was counting.

One morning, the owner walked up to me and said, "I can't f***ing believe it! Do you know who's been PISSING all over that urinal?! It's not plumbed up! I just set it there against the wall!" He stared right at me as I did my darndest to keep a straight face. It felt like having red and blue lights flash behind me on the highway—but I simultaneously thought this was extremely funny.

I didn't want to lie, but at the same time I wasn't about to admit to anything. So, I just kind of shrugged my shoulders and gave him my best, "I have no idea" face. I don't know what he thought. For all I know, he's telling stories about the time that *Flash 52* peed all over his plumbing supplies.

Back on the trail, I thought about how pleased I was to be able to hike for six days straight without over-stressing my injured leg. I thought I might be ready to bump up my daily mileage but would be cautious and make changes gradually.

Just after lunch, I met and walked with *Old Grouse*, a NOBO who was willing to hike with me at my pace. It sure was nice to have someone to talk with. *Old Grouse* told me about a couple of NOBOs, *Otis* and *Mongo*, whom he had met at The Captain's Place. Although the Captain wasn't there, they poked around on their own and found some frozen trout in the freezer. He said that *Otis* and *Mongo* told him, "The Captain must have caught these to give away to hikers."

Although he didn't admit to lifting any fish himself, *Old Grouse* seemed to like the idea of this, as he said he was low on food and getting a bit hungry. When we finally arrived at the War Spur Shelter, I got to meet *Otis* and *Mongo,* who were working away cooking up their newfound fish. They had made a large fire, cooked it down into red coals and then placed a large, flat rock on top of the coals followed by the first of several fish that they'd be cooking. "Yum, yum…" *Otis* said, "this one's called 'Little Jimmy.'"

Little Jimmy was just starting to smell good when, suddenly, the rock exploded. Little Jimmy catapulted into the air, *Mongo* leapt back from the fire in surprise, and Little Jimmy flopped down onto the dirt. *Mongo,* who was thrilled he wasn't injured by the exploding rock, retrieved Little Jimmy, cleaned him up, and shared the fish with the rest of us. I realize I could have written this differently to obscure my involvement, but I'm giving you the straight scoop here so, yes, I do confess to eating stolen fish. (Sorry about that, Captain.) It was delicious.

"The King" was next on the menu, and he was a much larger trout. The King was almost done when the replacement rock exploded as well—flinging The King twenty feet up in the air. *Mongo* almost caught him this time on the way down. *Otis* and *Mongo* made quite a pair laughing about the exploding rocks and flying fish. *Old Grouse* and I couldn't help but join in with the hilarity.

I made my dinner of lentils and mashed potatoes while sitting on the picnic table, enjoying the warm evening by the fire out in the wilderness. After it got dark, the wind picked up and was vigorously blowing through the trees in the forest when we heard the sound of a branch breaking up above us.

Instantly all four of us jumped up and ran into the shelter for cover. *Old Grouse* was moaning because in the dark he banged his shins into the edge of the shelter. I shouted out with glee, saying, "That's amazing! I haven't been able to run in three years!" I went to sleep thinking about how funny *Otis, Mongo*, and the exploding fish were. I didn't realize that my adventures with them had just begun.

The next day I went through several nice grassy pastures, which made for a nice change from hiking along the ridge tops or through the woods. At about 7:00 pm, I went past the Keffer Oak Tree, the second-largest oak tree on the Appalachian Trail. It's over three hundred years old. I noticed a nice green grassy campsite there with a bunch of firewood stacked up right by the fire pit and decided to stay there for the night.

It turned out that I was in a cow pasture. Several cows came by to check me out, including a smaller calf who was curious about the campfire and the meal I was cooking. During the night, an animal chewed on the hot chocolate residue on the edge of my cookpot top, which I'd left by the fire pit.

I used the following two days to gradually get up to a ridge where I reached the Audie Murphy Monument, overlooking a beautiful valley. Audie Murphy was an American soldier, actor, songwriter, and rancher. He was one of the most decorated American combat soldiers of World War II. He died in a plane crash near the monument's site when he was almost forty-six years old.

A few hours after this, I met a South Bounder, or SOBO, named *Mountain Man*. His name was fitting—he was short and had a long white beard that came down almost to his waist. He seemed pretty excited to tell me the story about a skunk attack he had witnessed the previous night. He was camping out with—who else—*Otis* and *Mongo*, the exploding fish guys. Here's what I found out from *Mountain Man* there on the trail and later when I caught up to *Mongo* at the next hostel.

It seems that a skunk had initially wandered into the camp while they were out by the fire, and they had shooed it away. When the fire died down, they all hit the sack. *Mongo* was sleeping outside on his mini cot (without a tent). *Mountain Man* and *Otis* saw the skunk come back and walk over to the foot of *Mongo's* cot.

They tried to wake *Mongo* up, but he said he was tired and buried his head in his pillow. Then the skunk jumped on *Mongo's* back and sunk its claws in. *Mongo*, who was now fully awake, leapt up and jumped around. "*Otis*! Get him off, get him off… *Otis*, get him off of me!"

"Ok, he's off, but he's not going away!"

"*Otis*, you've got to take care of this for me," *Mongo* pleaded. "I can't deal with this. Just smack him for me, will ya?"

After much yelling, poking with hiking sticks, a smack from a hiking boot, and a final mighty "Tiger Woods" swing with a large branch, the score was one dead skunk, and one seriously damaged *Mongo* foot. While *Mongo* was jumping up and down, he sliced the bottom of his foot open on a piece of shale. A skunk that acts like this is most likely rabid, so while I felt bad for the skunk, I was glad that no one was bitten.

Later that afternoon, I climbed up a series of ridges to get to Dragon's Tooth, which is a large rock formation on the top of a mountain which, of course, looks like a dragon's tooth. The climb up to the top included a fair amount of scrambling over rocks using my hands and feet. Once I got up there, I looked forward to what appeared on FarOut to be an easy downhill trail to take me to the Four Points Hostel.

As it turned out, there were several places where I had to find a way down fifteen to twenty-foot-high cliffs by stepping on ledges that were an inch or two wide. "I'm supposed to go down that?" I asked myself out loud. If I'd had a climbing rope, I would have rappelled down.

So, I reminded myself to go slowly and carefully as it was the end of the day. I was tired and alone. I took my pack off and used my bear bag rope to lower my pack down ahead of me, then I carefully climbed down while holding on with both hands.

I did fine for the first three or four drops but then found myself halfway down a cliff without a place to step down any further. My options were limited; my injured foot muscles were too weak to hold a grip on the tiny ledges.

I saw a small tree four feet out from the cliff, and without considering any other options, I leapt out and wrapped my arms around the tree, intending to slide down it. The tree bent downhill over steeply sloped terrain, and I suddenly realized I was seriously at risk. Fortunately, the tree was strong enough to spring back without breaking, and I slid down, gripping the bark with my gloves to slow my descent.

At this point, the trail leveled out, and I made my way down the hill while thinking about another time when I was in danger of losing my life. When I was twenty, I worked as a mechanic at a Texaco gas station. One of our good clients brought a VW Rabbit in and asked us to see if we could fix a loud whistling sound that occurred while he was driving. I used an air hose to blow compressed air over the front of the car but wasn't able to reproduce the sound.

So, then I told the other mechanic, "Tell you what, if you can drive up the back road at like 20 mph, I'll get on the hood and move the wipers and stuff around. If we can get the noise to come and go, we'll know where it's coming from." And we actually tried it! I couldn't hear anything, so I asked him to drive a little faster… then a little faster…

Suddenly, my brain kicked in, and I realized I was going 55 mph on the hood of a car. I shouted out, "Carefully… Gradually… Slow down and stop!" Clinging to that tree had reminded me that I'm capable of making serious mistakes in judgment.

When I reached the road, I turned right and limped my way up to the Four Pines Hostel. I ran into *Otis* and *Mongo at the hostel,* who gave me their version of the skunk attack story. I met *Big Cheese*, who told me about being stationed (and injured) in Iraq. After serving there for a year, he was 20 minutes away from leaving to go home when he was shot in the leg and arm, suffering nerve damage similar to my injury. Seeing him doing so well despite his serious injuries was quite motivating.

I had been looking forward to the hike up to McAfee Knob since the beginning of my Appalachian Trail journey last year. The most photographed spot on the Appalachian Trail, it is named for James McAfee, a Scots-Irish immigrant.

He settled here in the late 1730s. After crossing the road, I did the four-mile climb arriving at the top by 5:00 pm.

I wanted to get some good photos with my legs hanging over the edge but was afraid to get close to the edge. Finally, *Timeout*, another NOBO, offered to take some pictures and helped me get my courage up to sit right on the edge. After getting my photo taken, I tried to scoot back from the edge but couldn't move because my backpack was caught on a piece of the ledge. "Hey *Timeout*, can you *please* come over here and pull me in?" He was nice enough to come over and grab onto my pack and pull me back from the edge.

It was with a bit of regret that I finally left McAfee Knob with its gorgeous views and made my way less than a mile down to Campbell Shelter to spend the night. Two other hikers were there with me: *Old-Growth* and another NOBO named *Disfunkschwenal. She* was starting out on day one of her flip-flop hike of the Appalachian Trail beginning here at McAfee Knob. A flip-flop hike is where you start somewhere other than the top or bottom of the trail, hike to one end, and then "flip" down to where you started to complete the remaining section.

I enjoyed beautiful views in the morning as I made my way from Campbell Shelter down into Daleville—my longest day yet at just over fifteen miles. I kept stopping to look off the rocky ledges and enjoy the wonderful valley with its patchwork quilt of sunny and shaded spots spread out below.

I then took four days off to drive up to Maryland to see my beautiful wife. It felt bizarre to be off the trail and back in civilization for a few days. I was surprised to discover that

I still had a hard time walking around town. I was hiking so well on my leg that I assumed I'd be able to walk much better once I was off the trail. When I'm hiking, I have support from my hiking boots, various braces, and the support of my hiking poles, which help stabilize my gait.

While I was home resting, I did a lot of sitting around with my leg propped up only to find that my leg had stiffened up, and it was painful to walk even a short distance. I wondered if some part of me was holding back to make sure every step I took counted toward completing the Appalachian Trail.

One of the best parts of hiking the trail was that it made daily decision-making easier for me. My goal each day was to make it another ten or twelve miles north up the trail. Some days when I got up in the morning, my foot and leg hurt so much that I wondered if I'd even be able to walk. I would grab my hiking poles and take a few initial steps to loosen my foot up a bit. Then I would stretch out the calf on my injured leg because it got really tight.

The first mile or so could be painful for me, but I could push ahead for two reasons. First, I knew that once my leg loosened up a bit, the day would get better. The second reason was that I knew that if I could push myself through some discomfort, I'd, hopefully, be healed up and out of pain once I completed my hike.

After my four-day break, I headed south in my car to get back on the trail. It had felt strange to take a break from hiking, and then it felt very strange to be back on the trail again. My leg and foot were bothering me quite a bit, which was surprising since I'd taken a four-day rest. My first day back ended up being a little harder than a typical hiking day for me.

PETER E CONTI

I stopped at the Fullhardt Knob Shelter to try out the cistern water system, which worked great. Rainwater is collected on the roof of the shelter and runs down into a cistern. A pipe runs a bit further downhill ending at a spigot that opens to fill up your water bottle. It was a reasonably smooth trail for the day, which was nice since my leg was bothering me more than usual. I stopped again later to get more water when my oldest daughter called.

I was surprised that she reached me when I was surrounded by hills on all four sides. Since I was often hiking alone, it was extra special for me when I was able to text or talk with my family from the trail.

While I was home with my wife, she asked me what I think about all day long while I'm hiking, and I couldn't really explain it. So, I began to pay attention to my thoughts and discovered that much of the time, I simply enjoyed each moment of being out on the Appalachian Trail and hiking in the great outdoors. It sounds simple, but this may be one of the biggest benefits of going on an adventure like this—the ability to be fully present and enjoy each moment of the day.

Sometimes I thought about funny things that my kids did growing up or many of the awkward, stupid, or fun things that I had done throughout my life. The nice thing about having so much time just to be quiet and think is that I could process through and get a chance to enjoy, once more, many of the funny moments I've had. Or think through mistakes I've made and work my way towards forgiving myself for being less than perfect on occasion.

The next day my leg and foot began to feel better, so my new theory was that it takes a day of hiking to loosen

247

ONLY WHEN I STEP ON IT

things up. I didn't have far to go. The six miles were short and easy with a smooth downhill trail to get me back to my car at Jennings Creek Rd. While crossing the bridge, I saw *Last Chance* soaking his feet in the cool river. He started last year hiking north from Harper's Ferry to Katahdin. This year he was hiking the southern part of the trail. During this stretch, he had two different incidents that could have easily ended his hike.

The first was first and second-degree burns he suffered when he spilled boiling water on his leg. The second was a staph infection that infected an insect bite on his hip. At sixty-three years, *Last Chance* was eight years older than I was, hiked faster than I did (like most people), and had incredible persistence. I found it quite motivating to talk with him.

I then met with Stephanie, the news reporter from the Roanoke Times. I spent the night a few weeks ago at a shelter with some friends of hers, who introduced me as a possible news story. It was fun having a photographer snap photos of me and take some hiking videos while I filled her in on the details of my motorcycle racing accident three years ago.

My hope was that by sharing my story, I could encourage other people who deal with chronic pain or traumatic injuries that life can go on. It took me a good three years to accept that I was injured for life. While I can't run anymore, (unless a branch cracks above my head) I *can* hike the Appalachian Trail. And that's one of the secrets when you're hurt—don't focus on what you can't do. Focus on what you CAN do.

After meeting with Stephanie, I drove to the airport. Then I flew down to Florida for a few days, just as I had done the prior year, to watch my son play paintball in the Collegiate Paintball Nationals with his team from Clemson, SC. He was president of the team, and I enjoyed seeing him leading and encouraging his teammates. In years past, I'd gotten a hotel and a rental car. Having hiked the AT, I was used to getting by with less. So, I decided to Uber over and stay in my tent at the playing fields.

When I arrived at 11:00 pm, I discovered that the municipal fields were fenced and completely locked up this year. Rental car? Didn't need it. Hotel? Uh, maybe I should have gotten one. I found a secluded spot behind the brick entrance wall that wasn't quite big enough for my tent, but that would accommodate me "cowboy" style, out under the stars. I checked the weather, and it wasn't supposed to rain. So I blew up my sleeping pad, pulled out my sleeping bag, and went to sleep.

That is, I tried to go to sleep. I quickly discovered that it's way easier to sleep in the cool, quiet mountain air on the Appalachian Trail than twenty feet from a noisy highway in the hot, humid Florida night. When it began to rain, I felt.... well, like I was homeless. I decided to stay at the Marriott the following night.

The next day, I flew from Orlando to Lynchburg with a transfer in Charlotte, North Carolina. The Charlotte airport is enormous, and I managed to walk through the entire airport without any assistance. You'd think this would be easy for anyone who's hiking the Appalachian Trail. Still, a year and a half ago, I used a wheelchair in airports because I could not walk long distances.

Healing from a traumatic injury like this comes very slowly over time. One of the most frustrating parts of getting better is that your progress can be so slow it's hard to notice that you're improving. Walking through the airport without assistance made me realize that hiking the Appalachian Trail really was healing me.

After the airplane landed in Lynchburg, I drove back to the trail. I didn't get to the trailhead until just after 5:30 pm, so I breezed up the hill and hiked 3.8 miles as quickly as possible to get to the Bryant Ridge Shelter. This was one of the largest and fanciest shelters I'd seen on the trail. Even though it sleeps fourteen people and has three levels, I was the only one there. As I laid there looking out into the woods, I could hear the stream running nearby along with the other forest sounds of the night.

While hiking the next day, I met a SOBO hiker who told me to look for water about a third of a mile before reaching the Thunder Hill Shelter, where I planned to spend the night. Once I got near the shelter, I searched for the water source by walking up and down a fire road for forty-five minutes in the gathering darkness. I finally went back to the section of trail where I thought the spring should have been. *Ah-ha!* I was surprised to find a note written on a piece of paper that was held down by a rock—right where I'd walked by forty-five minutes before!

The note pointed out the spring, which was fifty yards downhill. I wondered how I managed to walk by this message when I was specifically looking for the spring. Turned out the spring was just a trickle, and I had to use a small plastic tube to create a mini waterspout so I could fill up my water bottle. At least I'd had water to make dinner. At the shelter, there were three other hikers there that night, and we had a nice campfire going.

When I got up the next day, I talked with *Keeper*, who runs the Unified Warrior Foundation. He was hiking in honor of PTSD vets who have committed suicide at the rate of twenty-two vets per day. He was carrying the name tags of forty-four deceased vets from Springer Mountain to Katahdin. After talking with him, I learned much about how we needed to provide better support and care for our returning vets. I spent a lot of time thinking about this and found another organization that does great work as well, Homes For Our Troops (www.hfotusa.org).

Later that afternoon, I was moving along an easy section of trail when I hooked a root with my injured foot and suddenly fell flat on my face. As I was getting up, I recalled falling while trying to use an escalator about two years ago when I was still using crutches. I thought about this and figured the difference is that if I fall on my face in the woods, there was less of a chance that anyone would see me.

When I woke up the next day, I could hear the birds singing through the morning mist. What sounded like intermittent rain against the outside of my tent was likely to be the remnants of last night's storm getting blown off the canopy of leaves overhead by the morning's breeze.

I began what had become my morning routine. Sliding my left leg out of my warm sleeping bag into the cool morning air. Crossing over the right leg, I reached out, grabbed onto my foot, and pumped my left ankle with my right hand. Extend, back, extend, back, pushing as far down and up as my limited range of motion allows. 19, 20... 30... 40... and finally 99... 100.

Next was "winding the clock," where I held the end of

my foot and turned my ankle clockwise 100 times. Then 100 times the other way. It's hard to know if all this really helped my foot or not. I told myself that it would help to reduce the pain I felt during the day.

Next, I put my leg up on my knee and drew little circles with my toes in the air. The first hundred looked mostly like circles, while the counterclockwise set looked more like fishhooks. *It all helps*, I told myself, remembering that one of the many "Fixing Your Pain" books I read said this helps reduce pain and improve healing.

The problem was that I wanted to be healed right then. Yesterday would have been even better. To finally be rid of the nagging hurt. That was my goal and was why I was out hiking the Appalachian Trail. To get rid of the pain. To heal myself.

After twenty or thirty minutes of swirling my foot around, I reached back and opened the valve in my air mattress so it could deflate while I got ready. I put on my camo tights, toe socks, ankle brace, and hiking socks. Then I stuffed my sleeping bag into its waterproof compression bag, pushing it down tight so that it took up as little space as possible.

I rolled up my air mattress, stowed it into the bottom of my pack next to my sleeping bag, followed by all the other odds and ends. Yesterday's socks got pinned to the back of my pack so they could dry while I was hiking.

Finally, as I put my boots on, I evaluated how my foot might be doing based on the initial sensations that resulted from pulling the laces tight. As I backed out of the tent, I was able to do another stretch, releasing some of the tightness in my left calf.

As I hobbled over to get my food bag down from its place on the bear line in a nearby tree, I couldn't help but grimace a bit with each step. If I didn't know that each day started like that, I would have wondered if I'd be able to make it another ten or twelve miles.

By the time I packed up the tent, ate my two Pop-Tarts, and got ready to go, the initial pain and stiffness had passed for the day. I swung my pack onto my back, buckled it up, and followed the blue-blazed path back to the AT. I turned northward and began my walk for another day.

It was 2:30 pm when I arrived at my target shelter for the day, so I decided to try to make it to the next shelter, which would be a total of fourteen miles. This would make it close to my longest day so far. Until recently, I'd always used a trash bag liner inside my pack to keep everything nice and dry. Because the weather had been so dry lately, I got into the bad habit of leaving this trash bag liner ignored in the bottom of my pack.

Around 4:30, the sky opened up, and it rained... hard. My pack cover, which I thought was waterproof, got soaked and then allowed the falling water to work its way through my entire pack. I thought of stopping a few different times to check my pack and retrieve my trash bag liner from the bottom where I had stashed it the week before. Each time I convinced myself that things would just get even wetter since it was raining so hard.

By the time I finally arrived at the Seeley-Woodworth Shelter, everything I had—all of my clothes, everything in my pack—was wet. Luckily, my sleeping bag was protected by a compression dry bag. I put up a clothesline, hung everything up, and went to bed wearing just a pair of rather damp shorts. After this experience, I decided to faithfully use my trash bag liner and carry a dry set of clothes to sleep in. I asked my wife to get me a Cuban fiber pack cover for my birthday. It's expensive, but as it's actually waterproof, I think it's certainly worth it.

In the morning the weather was warmer which made it easier to put my wet hiking clothes back on. Within a few hours, everything had completely dried out. It was 2:00 pm when I reached the Priest Shelter. The dozen other hikers there looked half settled. I noticed a few food bags hanging from a tree, and I wondered if they were getting a late start or had arrived early to spend the night.

Seam, the NOBO that I had spent last night with at the Seeley-Woodworth Shelter, showed up with another thru-hiker, and suddenly there wasn't enough room for everyone to sit down. This seemed strange to me after hiking for two and a half months and seeing only a handful of hikers each week.

A tradition on the trail is to "confess your hiker sins" at the Priest Shelter by making an entry in the shelter journal. I asked for forgiveness for the times that I'd burned trash in the campfire. You're not supposed to do this because any metal or plastic that doesn't combust completely is left behind.

Shortly after leaving the shelter, I started down the trail, which dropped over 3,000 feet to reach the Tye River Crossing. I sent a text with an ETA to my sister Lisa, who would be picking me up at the bottom of the hill and started down the mountain. The trail was steep and rocky, and I moved slowly down the hill as I looked for a relatively flat place to place my injured foot with each step.

I met a number of SOBO hikers who all looked pretty freaked out as they climbed up the steep grade past me. Each of them asked if it was much further to the top, and I tried to be encouraging without saying, "You're almost there." I wondered how much further I had to go when I was surprised to see my sister hiking up to meet me. We hiked the last half mile together and met my brother-in-law, who invited me to sit down in some camp chairs in the parking lot along Route 56.

I enjoyed a glass of wine along with a few chocolate chip cookies they had brought to feed me and the thru-hikers who showed up. I met *Rooster*, a really cool NOBO who had served in Iraq. He worked as a park ranger and took some time off to hike the AT. My brother-in-law invited *Rooster* to join us for the night, and I got to know him better as we enjoyed a gourmet dinner at Lisa and Chris's house nearby.

After a breakfast that outdid most bed and breakfast places, Lisa and Chris made good on their promise to come hike with me while I was on the trail near their house. Our plan was to take it easy and hike about three miles up to Harper's Creek Shelter, so we were able to make a leisurely start at about 3:30 pm. Chris and Lisa took the lead while I pushed along slightly faster than my usual pace to keep up with them.

It was wonderful to hang out on the AT with my own family. We had a good time talking around a nice fire that Chris had built, and when it began to get dark, it was time to go to sleep. There were several entries about aggressive mice in the logbook. One caught my attention that was from a hiker who claimed to have killed one mouse along with a warning to be on the lookout for another mouse who walked with a limp. I, of course, felt a certain kinship with the limping mouse and was happy and content to be in a nice shelter along with some of my amazingly supportive family.

The following morning, I said goodbye to Lisa and Chris as I headed up the mountain trail, and they returned back down the way we hiked yesterday. The climb up to Three Ridges Mountain was considerably steep and somewhat rocky at the top. My plan for the day was to hike about thirteen miles. I was pushing along the trail, trying to pick up my pace since my climb up the mountain had progressed at just one mile per hour. Then I got an unexpected (and incredible) text from Lisa:

We're doing trail magic for you at Reed's Gap.

Thrilled, I sent Lisa a text with my expected ETA and hurried down the trail. I was rewarded with ice-cold lemonade, hot chicken wings (I ate every single one), and a glass of Chardonnay. I was just starting to think about the remaining miles I had for the day when Chris said, "Why don't you come back to the house with us? I can drop you back off right here tomorrow morning."

"That sounds perfect."

Soon, I was back at their beautiful house. It has a view of the ridgeline where the Appalachian Trail runs, right from their front porch. They cooked up another amazing dinner. I was enjoying this part of the trek.

At 9:00 am the following day, my brother-in-law dropped me off at Reeds' Gap in a final gesture of what was some fantastic trail magic. I decided that I would try to enjoy hiking each day rather than falling into the trap of only focusing on how many miles I could traverse. The trail was decent, with a few smaller hills and some rocky sections that required me to slowly pick my way through as I looked for a flat spot to land my injured foot.

It rained on and off, so it felt good once I finally arrived at the Paul C. Wolfe shelter and changed into dry clothes. It got dark after about an hour, and I was the only one there. It became pitch black out and the rain was coming down so hard on the roof that it would be hard to have a conversation (if someone was there for me to talk to). I was glad to be inside the shelter as I wasn't sure that my tent would hold up with such a large water volume dumping down on it.

Suddenly there were three lightning strikes in quick succession, very close by. Each one announced itself with a blinding flash and an ear-splitting bang. I was half scared to death. The other half of me was resigned to being there, knowing that there wasn't much I could do other than pray I didn't get hit.

The following afternoon I was so excited to reach Rockfish Gap, the southern end of Shenandoah National Park. The previous fall and winter, I hiked almost all of Shenandoah National Park, through West Virginia, and most of Maryland. So, after walking 540 miles from Erwin, TN, to there, I was going to jump up to a point on the trail that is six miles shy of Pennsylvania. This would put me at the north end of all the miles I had hiked so far.

By jumping over the part of the trail I'd already hiked, I was clearly defined as a section hiker. I was no longer the more illustrious sounding thru-hiker that I had hoped (and admittedly still pretended) to be. At this point, after all I had been through, I was thrilled to even be out there. I reminded myself to focus on my own adventure without comparing myself to what other people could do.

During the next two days, I completed a twenty-mile section of the trail in Shenandoah National Park that I missed the previous winter when the road was closed. Since it was rainy and foggy with no views, it wasn't the best hiking I've experienced, but I wanted to get this done while I was in the area to make sure that I hiked every single mile of the trail.

I reached Elk Wallow Wayside right before it closed and got a burger and fries before going out to the road to see if I could hitch a ride back to my car. After waiting twenty minutes without a single car driving by in the fog, I decided to call the cab company listed in AWOLs guidebook. They hit me up for $90, but I was anxious to get home and didn't want to spend another night camping out, so I agreed to pay it.

I told the cab dispatcher that I would be out behind the wayside on a picnic bench. The problem was that the driver had never been in the park before and had no idea where the wayside was. I had been waiting over an hour when it became apparent that the cab was driving through the park, somewhere off in the fog, honking his horn, "Brreeep-beep-beep-beep-beep!"

I couldn't get a signal on my phone to call the cab company. All I could do was sit there and listen as the beeps faded in and out, at times getting louder and at other times becoming much softer. After twenty minutes of listening to these honks off in the fog, the driver finally pulled into the lot, and I climbed into the back of the cab. The driver said,

"I had no idea where you were. They told me you were by a picnic bench, so I kept honking whenever I saw another picnic bench." I have no idea how many picnic benches are in the park but I'm sure they must have hundreds of them.

Once we were moving, he turned his head back towards me and said, "Hey, are you into science?"

"Sure, I like science," I responded.

The cab driver explained how he watched "all these videos" on YouTube. He said they "proved" the world was flat and then went on to let me in on the "secret" that the government was trying to hide all of this from the public. As ridiculous as this sounded, I didn't attempt to correct anything I heard. I was soaking wet, dead tired, and just wanted to get home.

I'd experienced time slowing down at other points in my life when I was really tired. There were times when a nominal wait in line at a grocery store seemed like it was taking forever. My mind wandered from the endless yapping from the driver's seat, which had moved on to how the moon landings were obviously faked. Then I found myself staring out at the blasted 25 mph speed limit signs along Skyline Drive as we slowly made our way through the thick fog. We finally arrived at the overlook where I had left my car.

With this last section of Shenandoah National Park done, I'd completed all of the Appalachian Trail from Springer Mountain in Georgia up to a few miles shy of the Maryland/Pennsylvania border. As I drove for several hours home to Annapolis to take a break for a few days, I thought about everything I'd been through lately.

I looked back at all of the challenges I'd faced so far and

realized that every step I took was another small step forward in healing both my body and mind.

I also thought about some of the crazy things I had done over the past three years to try and overcome the pain I had been dealing with. Chronic pain is any pain that continues for longer than twelve weeks after getting treatment. People will keep trying anything to reduce chronic pain even if a new method is totally unproven.

I'd had quite a bit of massage work during my life to help relax tight muscles and heal various injuries from riding dirt bikes or competing in triathlons. I usually choose someone specializing in deep tissue work where they use their elbow to get down in and iron out all the sore spots in your muscles.

A few weeks after my injury, when I was in the rehab center, I found someone willing to travel to the center to give me a massage. Partway through, she suggested trying something called Reiki. This is where instead of touching you, the masseuse waves their hands through the air over you to "adjust your energy fields."

You can probably tell by the way that I describe this that I think this is a bunch of BS. Does it work for some people? Of course it does. The placebo effect can work with any type of treatment or medication by providing someone with an improvement if and when they expect to get one. The nice doctor in the white lab coat gives you some pills and says, "Take two of these each morning, and your pain should feel much better."

The medication that the doctor gives you could be nothing more than sugar pills. Still, if you really believe that you'll benefit from it, your brain finds a way to make at least some improvement come true. In double-blind studies, it's been proven that the placebo effect can provide as much as a 32 percent improvement. Because of this, for new drugs to be approved in the US, they need to test at a level that's higher than the 32 percent placebo level of improvement.

So, if I'd believed in Reiki, then I may have experienced some benefit from it, but I don't, so I didn't get anything out of the treatment. That said, I think it's interesting that when dealing with chronic pain, the temptation is to try almost anything, no matter how crazy it sounds. The hope is that maybe, just maybe, you'll be able to get some relief from your ongoing pain.

I went home from the rehab center to find a hospital bed that my wife had rented for me set up in my living room. I was getting around in a wheelchair and hired an assistant to drive me to my doctor appointments and help put my shoes and socks on for me since I couldn't bend down far enough to reach my feet on my own.

I had my assistant drive me into town to try out acupuncture. After signing in, I was led to a large room with dimmed lights where about a dozen other chronic pain patients were resting in lounge chairs. The nice lady stuck me with various pins, the most memorable being the one stuck in the end of my big toe on the injured side.

It was peaceful and quiet. I tried to think healing thoughts. After my time was up, I did feel better. I can't tell you what portion was due to lying still and breathing deeply vs. having pins stuck in my "energy centers." I discovered that any relief I did find was quickly blasted away by the experience of driving home. It's not that Kara, my assistant, was a lousy driver.

The problem was that for me, at that point, any tiny little bump in the road seemed like an earthquake to me. The one I remember most was going over the expansion joint onto the Severn River Bridge. Thousands of other people drive over this small bump every day without giving it a second thought.

Other things I've tried included dozens of different pain relief creams and balms. Most of them smelled pretty bad and didn't seem to help. I will admit that I was looking for a magic solution during the early stages of my experience with pain. I wanted to be able to take a pill, put on a salve, have a doctor pull my leg just the right way to make ALL of the pain go away and heal me up completely. Not very realistic, of course, but that's the way I was thinking back then.

This led me to a guy I'll call Dr. Joe. Most of my conversations with other people at this time focused on the high level of pain that I was dealing with. Sure, I should have probably asked people more about what their challenges were, but when you feel like an elephant is sitting on your leg, all I could talk about was, "How do I get this elephant off my leg?"

So, someone, and I don't remember who, suggested that I go see Joe. "He's sort of like a chiropractor. He's helped other people that I know." The first hint that this was an alternative treatment was Joe's voice mail. No business name or anything, just, "Hi, this is Joe, leave me a message." Hmm...

The second hint was when I arrived at Joe's "office." I pulled up to a house in a residential neighborhood and followed the instructions he'd given me. I limped down a path around the back of the house to a sliding door where I didn't see a sign of any type. I met Joe inside a room that appeared to be an ordinary family room with a few chairs, a sofa, and a chaise-type lounger. Joe didn't look like a doctor, but what the heck? I had come all the way here, and I was in pain.

He had me walk back and forth across the room and then asked me to lay face down on the chaise. Then he put his thumb on my tailbone, gave it a little push and wiggle for two seconds, and said, "There, try that. You'll feel much better." At least I didn't have to get undressed. He said, "My first treatment is free. The next one will be $40."

As I'm writing this, I hesitate to tell you that I went back a second time, but I did. I remember thinking, *Maybe Dr. Joe will do something more… maybe he'll be able to fix me.* I believe the ongoing pain drove me to keep looking and hoping for anything, no matter how outlandish it might sound. After a second visit with another two second treatment, I decided that I was done with Dr. Joe.

As crazy as all of this may sound to you, I know that our brains are able to control so many things depending on how we think about something. About twenty years ago, a business partner and I taught real estate investing seminars. One of the most significant factors that affects someone's success in real estate, or any other endeavor, is belief. I've heard it said that if you believe you can or if you believe you can't, either way, you're right.

Suppose you really honestly believe that you'll succeed in real estate or any other endeavor. In that case, you're about 1,000 times more likely to put in the effort and stick with it. If you don't believe you're going to succeed, then most people put in next to no effort to basically prove themselves right when nothing happens.

At our seminars, we would demonstrate this by teaching

the concept of "Spots." We explained that according to an ancient methodology, we all have a weak spot and a strong spot. Speaking in a strong, confident voice, we'd say, "Here's your strong spot right here," and demonstrate this by touching the center of our forehead.

"You also have a weak spot" (speaking in a softer, weaker voice). "It's located in the soft fleshly spot right here behind your ear." We again demonstrated and encouraged them to follow along. Then to give it a little emphasis, we added, "Careful, don't push it too much, or you'll get really weak!"

Then we said, "We'll show you how this actually works," and invited one of the stronger-looking participants up onto the stage. We'd touch the person in their "strong" spot and ask them to hold their arm straight out to the side. "Now I'm going to push down on your arm, and I want you to resist me as much as you can."

We'd push down with a decent amount of effort, and our client's arm would not budge down at all. "Now I'm going to touch your weak spot" (touching the person behind their ear). "And watch as I'm now able to push their arm completely down." The crazy thing is that no matter how hard the subject tries to hold their arm up, after touching their "weak" spot, it drops right down with much less effort than during the first attempt.

Then we said, "Now I want you to prove this to yourself. Pair up with the person next to you to test this out for yourself." The room would buzz with the sounds of people talking as they discovered that the strong and weak spots really did, for the most part, work. Then we would switch the spots.

"Isn't it crazy that just because we told you to push on the strong spot behind your ear, that made you really strong? And when we told you to push on the weak spot in the middle of your forehead, that made you really weak?" we'd say.

"No, no, you've got them backward!" the crowd would shout at us. At which point, we'd demonstrate that the spots worked just as well if you switched them, finally telling them, "We actually made all this up—but it works anyway!"

What you tell yourself and what you believe really does make a difference. I don't know if this helps to explain why I was hiking the Appalachian Trail. I was passionately committed to the belief that if I hiked the entire Appalachian Trail, then my foot and leg were going to *have* to be better. Each day that I hiked, with every mile further north that I went, heck, with every single step I took, I was reclaiming my life. I know that anything is possible. My adventure on the trail proved this to me each and every day.

14

MAY—FINDING A BUDDY

YOU CAN'T AVOID PAIN, BUT YOU
CAN CHOOSE TO OVERCOME IT.

—PAULO COELHO

Two and a half hours after leaving Shenandoah National Park, I arrived home. My wife gave me a huge hug and told me that she'd put together a "1,000 Miles on the AT" party for us to celebrate with family and friends. Once everyone arrived the following day, she made sure everyone had a glass of champagne and then made an incredibly nice toast to me.

She shared the story of how I was injured just over three years ago, the incredible pain I went through, and the challenges I had in getting off the opioid painkillers I was taking. How I'd seen the movie "Wild," where Reese Witherspoon's character hiked the Pacific Crest Trail, read a few AT books, and then started talking about hiking the Appalachian Trail.

She told everyone how she thought this was highly unlikely. "When he went on his test hike around the neighborhood, he barely made it one mile before calling me to pick him up because his leg hurt so much." She explained how I took the Amtrak train down to Georgia and started anyway, hiking just 3.6 miles the first day. And how since then, I've managed to hike a total of 1,057 miles.

I had tears in my eyes when she asked me to say a few words.

"It's been a long but absolutely amazing journey. And every step I've taken has been based on hope. Hope that I'll get better someday. Hope that I'm able to accept that I may never get completely better. Hope that I can grab on to each moment and enjoy it no matter what challenges I'm faced with."

At the time, I thanked her, but after thinking about it, here's what I *meant* to say:

"Joanna—you are the most incredible, beautiful person I've ever met. Thank you so much for supporting my idea of hiking the AT. By the time I finish (assuming I do), I'll have been away from home for almost an entire year. That takes an extraordinary wife, and I'm blessed to be your husband.

"For my kids—thank you so much. I love the plaque you got me and especially the texts that you send while I'm hiking. They give me a boost each time I see them."

Last but not least, I really do appreciate you, my reader. By reading my story, you have contributed to my ability to keep going. You see, whenever I have a tough day or a big hill to go up, I think of you and the other people who followed my journal and who are reading this book. I don't fully understand it, but I do know that I'm too proud (or something) to give up knowing that you'll be reading about my eventual failure or success.

It's because of this, along with my desire to heal myself, that I keep going, and I'm loving almost all of it.

A few days later, I left our comfortable house in Annapolis around 7:00 am. I stopped by to see my parents in Frederick, drove up into Pennsylvania, parked four days up the trail, and then shuttled down to my start point. By that time, it was already past 1:30 pm.

I began hiking at Raven Rock Rd, the furthest point north that I made while section hiking the previous winter. The trail started out with a nice uphill, but before long, the trail flattened out to make its way through the last six miles of Maryland woods that I would be seeing.

While I was home, I created an excel sheet that tallied up all my hiking days for the year.

- Total days hiking: 58
- Total days off (resting or visiting family): 31

- Average miles per hiking day: 9.7 miles
- Average distance traveled per day including rest days: 6.3 miles

If you were to compare this to an average thru-hiker, this would be horrible. I had basically hiked two days and then rested one. At this pace, it was going to be tight for me to get up to Maine and make it to the top of Katahdin before the mountain closes sometime in mid-October.

My plan at this point was to get in at least ten miles a day and preferably make it twelve miles, or maybe a bit more, each day. But with my late start, I was running out of daylight, and I didn't really want to be night hiking a section that can get a bit rocky at times. I stopped at Pen Mar Park to get water from a spigot and made dinner. While I was eating, a gentleman walked by, and upon learning that I was a thru-hiker (Yes, I'll admit that I told him that), cheered me on, wishing me good luck.

After dinner, I walked another mile passing the Mason Dixon Line into Pennsylvania. As it was getting dark out, I decided to set up my tent near a stream. I was the only one there, and it was nice to be close enough to be able to hear the water rushing down the creek bed.

I was disappointed to discover that my air mattress was no longer able to hold air. While I was home for the 1,000-mile party, I had noticed our cat doing something to my thermo-rest pad. I had optimistically convinced myself that it would be fine. It wasn't. In fact, it was completely flat on the ground. As I lay there, I tried to convince myself that it really wasn't that bad to sleep on the ground. Didn't cowboys sleep out on the ground all the time?

The next day I managed to hike 14 miles, which was a long day for me. I wanted to catch up on some miles I missed by starting so late the day before. This was an effort to get my average daily mileage up a bit so that I'd have a better chance to make it to Mt. Katahdin before it closed in mid-October. I also wanted to hike further that day so that I was able to reach the pre-planned point where I would meet Emily, my physical therapist, to hike with her in a few days.

I had gone over so many rocky-tricky sections that my foot was hollering at me when I finally made it into the shelter at about 8:00 pm. There were two shelters (Pennsylvania seems to have a number of double shelters like this), and both looked full. Because the forecast was for a rainy night, I asked if there was room for one more, and everyone scooted over a bit to make a spot for me.

I had stopped earlier at a stream to submerge my sleeping pad and found two holes. I did my best to patch them with repair tape that I carry. I hoped it would hold, but as soon as I settled down for the night, I felt the air leak out. One of the tricks to completing a journey like this is to convince yourself that "it's really not that uncomfortable" in situations like this. Let's just say that I didn't sleep very well.

I was used to my foot hurting each morning when I got up. I kept my hiking poles close by to support myself as I made my first tentative steps out of the shelter to the privy or a spot behind a close-by tree to relieve myself. It was actually more of a hobble at this point than steps. So, I'd put my foot down, knowing that it was stiff and would hurt a bunch until it began to loosen up. Sometimes I took five or ten steps to wake it up and get the initial pain out of the way to get the day started. Usually, once I started hiking, it still hurt but not as bad as it did when I first got up.

I had planned to go about thirteen miles, but after going several miles, my foot was still causing me to wince with every step. The rocky terrain didn't help as I stepped on rocks at various angles. And because of my nerve injury, I didn't have the control or strength in the small muscles in my foot and ankle to stabilize my foot placement.

Each of us has hundreds of muscles in our foot and ankle that help your foot step on and off uneven surfaces. Much like the shock absorbers in a car, these muscles (and the nerves that control them) work to ease your foot down. The muscles are engaged from the time that one side of the foot touches down until the other side is all the way down on an angled surface.

During the first year of my injury, I wasn't able to move my foot at all. Two different neurologists told me that I shouldn't expect to get any movement back. I left each time swearing under my breath that I would prove them wrong. Now I can move my foot, although my range of movement is limited.

Each step over rocky terrain added a minor insult to my ankle, and I discovered that I could only take so much. After several miles of hiking that day, combined with fourteen miles from the previous day, my foot felt like it was the end of the day rather than the beginning. When it began to rain, I thought about how I needed to replace my sleeping pad and decided to take a break from hiking.

I decided to head into the Trail of Hope Hostel, which was just down the road. I called them, and they were soon on the way over to pick me up. While waiting for my ride, I used my iPhone to order a new sleeping pad from Amazon.

With overnight delivery, it would arrive at the hostel the next day. I could sleep in the hostel for the night and then swing back by to pick up the new pad after hiking the following day.

About six months after the first physical therapy place kicked me out because they claimed I wasn't improving, I met my new physical therapist, Emily. I wanted to try out a medical device that would use an electrical stimulus to lift my foot up so that I wouldn't trip on it. The condition is called foot drop, and it means that the muscles or nerves are not doing their job of lifting the front of your foot up each time you take a step.

Up to this point, I'd used a clunky brace that stuck my foot and leg at a stationary 90-degree angle. While it kept me from tripping, walking with a brace like that is about as graceful as walking with a wooden leg (and foot). Anyway, I went to a local medical center to try out the new Med-o-electro-matic gizmo that might fix my foot drop. That's where I met Emily. She was cheerful and upbeat, asking me how I felt and how I'd gotten injured. When I inquired at the success rate of the medical device, she told me,

"It's worked for almost everyone I've tried it on."

That's what I wanted to hear.

But then once it was in place... nothing. My foot didn't move. To show me the device worked, Emily moved it over to my good leg and pressed a button. Boing! My foot lifted all the way up. Emily said, "Your nerves just need to regrow some more. Are you in physical therapy?"

"No, I was kicked out of physical therapy because I wasn't improving."

"That's strange, because your insurance will pay for another thirty sessions."

From that point forward, Emily became my physical therapist. Unlike most doctors I'd seen, Emily believed in my ability to get better. She seemed to always be in a good mood and was an ongoing cheerleader who encouraged me to keep trying to improve my strength, balance, and control. When I first mentioned that I was considering hiking the Appalachian Trail, she told me that she had hiked portions of the trail with her father. She thought I could do it.

Emily drove up to hike with me for the day. We were blessed with a nice ten-mile stretch with hardly any rocks, a *nice* change from some of the rocky sections I had seen lately. After lunch, we passed the official halfway point on the Appalachian Trail. I was halfway there!

It was great to have someone to talk with while hiking. The trail was friendly, and the miles seemed to zoom by. Before long, we arrived at the Pine Grove Furnace State Park, where there's a little grocery store. This is the site of the official half-gallon ice cream challenge.

Thru-hikers are supposed to eat a half-gallon of ice cream to celebrate making it halfway on the AT. I looked at the ice cream and didn't see any flavors that I cared for—so I decided to pass. Emily pulled out some Oreos she brought along for me, and I downed a bottle of Gatorade from the store.

We jumped in my car, which I had left there a few days ago, and drove Emily back to her car. Then I went to a Texas Roadhouse restaurant along I-80 to have a steak dinner. On the way back to the hostel, I stopped to get a pint of coffee ice cream. I enjoyed eating the whole thing. It wasn't a half-gallon, but it was my own way of celebrating being halfway done on the Appalachian Trail.

With some help from the shuttle driver at the Trail of Hope Hostel, the following day I decided to slackpack again. When I was home in Maryland for my party, I found a leg brace that Emily had helped me get about a year ago. At the time, the brace seemed to bother my foot. I had set it aside but thought I'd give it another try to find a way to support my foot and ankle as I made my way over all the rocks in Pennsylvania.

This fiberglass boot enclosed my foot and leg up to just below my knee. It has an open front and a hinge that helps lift my foot up so that my foot doesn't drag on the ground and trip me. I tried it out and discovered that I could hike more easily wearing the leg brace. However, by the time I got to the road crossing at the end of my day and walked another eight-tenths of a mile back to the hostel, my foot and calf were killing me.

I took some Advil and crashed on the sofa for a few hours, doing my best to try and ignore the pain. My best guess was that the brace helped to support my ankle but didn't allow for movement in my foot and leg, which caused it to tighten up. Fortunately, after resting my leg for a few hours, it started to feel better. I tossed the brace in the trunk of my car, thinking I'd probably never use it again.

I was worried at one point about making it through "Rocksylvania," which is what hikers call Pennsylvania because it's the rockiest state on the Appalachian Trail. I wondered at one point if I might need to skip Pennsylvania and then come back to fill it in once my leg was better and I'd finished everything else.

But after hiking without carrying all of my gear yesterday, I began thinking about a way to slackpack over *all* of

Pennsylvania's rocks. I parked my car just one day's hike up the trail at a small road crossing, grabbed my lunch, raincoat, and some water, then hiked southward back toward Pine Grove Furnace State Park. The Pine Grove Furnace was used in 1764 to make cast iron items by burning charcoal made from local trees and then later coal as its fuel.

I would have preferred to hike the entire trail while headed north. It can get a little confusing thinking about where you are when you hike in the opposite direction for a day. Hiking south for this one day made it easier to shuttle back to my car.

After worrying about all the rocks I'd have to traverse, I was rewarded with a mostly smooth, easy trail to hike on. As usual, my leg began bothering me more, starting at about 2:00 pm. This must have caused me to limp more noticeably because during the last stretch of the day, a SOBO lady came by and remarked:

"You look like an old man trying to come through here."

I mumbled something about an old injury and thought to myself, *Uh... is it that bad?* I didn't know how to respond but felt mad, sad, and angry while trying to convince myself that I was doing the best I could with the cards that I'd been dealt.

I texted back and forth with one of my daughters, trying to develop a funny response that would help me laugh instead of feeling hurt by such an inconsiderate comment. Here's what I came up with:

"Yeah, I got it caught in a tractor grinder about 2 miles back." After making it over 1,000 miles on the trail, I definitely don't feel old. Bold maybe, but not old.

I spent the night at the Ironmaster's Hostel. It was nice and clean and had a grand piano. I played a few songs I knew along with another hiker girl from Germany. I had dinner with *Hestia* and *Dave from Ireland* whom I hadn't seen since the early days of this year's hike down in Tennessee.

I got up early the following day to eat waffles provided by the Ironmaster's Hostel before catching a shuttle with Roger so that I could slackpack for another day. Since I'd been hiking sections heading south for the past few days, I'd been running into many of the same hikers each day who were hiking north. I was coming up to a section called "The Rock Maze" that other hikers told me was pretty rugged.

"You'll have to jump, but I think you can do it," was the advice I'd heard. I wasn't so sure that I'd be able to jump. I worried about this upcoming section as I made my way along the trail during the day. I finally made it to the Maze and was happy to find that I could hold on with my hands and lower myself down in the two places that another hiker with better legs might have jumped down.

Once I made it back to my car, I drove north up to Duncannon to stay at the Doyle Hotel for the night. The shuttle driver called it a rat trap, and it was undoubtedly old but didn't seem very dirty to me. I'd heard a podcast where *Baltimore Jack*, whom I'd met back in Georgia, told the story about when he stayed at the Doyle Hotel.

It seems that The Doyle was renting out rooms on a weekly basis for single older men, and one of them hadn't been seen for a few days. The manager checked, but couldn't get the door open. This was strange because The Doyle doesn't have locks that work. The manager convinced *Baltimore Jack* to put a ladder up to the window and climb up to see what was going on. "He doesn't look so good," *Jack* said. "I think he's dead—looks like he's leaning up against the door."

"Can you just climb in there and pull him away from the door so that I can get in?" responded the manager. *Jack* said something about how that was beyond his duties since he himself was a guest in the hotel. I'm not sure who went in to get the door open. After hearing this story and others about this old place, I decided to play it safe and slept on top of the bed in my sleeping bag for the night.

The following day I left my car parked behind the Doyle and shuttled back south to the point where I'd left off hiking the day before. At 4:00 pm, I arrived at the Darlington shelter and sat down to talk with *Johnny Cash*, a NOBO, and *No Worries*, a SOBO. I needed water to make my dinner, and I offered to make the hike down to the spring for them. *No Worries* took me up on my offer, and I walked downhill to get water from the piped spring. As I walked back up the hill, I rejoiced thinking of all the times a year ago that I either struggled in pain to get water for dinner or ended up asking another hiker to get water for me. My injured leg really was getting better!

While I made dinner, *Hestia*, *Rock Ever*, and a few other hikers made their way into the shelter area. It was nice to have some conversation and companionship with a few other hikers. After dinner, I packed up and hiked another four miles up the trail so that I could have a shorter hike the next day. The end of the day was quiet and beautiful as the trail made its way through the middle of some fields with tall green grass. I reached a campsite near a stream just as the last bit of the day's light faded out. It only took me about five minutes to put my tent up, and since I had already had dinner, all I needed to do was hang my food bag from a tree and go to sleep.

In the middle of the night, I was awoken by the sound of something walking nearby. Whatever it was, it was large enough to crack some of the bigger branches on the ground. I wondered if a bear was trying to reach my food bag hanging from a nearby tree. I realized I didn't have anything at all to protect myself. I'm not into guns, and because I was hiking light, I didn't even have a small knife. I thought of using my hiking poles, but they were busy holding up my tent.

I turned my headlamp on, but it just reflected the light back from the inside of the screen door on my tent so that I couldn't see anything outside. I thought of unzipping the screen so that my light would work better, but somehow, I didn't want to part with the psychological barrier the screen provided. I heard a few more cracks, and then it was quiet except for the sound of my heart, which was pounding.

I lay there, unable to go back to sleep for about an hour. I convinced myself that there really wasn't much of anything that I could do to stop a bear if it was determined to get me. Eventually, I went back to sleep. The "very rocky trail" mentioned in the guidebook had slowed me down a bit that day but wasn't nearly as bad as I had worried it might be.

It was almost noon the next day when I met *Boogie Pilgrim* on the way down to the trailhead. I offered to drive him over to a grocery store to resupply. Using my car like this helped me to better justify the luxury of bringing it along with me on my hike. I would make the three-hour drive back home to Maryland later that day to fly to Florida to see my granddaughter for the next few days. After visiting my daughter and her family, I planned to catch an early flight and drive back to Duncannon.

Four days later, I got up at 4:30 am to catch an early flight back up to Maryland. I got in my car at the Baltimore airport and headed north towards Duncannon, Pennsylvania, where I had left the trail on Thursday. I was hoping to get started hiking at about 12:30, but by the time I stopped for lunch, checked emails, updated my journal, and drove back to the trail, it was 3:00 pm. I tacked on another half hour by starting out without my knee brace before realizing I didn't have it, so I turned around to go back and get it.

I hiked south so that the long road walk into Duncannon would be at the end of the day when I'd be running out of daylight. This would also put me back at the Doyle Hotel, where I planned to spend the night again and get dinner so that I wouldn't have to carry my tent, pad, and sleeping bag with me for the day. It was almost 8:30 pm when I stepped out of the woods and crossed the railroad tracks to begin the two-mile road walk into town.

When I finally arrived at the Doyle Hotel, I was surprised to find the place completely dark and locked up. The sign showed the hours as "11:00 am to 10:00 pm?" I figured the question mark means that they close whenever the bar empties out. If I weren't slackpacking, I'd have my tent and sleeping gear with me and could have found a spot somewhere to spend the night. After feeling a little bit stuck with no place to go, I found another hotel about 10 miles away that had a room for me. I walked up the street to have pizza and Uber'ed to the hotel.

After a shuttle ride to PA 325, which was ten miles north

of the spot I left my car the day before, I hiked southward to get back to my car. Then I drove up to Route 501, spent the night on a little patch of grass I found just north of the road, and left my car at the trailhead in the morning before shuttling with *Trail Angel Mary* back down to PA 325 where I left off the day before. I told her I had started out thru-hiking last year, making it to Erwin, Tennessee, and then restarted in February this year.

"Oh, you're a Lasher" she responded.

"What's that?" I asked.

"It's a long-ass-section hiker," she said.

That didn't sound as cool as a thru-hiker, but did it really matter what category someone else might put me in? I was there to heal my leg and get my life back no matter how long it took me to hike the Appalachian Trail.

I walked during the morning with *Jim*, a NOBO who just retired from the Army. He was okay going along at my slower pace for a while. I asked him open-ended questions to get him talking while I scurried along behind, trying to keep up as we went up a few hills. This allowed me to focus on my breathing while slowing Jim down to my pace since he was talking rather than taking deep breaths like I was.

I didn't really feel like hiking and kept thinking about my visit with my granddaughter. I found myself wondering, *what am I doing slogging along the trail?* I mentioned this to my Dad, who suggested that I think about the trail as a "challenge" as opposed to a "slog."

At the end of the day, I turned off the AT to walk three-tenths of a mile to the Rausch Gap Shelter. I know that this doesn't sound like much, but for me, with my leg really hurting at the end of the day, all I could think about was the extra six-tenths of a mile that doesn't count toward my goal of 2,189 miles on the Appalachian Trail.

I spent the night with four serious thirty-something NOBO hikers who all smelled as bad or worse than me. They didn't talk much and seemed concerned about getting their next twenty-mile day done rather than engaging in conversation. The shelter did have an excellent water supply that ran into a stainless-steel trough right in front of the shelter. I went to sleep, hoping that I felt more excited about hiking soon.

I stopped the following day to rest by a stream that was a few miles south of I-81. Since the guidebook and app didn't show any water ahead, I filled up with a couple of extra liters of water from the stream to use for dinner. I headed north towards I-81, expecting to climb up a mountain towards the tent site that was my destination for the day.

I ran into an older SOBO hiker who told me that a small stream ahead crossed the trail right as the AT headed up the mountain. So, I dumped out the extra water that I was carrying so that I wouldn't have to haul the excess weight for the next two or three miles. I could get my water at the stream. Right after crossing under I-81, the trail crossed a small cement drainage ditch and headed uphill. *Is this the stream that he mentioned?* I asked myself. *It couldn't be. Or could it? It's probably full of all kinds of chemicals from the water that washes off the highway.*

I continued hiking without getting water and then wondered what I would do if there wasn't an actual stream ahead. So, I turned around and walked 50 steps back to the drainage ditch and filled up with water for dinner. I justified this to myself by thinking, *it's just one day, and there can't be THAT many chemicals in a few liters of water.*

Five minutes further up the mountain, I was happy to see a small stream crossing the trail. I dumped out my water for the second time that afternoon and refilled it from the stream. I thought, *this water is just going downhill into the drainage ditch that I just filled up from.* That was okay. I liked it better from there.

I found my campsite at 5:00 pm, set up my tent, and laid down to rest. I didn't make a fire or do any walking around other than hanging my bear bag because I wanted to rest up as much as possible. I made my dinner and went to sleep as soon as it got dark.

The next day I was feeling a little better. I was learning to find ways to enjoy hiking on all those rocks rather than mentally complaining to myself about them. The trail was narrow, with green plants growing on both sides. I stopped at a shelter to get some water and called my daughter to wish her a happy birthday.

I met a couple heading northbound who joined me to get water, and he reached out to shake my hand as he departed. I was too slow to distract him with a bow or knuckle bump and ended up shaking his hand as a reactionary habit. I immediately took my pack off and dug out soap to wash my hands since I didn't know if he washes his hands or how many other grubby hikers he'd shaken hands with lately.

About a half-hour later I met a SOBO hiker, who said he had just seen a bear about a quarter of a mile up the trail. I pulled my eyeglasses out of my pack then looked and listened carefully for the next hour but didn't see the bear. Then my daughter, the one with the birthday, sent me a text with a bear walking in her backyard. I should probably mention that she lives in Anchorage, Alaska.

When I got to Rt 501, I saw a flyer on the trail kiosk with information about a newly opened hostel which I'll refer to as the Ironman Inn. I decided to try it out, and it was awesome! The hosts were super friendly. It was nice and clean, had a hot shower, *and* you get home-cooked dinner and breakfast! I got to see *Disfunkschwenal* again, a NOBO that I had met at a shelter near McAfee Knob in Virginia. She's a doctor, has hiked the Pacific Crest Trail, and was interesting to talk with. She liked to slackpack, which is what I'd planned to do for the next few days with the hostel as my base.

The following day started out with rain coming down. However, by midday, I had my raincoat off and enjoyed a nice cool day of hiking under the clouds. Between hiking without my full pack as much as I could and changing the way I thought about them, I was getting better at hiking over all of those rocks. One of the biggest challenges with rocks, like many things in life, is how you think about them. I had been worrying about rocks, asking other hikers about rocks, and wondering how the rocks would affect my foot.

It turned out that the rocks were never as bad or as good as other people led me to believe. They did slow me down a bit, but they didn't seem to affect my injured foot too much unless they were really bad. I decided that I was going to enjoy hiking on the rocks... Well, as much as I could anyway.

Back at the Ironman Inn, I got cleaned up for dinner. *No Regrets* was there with his wife, who had broken the metatarsal bone in her foot and was catching a flight home the next day.

It sounded like this could happen just by stepping between two tightly spaced rocks with lighter-weight hiking shoes. Ouch! We heard a ton of funny stories from *Tony Stark*, the hostel owner, about his career as a Pennsylvania State Trooper. Both he and his wife were very friendly and eager to make sure we all enjoyed our stay.

For a few days, my routine was to wake up in time for a scrumptious breakfast made by *Tony's* wife *Judith* before heading out and dropping my car off at a trailhead another ten miles or so up the trail. *Tony* picked me up and shuttled me back south to the point I left off the day before. This allowed me to slackpack over the worst of the rocks in Pennsylvania.

I was working my way down a hill towards the end of the day when I noticed another hiker coming my way. I turned off the audiobook that I was listening to, *The Science of Power Generation*, so that I wouldn't disturb another hiker's wilderness experience. I looked up a few times to see where this other person was, but he wasn't getting any closer to me for some reason. I finally figured out that he must be going the same direction, northbound, like me.

I tried to hike a little faster to catch up to him, which just doesn't usually happen. The only hikers I had ever passed before were extremely out of shape people who were struggling to make their way up a steep hill. I finally caught up to this mystery man when he stopped to get water at a stream crossing. His name was *Dr Fix-it*. He was about ten years my senior and from Branson, Missouri. I talked with him and quickly realized that we had many things in common.

He, like me, was a slow hiker. We had the same brand packs, type of tent, sleeping pads, and we were both serious about keeping our gear light and doing what we could to make hiking easier on us. We had fun stuff to talk about, too. We both invested in real estate and had been professional speakers. I hoped he'd be willing to hike with me for a day or two.

We talked for thirty minutes or so and then came to Reservoir Road, where I turned off on a side trail to get back to my car. I told *Dr Fix-it* all about the Ironman Inn, hoping that perhaps he would join me in going there for the night. He thought about it for a moment but he had promised to meet two other hikers at a shelter further up the trail.

We exchanged phone numbers and agreed to meet up the next day either on the trail or at Hawk Mountain Road, which is about 10 miles north. *Dr Fix-it* explained that his body was high mileage, but he had low mileage legs. "They can only handle ten miles a day," he said. That sounded just like me.

After spending another night at the Ironman Inn, I shuttled back to the trail again. I decided that I would try to slackpack the entire way through Pennsylvania's rocks. I had been worried that my foot wouldn't handle going over so many rocks and thought that I might need to bypass Pennsylvania. So far, this was working out well. By hiking with less gear and doing fewer miles each day, I figured I might be able to pull this Rockslyvania thing off.

That afternoon I saw my first poisonous snake—a copperhead. Some other hikers were nice enough to point it out so that I wasn't surprised. I sent *Dr Fix-it* a text to let him know that I started late, so when I got to Hawk Mountain Road at the end of the day, I was delighted to see that he was sitting down right by the car. It was nice to see that he was willing to wait for me. We drove to the Ironman Inn, got cleaned up, and enjoyed a nice dinner that *Judith* cooked for us before sleeping in the bunkhouse for the night.

We woke up the following day with *Tony Stark* bringing out hot coffee for us, followed by another good breakfast including fresh-cut fruit and orange juice. We dropped my car off at a trailhead about eight miles further up the trail, then *Tony* shuttled us back to Hawk Mountain Road, where we started hiking for the day.

An old building stood there, which served as an inn during the 1800s. Dr Fix-it told me that, years ago, a serial killer named Mathias Schaumbacher operated the inn. Some of the travelers who stayed there were never seen again. He confessed on his death bed to killing over a dozen people and let people know to look for their remains in his well. It's reported that the undertaker and minister had to run for cover in the cemetery because lightning kept striking the serial killer's headstone while they were trying to bury him. It's now a personal residence for someone crazy enough to live there.

It was great having someone to talk with for a change. My usual solitary walk was peppered with an occasional "Hi—goodbye" as other hikers made their way past me. *Dr Fix-it* and I had plenty to talk about as we made our way up the first hill of the day. Before long, we were into a seriously rocky section—and then it got even rockier. We slowly picked our way along, taking turns coming up with things to say to keep us in good spirits.

"Each step takes us a little closer to the end of Pennsylvania."

"This isn't as bad as I thought it would be."

"Once we conquer this, we'll be able to do anything."

And later in the day when the trail smoothed out for a bit…

"Hey *Flash*, we're getting credit for Pennsylvania miles on this section too!"

Before long, the trail improved dramatically as the AT turned down an old fire road. The last few miles were smooth, so I turned up my speed to a whopping two mph, which is still slower than most of the younger hikers go even through rougher sections.

Before long, we were back to the car, drove "home" to the Ironman Inn, and enjoyed a nice hot shower in preparation for dinner. That night's meal, once again, was superb. *Tony Stark* had gotten a deer during the hunting season and made a venison stew. To make it even more memorable, we invited the deer himself. Well, actually, just the deer's head. *Tony* still had the white skull from the deer with antlers on it, so we propped it up to sit in a chair at the table with us while we had dinner in the deer's honor.

We were somewhat concerned about the next day's hike after reading the comments about an upcoming section called the Knife's Edge. When *Tony* dropped us off, he walked a few feet into the woods and said, "The trail looks great from here!"

He was right. The trail did start out friendly enough but then got pretty rocky, and before long, we arrived at the Knife's Edge. I went first, trying to make my way before stopping to put my hiking poles up on my pack and then proceeding like a monkey walking on my hands and feet. While this helped alleviate my fear of falling, I hadn't traversed like this since I was four or five years old, so I felt like a fish out of water. (An *old fish* out of water.)

After Knife's Edge, it was rocks, more rocks, and even

more rocks. Then we came to another big rock pile to climb over. It wasn't as long as Knife's Edge, but it required the same type of clambering. After that, it was—you guessed it—more rocks. What a day!

Luckily, the last few miles were okay. We knew that we were getting close to the end of the day. All we had to do was make it across a power line to get to the car. The power line, of course, ended up being another boulder field. The upside to all of this was that both of us felt that if we could make it through this type of terrain, we could handle anything. *Dr Fix-it* said, "Look out, Maine, here we come!"

The following day, I was sitting at the picnic table with a few other hikers getting my gear ready to go for the day. A female hiker from Germany that I recognized pulled her car in the driveway, and *Pork* and *Sausage* climbed out. Like many hikers, they looked a little scruffy around the edges. I figured they were there to get a shower and maybe rest for the day. I invited them to sit down and told them where to find the bathroom and the water spigot. *Pork* asked about a package that he had sent to the hostel, and I told him to look on the shelf in the garage.

About 15 minutes later, *Tony Stark* walked out, and he didn't look like his usual happy self. He later told me that he'd received a suspicious package because it didn't weigh much at all. He said that most packages weighed more because they were full of food and supplies.

He'd just found the remains of this opened package on top of his trash can, which smelled really strongly of marijuana, and there was a little smoking pipe in the bottom of the box. I should probably mention that *Tony* has a law enforcement background, and he's over six feet tall. He could easily work as a bouncer if that gives you an idea of what he looks like.

Tony strode up, dropped the box and packing materials on the picnic table, and said, *"Hey, who shipped marijuana to my house?"* He got a blank stare from *Sausage*. *Pork* actually smiled at him. *Tony* took a few steps over towards the two of them and shouted, drill-sergeant style, "WHO SHIPPED WEED TO MY HOUSE?!" *Pork* and *Sausage* still didn't say anything. *Tony* said, *"You need to leave. Right. NOW!"*

Pork said, "Are you serious?" At which point *Tony* reached over and grabbed him by the front of his shirt. With one hand, he lifted *Pork* up in the air so that his face was two inches away from him.

"DO I SOUND LIKE I'M SERIOUS! *I WANT YOU OUT OF HERE NOW!"*

They looked like they were ready to crap their pants and started to slowly put their backpacks on. *Tony* followed up with, *"I'm going in the house to contact law enforcement! I want you to MOVE IT!"* *Pork* and *Sausage* began walking down the driveway.

One of the other hikers said, *"You better run!"* and they started trotting. *Tony* yelled, *"You're not running fast enough!"*

Last that *Dr Fix-it* and I saw them, they were sprinting full speed down the road.

Our hike for the day was far enough north that we got in touch with another shuttle driver rather than relying on *Tony* to keep shuttling us further and further north. Our new shuttle driver was known by his old trail name, *The Mechanic*. I'm hesitant to write this about someone willing to help hikers along the trail, but this guy seemed to have, uh… issues.

While driving us, *The Mechanic* talked non-stop in a slightly too loud voice and took an aggressive stance on most everything. He also brought his Doberman along for the ride. We stopped to drop a few other hikers off at a trailhead, and the Doberman jumped out of the car, raced out, and started growling and barking at another hiker who was coming out of the woods. The hiker, without breaking his stride, said, "Call off your dog, or I'll shoot it!"

The Mechanic hollered at his dog, and it ran away from the hiker but headed straight for my pack. The Doberman stuck his snout in the side pocket and promptly gobbled down my breakfast sandwich. Very nice. Very nice. When we drove away (in the car where the other hiker couldn't hear him), *The Mechanic* said, "That guy's crazy! If you shoot my dog, I'll shoot you! You shoot my dog. I'll shoot you!"

Despite the dramatic morning, our hike was excellent. Plenty more rocks, but I was starting to—almost—enjoy them. I just went very slowly, at times pretending that I was doing Tai Chi from one rock to the next.

I heard that the climb up out of Palmerton was really steep, and the following day we discovered that claim to be valid. The area is unique because there was a zinc mining and smelting operation at this location for over a hundred years. The zinc and pollution from the smelting killed all the vegetation in the area and had polluted the water with heavy metals. It looked as if some efforts have been made to reclaim the place as one area was completely fenced off and some vegetation was coming back.

The hike started off okay, but we quickly came to a point where the white-blazed Appalachian Trail went straight up, and a blue-blazed "bad weather" trail turned off to the left. These blue blaze trails are provided for use in poor weather conditions or for hikers who might want an easier way around an obstacle such as the one we were about to face.

Dr Fix-it said, "It's too dangerous. Let's take the blue blaze."

"Naw… I'm going this way," I said, indicating the AT. "I've come this far, and I want to hike the entire Appalachian Trail." Don't get me wrong, I'm not a purist. I'll take the blue blaze trails in and out of a shelter, but my goal is to do the whole thing.

"You can take the blue blaze, and I'll meet you up the trail," I suggested.

Dr Fix-it responded with "That's okay; I'll go with you."

The climb became steeper until it reached a point where the only way to make it any further was to put my poles on my pack and climb up using my hands and feet. There was one part where I was downright scared, terrified actually. I was holding on by my fingertips while trying to grip the rock face with one good foot combined with whatever contributions my injured foot was able to muster.

I couldn't make a toe hold work with my injured foot, so I had to look for cracks or spots that were wide enough to turn my foot sideways to get some grip on the rock surface. It was steep enough that if I fell, I don't know that it would kill me, but it wouldn't be pretty. With some help from *Dr Fix-it,* who placed my injured foot in the right spot a few times, I managed to work through the fear and make my way slowly but surely up the rock face.

Once I was past the most challenging point, I looked back to see *Dr Fix-it*, and he looked terrified. He was sweating so much that his shirt was soaked, getting his phone so wet it wouldn't work when he tried to take a photo. He was determined to make it up no matter what. I was highly impressed with this guy.

About a year later, *Dr Fix-it* told me why he wanted to take the blue blaze. "I have an inner ear problem that can cause me to completely lose my sense of balance," he admitted. It meant a lot to me at the time to see him struggle up that steep rock face. It means even more to me now that I know the real risks that he took that day just so we could hike together.

We were almost back to the car where the day's adventure would conclude when we met *D Squared*, who was headed slacking southbound. He told us that he'd seen a couple of rattlesnakes up ahead, so we should keep an eye out. He said that the first hiker who comes along wakes the snake up, the second hiker who comes along makes him mad, and the third hiker is the one who gets bit. It's a good thing there were only two of us.

After such a challenging day, we decided to spring for a motel to recover for the night. It felt great to be resting at a decent motel after such a long, hot, rocky day. *Dr Fix-it* was getting cramps in his legs, so I ran out to get some potassium tablets along with some cool Gatorade and some ice-cream. I felt pretty lucky to have met *Dr Fix-it*. We seemed to make a good hiking team.

We debated whether or not we should shuttle with *The Mechanic* again the next day and decided to give him a chance to redeem himself. He was much more mellow and almost pleasant to be around this time. Yes, we were still using a shuttle each day to slackpack our way through the Pennsylvania rocks. When I mentioned this to my wife she said, "Isn't that cheating?"

Coming up with ways to not carry your full pack is considered by some purist hikers to be a lazy hiker's method, but I haven't heard anyone call it cheating (other than my wife, that is). Slacking every day like we were is overdoing it a bit, but still, I was worried that I might have to skip or bypass Pennsylvania altogether, so I was thrilled at our progress. *Dr Fix-it* said that "hiking your own hike" applied especially well here.

Once we made it back to the car at Wind Gap, we drove up to Delaware Water Gap to check out the church hostel in town. *Dr Fix-it* said that the hostel smelled really bad when he went inside, but I didn't notice anything. There was a shelter out behind the church where we decided to spend the night.

That night, the bugs were biting so much that I zipped up inside my sleeping bag. Unfortunately, the temperature was up in the 70s somewhere, and I sweated so much that my bag was soaked when I got up. I decided that next time I would set up my tent instead.

We spent the last few days finishing up the last of the Appalachian Trail's miles in Pennsylvania. The last bit wasn't very rocky. We were used to the rocks by then, so hiking through a few sections of them wasn't such a big deal anymore. Before our journey through this part of Pennsylvania, many hikers had warned us about all of the rocks here. "It's horrible," was the consensus. I even saw multiple entries in some of the shelter journals where hikers used foul language describing how bad the rocks were.

We found that most hikers embellish their stories a bit to make it sound a little worse than it really was. As a result, I would worry about a challenging section coming up and would make it harder or rockier somehow in my head before getting there. The best advice I got was from Dad, who suggested thinking of it as a big challenge. This worked so much better than just hiking along hating the rocks. I actually learned to love…well… *appreciate* the rocks.

We were finally done with Pennsylvania.

15

JUNE—ANOTHER CLOSE CALL

YOU EITHER GET BETTER OR YOU
GET BITTER. TAKE WHAT'S BEEN
DEALT TO YOU AND ALLOW IT TO
MAKE YOU A BETTER PERSON OR
ALLOW IT TO TEAR YOU DOWN.
THE CHOICE BELONGS TO YOU.

—JOSH SHIPP

We left the car in what appeared to be a safe parking lot and hiked through town to cross the Delaware River Bridge into New Jersey. My biggest surprise about New Jersey was that it was beautiful, at least along the Appalachian

Trail. The only comparison I had was what I had seen while driving along the New Jersey Turnpike, and I liked what I saw on the AT much better. The trees were smaller, and the forest's undergrowth and bushes were thriving. At times I had to push the bushes back to make room to get by on the trail.

We camped along a ridge that looked out to the east over a beautiful body of water. We found a couple of rocks to sit on while making our dinners. I marveled at the ingenuity that *Dr Fix-it* put into creating his own hiking gear. He had a tiny little alcohol fuel stove, a titanium pot, and a homemade cozy that kept his food warm—all of which weighed next to nothing. He obviously spent an enormous amount of time planning, researching, and getting ready for his hike.

Dr Fix-it got his trail name because of his odd habit of fixing things everywhere that he went. He helps other hikers with broken gear, fixed things at the hostels he visited; he even came up with unique ways to resolve business challenges. This guy was incredibly creative and intelligent. His trail name was *Mr. Fix-it* until another hiker said, "You're not a Mister, you're a *Doctor Fix-it*. He even helped a hostel owner in Harper's Ferry figure out how to sell his business to a family member. When people asked him where he got his degree, he responded, "Oh, it's a DIY degree."

One of the nice things about being out hiking was that I could step back and remember a bunch of the good times in my life, along with many of the mistakes that I had made along the way. It was great to talk things through with *Dr Fix-it* and get his perspective.

I told him about my background doing consulting with hundreds of commercial real estate investing clients at a time.

I explained how I had built a big company with thirty-five employees and seventeen coaches working for me. This was before I sold the company to a business partner so I could focus on recovering from my injury.

It took me a while to describe it to him, and eventually, I explained that while this was working out fine financially, I just wasn't happy. Something just didn't feel right. That's when I told him I really missed the times when I used to mentor clients personally.

"I love the excitement of helping someone to get their first property. I know what it's like to go through that scary part in the beginning. When I help someone overcome that initial roadblock, I feel like I'm making a difference that really counts."

"Then why don't you do that?" *Dr Fix-it* said.

"What do you mean?"

"Raise your fees if needed but find a way to work directly with your clients instead of outsourcing the part that you love to someone else."

This sounded like a great idea. I decided to try it out when I was done hiking, and that's exactly what I did. (If you'd like to find out more about how to buy commercial properties by working together in a small team environment, go to: CommercialLeaseOptions.com.)

Later in the afternoon, a cold front provided us with welcome breezes and fortunately, only a few drops of rain. At right about twelve miles for the day, we found a campsite by the trail with just enough room for both of our tents.

It was about 10:00 AM the following day when we stopped in at the Mohican Center for a breakfast of pancakes, eggs, bacon, and coffee. We hiked along throughout the day, hitting both rocky sections and some nice smooth areas of trail. We planned to end the day near a stream where we would have water to make dinner. However, a mile before we reached the stream, *Dr Fix-it* realized that we were higher up along the ridge where there was a slight breeze, and he thought there would be fewer mosquitoes.

He explained that mosquitoes like to be around water, and they also tend to be more prevalent at lower elevations. I had never known this, but fewer mosquitoes sounded great to me, so we went ahead and camped up on the ridge. His prediction proved accurate, as I didn't see a single mosquito that night.

The next day, all we could think about was reaching the Appalachian Trail Deli in Branchville, New Jersey. Other than the trail towns I'd been through further south, this was the first place to get real food right on the trail, so I was excited. When we finally arrived at the deli that afternoon, we were disappointed to discover it was no longer in business.

We walked down the road and found a bar called The Gap Tavern. There was a sign out front that instructed hikers to walk around back rather than use the front door. At this point, I was thrilled to find a place with food and drink that was open and still in business. I didn't mind that I was one of the stinky hikers who was asked to go around back. We joined about a dozen other hikers and sat on the patio looking out over a gorgeous lake. We satisfied our hiker hunger with French fries, a burger, pizza, and three soda refills. We then hiked up a few miles to the top of the next ridge, where we camped for the night.

I realized at the time that this was my twelfth day of hiking without taking a zero. This was a new world record for me! *Dr Fix-it* was great at providing encouragement when I needed it later in the day, especially when my leg was really bothering me. He also helped rein me in when I was having a good day and wanted to go further than ten or twelve miles, which was about my daily limit at this point.

By the way, that "world record" thing comes from growing up with my brothers. In the winter, we ice skated on a rink our Dad made for us in the backyard. In the summer, we played field hockey in the yard with a tennis ball, and year-round we played ping pong. Everything was competitive, but I remember how a series of ping pong games would always conclude in a "world championship" even though it was just the three of us. As I lay there falling asleep that night, I could hear the rain start to fall on my tent along with the last few bird calls of the day. Life was good.

We left our campsite at the Culver fire tower base and headed into the morning mist. We hiked along for about three hours before coming to the Sunrise Mountain Pavilion. We decided to rest for a moment and eat an early lunch. Just as we sat down, the sky opened up, and it rained like crazy. We enjoyed staying dry while watching the rain pour down, contentedly eating tortillas and peanut butter. Several minutes later, the rain stopped, and we joked and congratulated ourselves about how perfect our timing was. "I sure wouldn't want to be caught out in a downpour like that," I said.

We continued hiking through the day, working our way over a never-ending series of ledge rocks that the trail was routed upon. It was like walking in gymnastics class from one balance beam to the next. At about 5:30 pm, I said, "It seems to be getting dark early today, doesn't it?"

Then we heard the sound of thunder.

Several minutes later, as we were starting to traverse down a series of small cliffs, the skies opened up, and the rain came down much harder than it did this morning. It was raining cats and dogs, frogs and toads, catfish, and salmon!

We got completely drenched as we made our way down the trail that wandered down the mountainside. The water rushing down the trail was about six to eight inches deep, furiously washing over my boots and the bottom of my legs. I gave up trying to keep any semblance of staying dry and sloshed along through the middle of mud puddles for the rest of the day.

We ended the day's hike by checking into a Super Eight Hotel and hanging our gear up so that it covered almost everything in the room. Then it was off to Friendly's for milkshakes and a couple of sandwiches before going to Walmart to resupply our food for the next five days.

The following day we swung by a local outfitter to get a new set of hiking poles for *Dr Fix-it*. His old pair had developed a strange clicking sound, which even he was unable to fix despite much pounding with a rock on the side of the trail. They didn't have a pair that *Dr Fix-it* liked, but I found a new set for myself. I had been looking for hiking poles with a bigger handle since I tended to put a bunch of weight on my hands when going downhill. The top of these poles looked like a cane, so other than not looking cool, they met my needs exactly.

Since *Dr Fix-it* didn't find a hiking pole set that he liked, he started using my old Leki poles and offered to buy them from me. I told him they were worth more than the new price since they were already broken in, but ended up just giving them to him. We headed to High Point State Park and planned to leave the car there and hike north. But then we met Mason, a ridge runner, who offered to shuttle us further north thirty miles so we could drop the car and hike back to it over the next three days.

A ridge runner is someone who's paid to hike a portion of the trail and provide guidance and advice to hikers. He told us about when a bear grabbed his backpack from right outside his tent and ran off with everything in his pack, including his driver's license and credit cards.

We made it to the Jim Murray private shelter, a little retreat right off the trail. There's a water spigot to get drinking water, showers, and one of the most excellent shelters I've seen anywhere on the trail. It even has electricity inside. We decided to stay in our tents even though the shelter looked really cool. From my tent, I could hear a little bit of rain coming down. The view from where we had put up our tents really was beautiful.

The following morning, we came to a road crossing near Unionville, New York. *Dr Fix*-it said, "Let's walk the half-mile over to the deli." As you know by now, I dreaded hiking any bonus miles, but hiking with a partner requires concessions.

When we walked into Horler's Store and deli, *Dr Fix-it* said hello to the lady at the counter and went right into a story about a place where you could order off the menu or you could take the chef's challenge.

"The chef had a pretty good pantry," he said to this lady we just met thirty seconds ago. "And he'll make you anything at all—whatever you want for $75. In fact, the waitress said, If he can't make it, he'll pay you $200. So I said, I'll have the elephant trunk roast with lettuce and tomato on rye. A minute later, the waitress walks out and puts two hundred-dollar bills on the table. Couldn't do it, huh?, I asked. And she said, Nope, I was shocked…This is the first time I've ever seen him out of rye bread."

Everyone had a good laugh, and we ordered our food. The food sure hit the spot, and my leg didn't mind the extra mile. It was worth it. The funny thing was that hiking along that afternoon, I started to remember the story as if the deli we went to really did have elephant trunk roast.

Later in the afternoon, the sky suddenly got dark, and the wind picked up. I suggested putting our tents up to avoid getting wet in the rain. "Okay," said *Dr Fix-it*. "Here's a campsite right over here." At first, I thought he was reacting too quickly, but then I heard thunder and felt the first drops of rain. Both of us whipped our tents up in 30 seconds. We quickly got inside, laughing at the situation but managing to stay dry. The storm passed by within 15 or 20 minutes, and we packed up to continue hiking.

That evening we camped in an unofficial site, and *Dr Fix-it* got his bear bag rope stuck way up in a tree. He used something he called the Pacific Crest Trail method. He would throw a rope over an extremely high limb, pull the bag up in the air, and then put a stick in the line, which keeps the bear bag up in the air without having to tie it to another tree.

Some bears have learned that if they smell food, they can go around and scratch at all nearby trees. Suppose you've put up your bag using the traditional method of tying the rope to another tree. In that case, the bear eventually breaks the rope, and the food bag comes down. With the Pacific Crest Trail method, they can't do anything except try to pull on the rope, which is impossible for them to do with their big bear paws.

To hang his bear bag, *Dr Fix-it* put a rock into his Cuban fiber rope bag, which he had handcrafted at home, by the way. Then, he tossed the rock higher in the air than I've seen some fireworks go. I don't know how he managed to do it because he told me the rope was only forty-five feet long, but he hooked the bag over the limb of a tree, which looked like it was at least seventy-five feet high. That's when his lightweight rock bag wrapped around the limb and got stuck.

He pulled on it for a while before giving up. He walked over to start getting dinner ready while lamenting that he had lost his favorite bear bag rope along with the nifty little Cuban fiber bag. Once I had my tent up, I went over to give it a try myself. After pulling on it for five or ten minutes without success, I was ready to give up. Finally, I pulled all the slack down and then put a loop in the rope and carefully stepped up with my good leg (of course) into the loop and thrust all of my bodyweight down on the loop. The tree limb reluctantly let go, and *Dr Fix-it's* rope and the little bag came rocketing down to the ground.

I was thrilled to find at the end of the day that my leg and foot felt really good—better than any other days so far on the trail. The Appalachian Trail really was healing me.

At 11:30 the next morning, as we arrived at a road crossing, I asked, "Does this road have food?" *Dr Fix-it* replied that any road will lead you to food if you're willing to walk far enough. I pulled up the guidebook to discover that Heaven Hill Farm

ONLY WHEN I STEP ON IT

was just 800 feet down the road. They had quite good apple cider, coffee, and donuts.

That afternoon, *Dr Fix-it* told me a story about when he was called in to turn around a machining company. It had been mismanaged for years, and the employee's attitudes were horrible as a result. For several hours as we hiked, he explained how he went in and worked alongside the workers to help them develop all of the ideas that he wanted to implement. As he told the story, he cocked his head to the side, looked at me with piercing eyes, and asked me the same questions he used to draw in his workers some thirty years ago.

I found his engaging and dynamic style to be the perfect recipe for distracting my mind from its usual focus—thinking how much my leg bothered me. Every challenge he faced was overcome with just the right mix of creativity, intelligence, and psychiatry. I wondered if the story may have gained some embellishment with each retelling over the years. Despite this, I enjoyed the telling thoroughly, and I sensed that *Dr Fix-it* really cared about coming up with solutions and doing things the right way.

There's a unique intensity about him that's hard to describe. For example, a few days before a tree fell down during the night by the shelter. Two women were scared out of their wits by this. *Dr Fix-it* went into a long diatribe about how the Sasquatch has kept its presence a secret for centuries by not making any sounds.

He went on, looking and sounding serious as a heart attack, like it's the most important thing in the world. He explained in minute detail how the Sasquatch had to come up with a way to get its mate's attention without making any noise that would reveal its presence. "So, it moves through the woods, pushing on trees until it finds one that feels weak enough. Then with one mighty shove in the middle of the night, the tree comes down. *That's* how Big Foot is able to attract his mate."

Dr Fix-it delivered this outlandish story from start to finish with a consistently serious look on his face. I'm not sure how he did it, but as he told it he seemed sincere. The logical part of me knew that he couldn't really believe it, but he was pretty convincing. The two women laughed and felt so much better after learning that it was just Big Foot looking for a mate instead of an old tree that almost fell on them.

Dr Fix-it was either insane or a genius. I just couldn't figure out which.

After crisscrossing the border for a few days, we officially crossed from New Jersey into New York and climbed up to Prospect Rock, the state's highest point. I felt proud to see an American flag flying in the breeze. We live in a great country, and the Appalachian Trail truly is one of our nation's treasures. *Dr Fix-it* said he'd pay for a hotel to stay in for the night if I was okay with it. "Beats sleeping in a shelter!"

Upon rising the next day, we realized that the taxi service we used to get to the hotel the day before didn't start running again until four in the afternoon. It was four miles to get back to the trail, and since neither of us wanted to walk that far, we had to figure out what to do. We eventually found a nice guy named Mike who helped out at a local church who offered to give us a ride.

I had my first hint of concern when I noticed the older beaten-up car with an interior filled half full of trash and other odds and ends. I pushed some stuff out of the way and sat upfront while *Dr Fix-it* dug out a spot in the back seat. Mike asked me to reach over to open his door from the inside. This was because the outside door handle on his side was broken.

Then, I noticed the mirror on my side of the car. It was broken off, hanging down, and secured with duct tape to the side of the car. I tried putting my seatbelt on, but it wouldn't buckle. After we took off, the seatbelt signal started beeping, and I continued to try and fasten my seatbelt. "Can you buckle your seat belt there?" Mike asked.

"I'm trying, but it won't go in," I responded.

I had it lined up correctly, I was pushing it as hard as possible, and it just would not click in. I even flipped it around several times to make sure I wasn't doing it wrong. After thirty or forty seconds of beeping, Mike said, "Can't you do something with that? It's driving me crazy!"

"I'm trying, I'm trying!"

Mike told me to just hold the buckle in as best as possible, and that would stop the noise. That's what I did, but of course, it didn't make any difference. We made our way up the mountain to the trailhead at the top of the hill. As Mike started to slow down to make the left turn into the parking lot, I noticed a car heading toward us from around the curve in the road. Mike hesitated a second before pulling out right in front of the oncoming vehicle.

I looked out my window at the front of the car that was barreling straight toward us. From the backseat, *Dr Fix-it* yelled, *"Go! Go! Go!"* and Mike stomped on the gas. The car sprang off the edge of the road, lurched over some potholes before coming to a bouncing, dusty stop in the middle of the parking lot. We quickly exited the car and told Mike how much we appreciated the ride. We were even more grateful to have survived it.

There were four or five places that day where the trail went up over obstacles that seemed to pop up out of nowhere from the forest floor. Late in the afternoon, we came to a point where it wasn't clear which direction the trail went. Right in front of us rose the side of a ridge that seemed to go almost straight up. Obviously, the trail wouldn't go up something like that, so we explored off to either side, looking for a white blaze or a path that would indicate where the Appalachian Trail went.

After searching both to the left and right without finding anything, we looked back up at the wall in front of us and found a few boot prints headed upward. *Dr Fix-it* looked further up the hill and said he could barely make out a white blaze about 20 yards further up.

This appeared to be a section of the trail that's been rerouted from its old location. Most hikers will tell you that a reroute is always harder, steeper, or more treacherous than the old route. That certainly appeared to be the case here. The reroute looked brand new because it was on fresh dirt rather than worn down to hardpack or rock as the trail is in many places.

Because of that, it wasn't obvious where to go or where to climb. After taking a moment to put my hiking poles up on my pack, I went first and got up to where I was pulling myself up the side of the hill by holding onto tree roots with my hands. I inched up my knee to reach a rock at waist level to see if I could get some leverage off of it to move me up higher.

I thought this would work, but it left me without another limb to reach up any further. My hands were busy clinging to the tree roots, and my right knee had found its way to the rock but was unable to push up any higher. That left me trying to use my injured leg, which was okay at walking, but not qualified at this point to do any mountain climbing.

I panicked and felt my heart rate increasing. I couldn't go any further up and didn't know what to do. I stayed there for a few minutes, trying to deal with the fear in my head. Then, I heard the reassuring voice of *Dr Fix-it*. "It's like a staircase, except you have many more options."

This helped me to relax, take a breath and realize that -yes—I could move around, wiggle a little bit, and find some more options. I slid my knee off the rock to back down a bit and found another place to put it so that I could push up high enough for my arms to reach the next tree root.

Thank you, *Dr Fix-it*. I had heard stories from other hikers who reached a point where they realized they couldn't safely hike the trail by themselves, and they quit and went home. I hope that I wouldn't have given up on this day, but I'm sure glad *Dr Fix-it* was there to help with his encouragement and advice.

We hiked through the Lemon Squeezer, which is a slot that gets narrower as you go through it. It got so thin that I had to take my pack off to avoid getting stuck. Right after that, the trail went up and over a twenty-five-foot cliff, which I wasn't sure we'd be able to climb. We were about to take the blue blaze trail around it when another hiker came by and went right up without any hesitation, which gave us an idea of how we might climb it. It took the two of us about 10 or

15 minutes to scale the rock face, and both of us admitted that it scared us.

That same night we camped out down the hill from a shelter where, from the sounds of it, another hiker was sick all night long. I'd been religiously following my practice of avoiding shaking hands with anyone, washing my hands with soap and water after using the privy and every single time before I ate. It was not unusual for thru-hikers to get sick while hiking. I was doing everything I could to avoid this.

Two days later, we hiked up to Bear Mountain Park and started down the other side, heading towards the bottom where the trail goes right through a zoo. On the way down there were hundreds of steps fashioned out of blocks of stone. Each block's edge appeared to have been split using a series of holes drilled in a straight line. I mentioned that the holes were probably made using a big hammer drill and *Dr Fix-it* said, "Oh no, they weren't."

Then he launched into a long, detailed story about how they use chicken feathers and a spike to split the stone blocks. As I listened to him, I thought, he's got to be making that up. There's no way this crazy tale is accurate. When he was done, I said, "That doesn't sound very likely to me."

So, he stopped walking, looked right at me, turning his head slightly to the side, saying, "That's exactly the way they did it. It's called plug and feather, you'll see." I wondered if this guy knows everything or just *thinks* that he knows everything. So, then we get to the bottom, and I saw some placards by the side of the trail. "Using Plug & Feather to Split Rocks."

What can I say? This guy was impressive.

We stayed in a nearby motel and then returned the

following day to continue our journey. I was looking forward to going through the zoo for two reasons: First, at 124 feet above sea level, it's the lowest elevation point on the AT. Second, I texted my kids, letting them know that I would see a bear that day. Unfortunately, we arrived before the zoo opened. So, no bear sightings as we ended up taking the overgrown and obviously little-used blue-blazed trail around the zoo.

After that, we walked over Bear Mountain Bridge to cross the Hudson River. As I took a selfie, I remembered seeing a photo of *AWOL* going across this bridge in his book, "AWOL on the Appalachian Trail." I read this book right before deciding to embark on my adventure. As I walked across the bridge in a cool breeze, I enjoyed the feeling of *"Wow, I'm really doing it!"* I was so lucky to be able to hike the Appalachian Trail.

Several days that week, the temperature climbed into the low 90s, and we slowed down to a crawl during the hottest hours in the middle of the day. For two blistering days, we tried taking a siesta in the shade for an hour or so right after lunch. I had a hard time dealing with the heat and needed to make sure it didn't wear me out.

The next few days, we stayed at The Spiritual Center and slackpacked by dropping my car off up the trail and then paying for a shuttle back to where we left off the day before. When we couldn't find a shuttle driver the following day, we did what's known as a key swap. I dropped *Dr Fix-it* off on the south end of the twelve miles we were hiking for the day, and then I drove up to the north end of the section. I hiked south and handed the car keys to *Dr Fix-it* when we crossed paths in the middle of the day.

At the end of the day, we were right near the well-built

RPH shelter and decided to tent there for the night. We had to hunt around for a place to park the car since no parking signs were posted nearby to discourage partying locals from driving there and using the shelter. We parked the car about a half-mile away and walked back to the shelter in the dark, where we put up our tents and slept well for the night.

The following day, which happened to be my birthday, the weather was cooler. We came to a lake and marshy area where a several-mile-long wooden boardwalk took us past the lake. It went through a cattail-filled swamp ending up right near a hiker-friendly landscaping business.

They had a rack with fuel, protein bars, and some hiker food. They also allowed us to get water from an outdoor spigot. We heard about a lunch truck just down the road, and food tends to motivate hikers, so that's where we headed. The new owners had opened their business two days ago. They proudly cooked up hamburgers and French fries that were crispy, hot, and perfectly salted.

We then headed out across some beautiful hayfields, picking up the pace so that we could reach the road where my wife would come by and pick us up. She surprised me yesterday by announcing that she was coming up to visit me for my birthday. It was supposed to be a surprise, but she ended up telling me to make it easier to find us on the trail.

Joanna and I went to a beautiful bed-and-breakfast while *Dr Fix-it* took the car to check out a local hiker motel. He said it was a decent place to stay but didn't appreciate that they advertised $85 a night in the guidebook but ended up charging him $120 instead. It was wonderful to see my wife, and I felt quite cared for by her. The idea to surprise me on the trail like this was really special.

Joanna had wanted to hike part of the trail with us, and fortunately, the route we took the next day wasn't too long, too steep or too rocky. In *AWOL's* book, he described taking his wife out for twenty-one miles the first day she joined him (which didn't turn out well). So, I made sure to keep the distance short by planning a five-mile day. Joanna was a good sport but admitted later that she felt she had her fill with hiking about a mile and a half into the five-mile day. During the hike, we stopped by the river to rest, and Joanna took the opportunity to sit and enjoy the experience of being right by the water. It was fantastic to have my wife here with us and to be able to share a small portion of the trail with her.

We got a late start the next day, and the trail took us uphill in the heat. It probably wasn't a great idea to start a hot day like this so late in the morning, but that's what we did. I discovered that I didn't have much energy in the heat, which caused me to move along lethargically. It was Father's Day, and each of my kids called to say "Hi." I enjoyed hearing from each of them and appreciated having a reason to sit down and rest while talking with them.

Because of the late start, the heat, and the Father's Day phone calls, we didn't do too well on mileage for the day. *Dr Fix-it* said, "This is just one day out of many, and it's okay to have some shorter days." I appreciated his ability to keep me focused on our hike's positive aspects.

The next day was hot as well, and I struggled to move along as we went up several good-sized climbs with the temperature in the 80s. I hung my shirt in the sun to dry out during our mid-day siesta. Within 30 minutes of restarting, my shirt was soaking wet again. The afternoon became more leisurely on the flat, smooth trail along the Housatonic River. Despite this, I found myself thinking, *What the heck am I doing out here? I could be home taking it easy. This trail is starting to look all the same.*

I was ready to call it quits that day. I was hot, tired, and worn out. I tried to remind myself that any long journey must include days like this. At the end of the day, we climbed up 400 feet to reach Silver Hill Campsite. It had a water pump that provided a nice stream of cool water if you pumped the handle thirty or forty times. I was just finishing cooking my dinner as *Dr Fix-it* sat on a porch-type swing talking with his wife. There was a gentle cool breeze, which felt incredible after the day's heat.

We got up early the next morning and started hiking by 6:30 am. Our plan was to get some miles in before it heated up. We packed up on a countertop under the pavilion as we discussed the virtues of hiking au naturale. Rumor had it that on the summer solstice, which was that day, hikers on the AT hike naked. But both of us were fully dressed as we left camp. Forty-five minutes later, I heard someone coming up behind us.

"Excuse me. Naked hiker coming through."

Top Knot walked past wearing his pack, hiking shoes, and a strategically placed sock, which appeared to be enhanced with stuffing. I struggled to come up with an appropriate compliment.

"Way to play full out," I finally said. He was the only bare hiker we saw that day, and that's the buck naked truth.

Later in the day, *Dr Fix-it* was ahead of me and sent me a text saying that he was missing his tent and his food bag. "Not in my pack—keep your eyes out." I stopped to put my glasses on so that I'd have a better chance of seeing his camo tent bag somewhere along the side of the trail. As I walked along looking for it, I couldn't figure out how in the world his tent and food bag could have jumped up and out of his pack, even if it was undone at the top.

"Maybe your tent came out when you slipped and fell this morning," I texted him an hour later. "No, I left it at the campsite this morning," he replied, followed by ten sad crying-face emojis. It was an excellent Zpacks Duplex tent, just like mine, except he had the camo color rather than light blue.

I called him and tried to cheer him up by suggesting we go back and get it. "No, it's gone by now," he replied despondently. Hudson, who owned the hostel we had stayed at, had helpfully searched for the tent. He thought a nice tent like this would be quickly taken by another hiker, but he still drove us around to check the trailheads and other spots where another hiker may have brought the tent out of the woods to leave it for its owner.

Hudson even drove to the road three-quarters of a mile downhill from the campsite where we left the tent. He grabbed his headlamp, jumped out of the truck, and sprinted up the trail looking like a white-tailed deer. Less than thirty minutes later, he was back with bad news. No tent or food bag. *Dr Fix-it's* food bag also had his really cool homemade alcohol stove and super-light titanium cook pot in it.

Our usual routine each morning was to double-check for items left behind on the ground by doing a final look around right before heading out for the day. *Dr Fix-it* said that he had done that but that he failed to check on the counter in the pavilion, where we loaded up our packs. He emailed Zpacks to see if they might be able to replace his tent without the usual six-week lead time. (By the way, the hostel at Bearded Woods Bunk and Dine was fantastic. Clean beds, shower, laundry, home-cooked food, and Hudson, having thru-hiked the AT, was a walking encyclopedia.)

As we came downhill that afternoon, I could hear the rushing water from Great Falls. I climbed out on the rocks to take a few photos using an app that blurs the water so that it looks like it's moving. Since it wasn't as hot and the humidity was down, I felt much better. The waterfall was incredible, and I was no longer thinking about quitting my hike.

The next day, I decided to try hiking without the Elevate Foot Drop Brace. The brace held my foot up and limited how far my foot could move, which helped avoid excessive strain. But my foot muscles were slowly getting stronger.

We hiked over quite a few glacier scraped dolomite rocks, many of which curved like a whale's back. Since these rocks didn't have many flat places to step on, my foot was starting to really hurt by mid-day. "Why don't you put your brace back on," *Dr Fix-it* suggested.

"Great idea," I responded. I had been thinking of doing that for a while, but kept thinking, "I'll just keep going." Maybe I was overly optimistic. I felt that if I could hike without the brace, I was closer to being healed. Fortunately, *Dr Fix-it* was there to talk some sense into me. I stopped, put the brace back on, and my foot really did feel better after that.

Over the past few miles, the trail crisscrossed the

New York-Connecticut border before we were finally in Connecticut for good. As we headed downhill, I looked out over the countryside and felt a cool breeze coming up the mountain. I stopped to stand there and take a few minutes to soak in the experience. I could take a photo or video, but there was something ethereal about moments like this that couldn't be captured. I knew that as much as I tried to save this experience in my head, I could only enjoy it fully right there, that day. I wanted to live all of my life like this. Taking in each moment, appreciating the people and experiences around me, knowing that I couldn't save or fully recreate any part of my life.

In Falls Village, we spent the night camped out behind Toymaker's cafe, a hiker-friendly breakfast place. *Dr Fix-it* said Zpacks was sending him another tent with a slight blemish in color without the usual wait. I offered to let him use the little one-person tent that I used last year—it's lightweight, but relatively small. *Dr Fix-it* is much taller than me, though, so on second thought I offered to let him use my two-person Zpacks tent instead. The little one had gotten me all the way to Southern Virginia, after all.

"Oh, no, I'll be fine," *Dr Fix-it* replied.

We had just settled down for the night when I heard *Dr Fix-it* say, "Hey, Flash. I'm wearing the tent." It was a pretty tight squeeze. The following morning, he said his head and feet hit the ends, and his face would hit the sides unless he looked straight up. While we were hiking, he searched on his phone for an inexpensive hostel where we could stay until his replacement tent arrived.

While some parts of the AT have plenty of water sources

to choose from, water had been scarce the past few days. At one point, I was so thirsty that I eyed a cow trough considering whether or not I should filter some water out of it. I decided to skip the cow trough, and an hour later, I arrived at a trailhead teeming with trail magic: water, in gallon jugs. Trail angels blessed us again! I called Mom late in the day, and while I was talking with her, I saw a baby fox running across the field.

The place we stayed next, a silent spiritual retreat center, didn't allow any music or talking, even when checking in. The price was right at $10 a night for a shower and a mattress on the floor with clean sheets. However, everything was worn out and threadbare. The washer and dryer were broken, and the towels had holes in them. This was another unique experience on our Appalachian Trail adventure.

On the way to breakfast the following morning, we picked up a hiker from Holland named *Oompa,* heading into town. He joined us for breakfast, and we had a good time learning about his country. We had to struggle to make room for *Oompa* in the back seat of the car due to all of the "hiker stuff" that had piled up over time, so we decided to clean out the car. It had gotten so full of various items that I couldn't find things when I was looking for them.

I pulled the car up next to a dumpster, pulled everything out, organized it, and created a good-sized pile of trash. *Dr Fix-it* went inside the business to ask if it was okay to use the dumpster. When he came back out, he said, "Back up the car and get ready to tear out." He could keep a pretty straight face when he was pulling my leg. I couldn't tell when he was kidding. I was pretty sure the guy said it was okay to use the dumpster, but I was still looking over my shoulder to see if someone was going to come running out and yell at us.

That was the thing with *Dr Fix-it*. He always had something going on. Yesterday, when I got to the car at the end of the day, he said that he added a new feature to my Honda Accord while waiting for me. He said he changed the wiring so that if I turned the key in the door three times in a row, the windows would all go down. "Sure, they will." I responded. I mean, I didn't think he really did anything with the wiring, and I've owned this car for over ten years. If there were some trick like this, I'd surely have known about it.

Later (when he wasn't watching), I tried it and presto— all four windows went down. I didn't know what to think. *Dr Fix-it* kept me guessing. Since I like surprises, that was probably a good thing. Hobbling around town, I was having a hard time believing that I was out hiking the Appalachian Trail. But there I was, and *Dr Fix-it* surely had made it less lonely.

While it does happen, it's hard to get lost while hiking the Appalachian Trail. There are white blazes painted on trees or rocks in most sections, often enough that you'll usually see a blaze every five minutes or so. If I suspected that I was off the trail or hadn't seen a white blaze in a while, the first thing I did was look back over my shoulder to look for a southbound-facing blaze.

If this didn't confirm that I was on the trail, I would walk, at most, another few minutes to try to see another blaze, and if I didn't see one, I'd turn around and backtrack until I found a white blaze to confirm that I was still on the trail. At intersections with other pathways, hikers or trail maintainers will often place small logs or branches across the "wrong" path to help keep people on the AT. Despite this, I'd stepped right over such diversions because I was daydreaming or simply not watching closely enough.

The app I used, FarOut, provided a GPS-enabled map for those occasions when a quick backtrack didn't get me back on the trail. Amazingly, it worked even without a cell phone signal, showing my position and the nearby trail route. Emergency locator beacons like the Spot device are also available and used by many hikers. I probably should have had a locator beacon with me, but I didn't carry one.

One morning, I had stopped to eat a protein bar and began hiking again, trying to catch up to *Dr Fix-it*. I went past an overlook when the trail looped back into the same path that I had just walked by five minutes earlier. The AT had taken me in a circle! Feeling a bit lost, I checked FarOut, hiked around the loop another time for good measure, and finally found where the trail went downhill past the viewpoint. Most of the other times I had gotten off the trail accidentally occurred while I talked on the phone. I wasn't looking carefully for clues such as branches across the trail or which pathway appeared to be the most walked upon.

We had left the car at the trailhead near Great Barrington earlier in the morning, planning on another day with less weight to carry by bringing just water, a raincoat, and lunch. We hiked north after arranging with a local shuttle driver to pick us up where the Appalachian Trail crossed Beartown Mountain Rd at 5:00 pm. When we arrived just before 5:00 pm, we discovered this was a narrow gravel road, and our shuttle driver wasn't there. After waiting fifteen or twenty minutes, *Dr Fix-it* hiked back up the hill to see if he could get a cell phone signal. I checked the guidebook and was surprised to see that there were actually two Beartown Mountain Roads that crossed the AT. The other crossing was five miles south of us.

Dr Fix-it got a call through to the shuttle driver and because he seemed somewhat confused, gave him turn-by-turn directions to get to us. It was something like "go straight ahead, turn left on this road, then left again on the other Beartown Mountain Road." I stayed down on the road to look for our driver while *Dr Fix-it* went back up the hill in case the driver tried calling us back. It should have taken ten minutes for him to reach us, but ten minutes came and went. As we waited, I could see the sun getting closer to the horizon through the trees in the forest.

Since we were slackpacking, we didn't have our tents, sleeping bags, pads, or even dinner with us, for that matter. I had a couple of protein bars, and *Dr Fix-it* had one granola bar. We could have hiked back a mile and slept in a shelter; however, the idea of sleeping on a wooden floor without a pad or even a sleeping bag didn't appeal to us.

There was a big rock right there that I could have sat down on. Still, for some reason, I chose to stand out in the middle of the road looking forlornly in the direction I expected to see our shuttle driver. I kept thinking he'd be there any minute. It began to get dark, and the clock kept ticking with no sign of our driver. Finally, another car came by and stopped. Well, they had to stop, because I was in the middle of the road. I explained our predicament and hinted strongly about giving us a lift, but with two kids in the car, they didn't have room and likely didn't trust this stranger out in the middle of nowhere.

It was past eight o'clock when I finally heard a vehicle approaching. A shiny new van with an older-looking driver pulled up to a stop. He looked over at me with a stupefied grin on his face.

"I can't believe I made it," the driver said. "It's a miracle! I was going to keep driving until dark, and then I was going to go home." I hollered for *Dr Fix-it* to come down the hill and started loading my poles and pack into the van. Joel was 80 years old, brand new to the shuttle business, and had some serious trouble navigating. One of the reasons for this, I imagine, was that Joel was using an AT wall map. This twelve-inch-wide strip shows an overview of the Appalachian Trail from Georgia to Maine. He was using this to try and find us on a gravel mountain road. *Dr Fix-it* said that he was going to get Joel a globe to navigate with next time.

Once we made it back to our car, we drove over to the hostel, and spent the night there. The following morning, we moved the car several days up the trail and had a *different* shuttle driver take us back to Beartown Mountain Road, where we resumed our hike.

That afternoon, I caught up to *Dr Fix-it* as he was taking a break, passed him and continued down the trail ahead of him. It may have been my competitive nature, or perhaps the fact that I was so much slower than all the other hikers, but I discovered I preferred to be in front of *Dr Fix-it*. He noticed this and started bugging me about it.

"I'm catching up to you…"

I stepped up my pace and walked a little faster.

"I'm going to pass you…"

I pushed it a little harder as I headed down the hill to try to stay ahead, even though I knew that he could probably still catch me.

"You know, I'm going to catch you when you stop to relieve yourself," taunted the Doctor as I tried to go even faster.

"In fact, you probably have to go now," he added.

"Your bladder is getting really full, isn't it?"

"Is that a rushing waterfall that I can hear just ahead?"

Amazingly, his suggestive powers worked on me, and I really had to go. I waited until the trail narrowed through an area with bushes on both sides, then stopped in the middle of the path to take a leak. To further enforce the "No Passing" zone, I turned uphill, spraying back and forth like a lawn sprinkler so that there was no way *Dr Fix-it* could get by me.

Then I heard him say, "Hi, this is *Dr Fix-it* here on the Appalachian Trail." I looked up to see him taking a video with his phone. "And this is *Flash 52* blocking the trail."

I don't think he was *really* taking a video, at least I sure hope not. But with *Dr Fix-it* you never really know. Anyway, we made it to the Upper Goose Pond Cabin in time to get bunks for both of us. There were about a dozen hikers there, along with the caretaker. I could hear the rain coming down on the roof overhead, which was a sound I had learned to love. Inside, warm and dry, was a good place to be for the night.

We met a lady the next morning who was getting off the trail because her knees were hurting so much. *Dr Fix-it* pointed out the oversized knee brace that I wear (on my good leg) and came up with this tale about how I went to see a doctor about my knee.

"There's no question about it. If you keep hiking, then your leg will probably fall off." He quoted the imaginary Doctor warning me. Then he added, for good measure, "The worst part is now I have to carry dry ice to keep his leg fresh if it does fall off." This lady looked at me sideways, wondering if *my* story was true or if this guy was crazy, and of course, I was expected to play along with it. I simply gave her a smile, wished her the best of luck, and turned to head up the trail.

16

JULY—HELP FROM TIM FERRIS

SUCCESS IS NOT FINAL, FAILURE
IS NOT FATAL. IT IS THE COURAGE
TO CONTINUE THAT COUNTS.

—WINSTON CHURCHILL

I took a few days off from hiking to head to Denver to see my oldest daughter get married. We drove to Albany, New York to stay in a hotel, and the plan was to fly out in the morning. *Dr Fix-it* decided that he would fly home to see his wife, and then reconnect with me in five days to continue our adventure together rather than keep hiking and get ahead of me.

I didn't have a suitcase, so I took most of my hiking gear out of my backpack to use it as my travel bag. (My wife was bringing my suit.) I thought that *Dr Fix-it* was doing the same thing, but he packed up every bit of his hiking gear except for some food items he put in a pile on the back seat.

"Why are you doing that?" I asked.

"Oh, in case I don't come back."

That's strange, I thought. *Dr Fix-it's* original plan was to hike about 400 miles from Harper's Ferry to Pawling, New York, where he would catch the train to get back home to Branson, Missouri. After meeting me in Pennsylvania and hiking together for a few weeks, he started talking about continuing his hike and going all the way to reach Mt. Katahdin in Maine with me. I told him that would be great, and I'd really appreciate his company, but that I'd made it most of the way on my own, so whatever he decided was fine with me. But at this point, I was wondering what was going on.

You see, over the past month, the conversation had gradually progressed from statements such as "Maybe I should keep hiking with you," to, "I'm going to Katahdin with you." Then there were more emphatic pronouncements such as, "I just bought my replacement tent, so now I'll have to go all the way to Maine with you." And even, "Yup, I just bought a non-refundable ticket back to Albany, so I'm definitely coming back."

When I was on the plane flying to Denver for the wedding, I had this nagging thought in my head about his "In case I don't come back" comment. I guess I could have asked him about it, but he joked so much that it was hard for me to get

ONLY WHEN I STEP ON IT

a straight answer out of him. I couldn't tell when he was really saying something or just making something up to be funny.

The wedding was incredible, and it was great to see Joanna and all of the kids at such a happy time. I would fly back to Albany the next day and was looking forward to continuing my journey with *Dr Fix-it*. As far as I knew at this point, he would meet me at the airport in Albany as planned.

I'd called in to a live radio show interview that *Dr Fix-it* had set up for the two of us. The host wanted to hear some of our stories from the trail. During the interview, *Dr Fix-it* off-handedly mentioned that he wasn't coming back to hike with *Flash 52* because he had a few things to take care of. This knocked my feet out from under me; it caught me completely off guard. I had my suspicions, but I figured that if my trail buddy wasn't going to come back and continue hiking with me, he'd call to tell me himself. I did my best to complete the interview even though I felt hurt and confused.

After ending the call, I told myself *I'm perfectly fine hiking by myself. I don't need him.* The truth was that I'd come to rely on *Dr Fix-it*, and I really liked his companionship. He's one of the funniest and most intriguing persons I've ever met. We had looked after each other for six weeks. We had helped each other out both physically and mentally through an extremely rocky part of the trail that I didn't think I'd be able to traverse. My expectation was that he was still going to be there for me, and then suddenly, he wasn't.

I also felt stupid. Perhaps I believed his over-the-top comments like "I'm definitely going to Katahdin with you" because I wanted him to stay with me as my hiking partner. This would take me some time to process. Fortunately, hiking all day long provides plenty of time for introspection, so I figured I'd be able to work through my hurt feelings. I'm honored to have met *Dr Fix-it*, spent time with him, and I know we'll remain friends for life. I knew for sure that I was really going to miss him.

Joanna and I were on the same flight from Denver to Baltimore, where I was catching a second flight to take me back to Albany, New York. We got off the plane together and walked to the gate for my flight. As we were saying goodbye, I noticed tears rolling down her cheeks. In the twenty-six years I've known Joanna, I've actually only seen her cry a few times. I think this is because she's super smart and processes everything really quickly. If she's concerned about something, she gets it out on the table, talks about things to settle the problem, and then moves on.

I wanted more than anything to hold and comfort her and find a way to help her feel better, but my flight was boarding, and I had to go. I'd made it three-quarters of the way up the Appalachian Trail, and I was determined to finish it. I was tired of all the pain I had been through over the past three and a half years and I was convinced from my progress so far that once I reached Mt. Katahdin, my leg would be healed. I gave her one last hug, gritted my teeth, and walked down the ramp onto the plane.

My wife let me know the next morning that she cried all the way home from the airport. I was devastated to hear this and fretted about it all day. I hoped she knew how much I loved her and would understand that I had to do this, to reclaim my life. In hindsight, I should have gone home, at least for a few weeks. Instead, I remained steadfastly focused on continuing up the trail. It wasn't until much later that I (once again) begged for her forgiveness and fortunately received it.

The following night, I met *Tator Tot* in the basement of a church that helps out hikers. He had an injury similar to mine twelve years ago. He has a spinal implant to help with nerve pain. This is an electrical device that a surgeon puts into your back, which sends tiny electrical signals into the nerves to distract your brain. If it works correctly, the idea is that your brain will pay attention to the light buzzing sensation while ignoring or paying less attention to the pain signals.

During the first two years of my injury, I used a TENS (transcutaneous electrical nerve stimulation) unit, which has similarities to a spinal implant. The TENS unit is an external device with a control unit, two wire leads, and a couple of sticky pads. To use it, I put a sticky pad on either side of my ankle and snapped a wire lead from the device to each sticky pad. I then chose from various patterns of signals to find a setting that was noticeable but not so strong that it was uncomfortable. I would feel a light electrical current in my leg, which served as a welcome distraction to the ongoing pain I usually felt. This helped me through some of the most challenging times when the pain was so overwhelming that I couldn't think of anything else.

You may be wondering why I didn't have a spinal implant. There are two reasons, the first being that I'm a big chicken when it comes to having surgery. While the odds are reasonable, you run the risk of complications such as infection with any procedure. There have even been cases with spinal implants where the patient ended up paralyzed due to mistakes that were made. From my personal experience, I'm glad the surgeons were able to piece my hip back together after my accident (I have 14 pins and 3 plates holding my hip together). But I really wish they hadn't mistakenly crushed the nerve in my leg while working on me. Stuff happens.

The other reason I didn't have a spinal implant is because my goal was to find a way to heal myself rather than attempt to cover up the pain. I had been on a lot of pain killers, which cover up the pain, but don't get rid of it. Even the most potent opioids couldn't eliminate the pain. They reduced it to make things more manageable, but the pain was still there.

I think of dealing with chronic pain as similar to pushing a beach ball underwater in a pool. You can use drugs (or a spinal implant) to push the pain down, but it doesn't go away. It's right there, ready to pop back up into your awareness once your brain adapts to the drugs or the leads on the spinal implant move a little bit in your back when you bend over or something.

By hiking the trail, I was doing two things to improve my condition. First, I was teaching my brain that it was okay to step on my leg. A typical injury would heal within six to eight weeks, with the pain slowly diminishing during that time. Obviously, at this point, something else was going on with me.

All I knew at this point was that I had nerve damage, and I tried to relax instead of tightening up. I wanted my brain to know that it was okay to step on my foot. I wanted my brain to be okay with the signals coming from my leg rather than fighting them off.

I was also increasing the strength and function of my leg and foot. Sure, it hurts to walk on it, but not using it made things even worse. If I just sat around, it would tighten up and hurt even more. When my nerve was damaged, I lost all connection between my brain and lower leg muscles. I couldn't move my foot at all for an entire year. So now, just like a stroke victim, I was working overtime to try and gain back that connection, the ability to lift my foot, to control the muscles in my lower leg and foot.

The trail had been perfect for this. I knew each day that I had to walk another ten to twelve miles. I knew which direction I was going—north. There was no option to sit down and feel sorry for myself. When my leg hurt, when it rained or when I had to climb a big hill, I thought about the challenge of the journey I was on rather than focusing on how much my leg might be bothering me. When I looked back to see how far I had hiked, I was hopeful for a future in which I'd eventually be healed. I'd gone from sitting on the couch most of the day to where I was now. And that felt good through to my core.

Having recently crossed into Massachusetts, I headed north out of Dalton. I was only hiking eight miles because I found that my leg usually hurt me more when I started back after a break. You'd think that a five-day rest would be good for my leg, but it was squawking at me all day. I felt out of sorts as I got used to hiking by myself and being back on the trail. It usually takes me a few days to get back in the swing of things.

The following day I was up by 5:30 and out hiking by 6:30 am to avoid the middle of the day heat while hiking up Mt. Greylock. I felt lethargic, and my injured foot was killing me, so I was moving pretty slowly coming up the hill. I often thought about quitting—my leg hurt, I missed my wife. *What the heck am I doing out here?*

I reached Bascom Lodge at the summit of Mt. Greylock

in time to get a hamburger before the restaurant closed for lunch. I took a nap, showered, and joined three other hikers for a nice dinner. I finished watching a movie on Netflix and got a good night's rest.

The other hikers and I came down the following day and mingled in with a room full of tourists who were also guests at the lodge. Instead of the typical hostel breakfast of eggs, sausage, and pancakes, I was disappointed to see that we were getting just muffins and coffee for breakfast. As it turned out, the muffins were stuffed with blueberries and tasted great.

I ate as many as I could while trying to not look like a total hog. I used the technique of casually taking two or three at a time while making sure not to grab the last one. This reminded me of growing up with seven kids in the family. If Mom made a pecan pie, we would take a slice, eat it, and then get another piece until the pie was gone. I think we learned how to be selfish as a survival mechanism. This selfishness expanded to where it affected things like the water jug that was in the refrigerator. If you took half of the water, no matter how low it got, then you didn't have to fill it up.

A SOBO yesterday complained about how steep his climb up the north side of Mt. Greylock had been, and I thought he was being wimpy. I discovered that he wasn't kidding—the terrain was steep and long coming down from Mt. Greylock. I did portions of it hiking backwards down the hills to protect my knees. This may have looked strange, but I found that it really worked.

I was giving a lot of thought to quitting—my leg hurt, I missed my wife, and my spirits were flagging. Further up the hill, I came to a sign marking the Massachusetts / Vermont border. I couldn't believe that I had made it to Vermont, which should have excited me. Instead, I was just tired. My adventure was wearing me out.

After hiking through the town of North Adams, I passed a house and noticed a water hose with a sign that said, "For AT hikers." I sprayed cool water over my head and arms and rinsed off my upper body before filling up my water supply. I was so thankful for all of the trail angels like this. They were such wonderful people to go out of their way to help folks like me on the AT. It really made a difference.

I reached Pete's Spring campsite with some gas still in the tank. After struggling the last few days to remember why I was hiking the AT, as I was falling asleep, I looked out at the night sky through the forest and realized that was it. That's why I was there. To savor and remember the images, the feelings, and emotions that were there for just a moment in time.

During the night, I noticed a light moving through the forest. After watching it for a bit, I could tell that a hiker was coming up the trail using a headlamp. I looked at my watch. 3:15 am. Weird... It must be someone who's trying to stay cooler by night hiking. In the morning, I asked the hikers who had camped there if anyone knew about the night hiker.

"Yeah, it was me," said *Bigfoot*, a NOBO that I had met during my stay the night before on Mt. Greylock. "I was in a bar in North Adams, and a lady offered to let me stay in a spare room at her house," he explained. "Everything was going fine until she started swearing loudly at herself, then she overflowed the bathtub. The neighbor in the unit below called the police, and then the landlord showed up. I had enough and decided to head to the woods for the rest of the night."

I don't get to hear stories like this from my neighbors, maybe because I'm married and live in the suburbs. It's been fun to talk with other hikers on the trail and get to know a broader spectrum of people. While hiking the next day, I found the trail was friendlier, and my foot let me know about it by feeling better than it had the last two days. I felt stronger and more energetic going up the hills in the afternoon for the first time since getting back from my trip to my daughter's wedding.

While crossing a powerline, I noticed a nice breeze and stopped for 30 minutes to dry my shirt out on my hiking poles. I pulled off my knee brace so the wind could dry my compression tights out in the breeze. When I started moving again, my clothes weren't completely dried out, but I felt so much better than I did when I arrived, soaking wet and hot.

I found a perfect campsite on top of Consultation Mountain that put me at just the right distance for the day. Just as I arrived, it started to sprinkle, so I quickly put up my tent and brought all my gear inside. While waiting to see what the rain was going to do, I blew up my air mattress and laid down for a moment with my boots still on. I immediately fell asleep and rested for an hour before realizing that I had dozed off.

It was still light out when I woke up, and the rain had stopped. I used my hiker's stove to make my old standby, lentils, and mashed potatoes. I considered dinner options that didn't need to be cooked so that I could leave my cookstove, fuel, and cook pot behind. Other hikers have told me that they carried less gear as they got closer to Maine. At this point, anything that was not absolutely critical was just extra weight.

The following day I did my stretching routine, got my bear bag down, packed up, and started hiking by 6:00 am. It had stopped raining, but the vegetation along the sides of the trail was still wet. I struggled to see the path in front of me, blinking my eyes to focus. I felt like I wasn't awake yet because I didn't have any coffee or any processing time to get my mind going. In addition to this, due to the thick cloud cover, it was still dark out. The trail and surrounding forest had a sinister, wet, remote feeling to it.

My hike that morning was not enjoyable. The trail wasn't too bad; while it had plenty of rocks and roots to step over, the lack of sun combined with the aches and pains in my body had me feeling less than enthusiastic. I had been hiking since February 5th—just over five months, although I took a few breaks here and there. I was tired. Physically and mentally. My legs, toes, and feet hurt. I didn't have much interest in getting to know other hikers at this point other than to get information about where I could find the next water source.

If I weren't pushing a timeline to get to Katahdin before it closed on October 15th, I would have taken a week off to rest up and recharge. I needed to find a way to increase my "get up and go" without taking too many days off from hiking.

I used to teach clients at my real estate seminars how to use "Green Hat" thinking to brainstorm ideas. To practice it, you come up with as many potential solutions as possible, no matter how crazy or impractical they may sound. The purpose is to get as many ideas down as possible in the hopes that you might discover something useful or valuable in the list. Here's what I came up with:

Peter's Green Hat Ideas on how to recharge my batteries & recommit to making it all the way to Mt. Katahdin

- Go walk in a pool
- Get a full body massage
- Foot reflexology (foot massage)
- Go see a movie
- Eat a nice dinner at an authentic restaurant
- Go visit my parents in Maine for a few days
- Go home
- Quit (hey, these are just green hat ideas, okay?)
- Clean my clothes
- Stay at a nice hotel
- Stay at a hostel, hang around and enjoy resting and talking with other hikers.
- Go shorter distances, 6—8 miles a day
- Slackpack
- Hire a Sherpa to carry my gear
- Get someone to rent an RV and meet me at days end at road crossings
- Hike with less gear/weight
- Try new shoes
- Get new sock liners
- Try moleskin type cushions around my toes
- Soak in a hot tub
- Go home and soak in OUR hot tub
- Hug my wife
- Pet my dog
- Eat a rice crispy treat

- Drain my legs (Lay on the floor
  with legs up on the wall)
- Write one page on why I want to finish the AT
- Write one page on how horrible it will be if I quit
- Get some new audiobooks
- Download some podcasts so I can listen
  when I don't have coverage to stream
- Find some new music to listen to while hiking

Over the next several days, I tried out a few of these ideas. I went to a laundromat and washed my hiking clothes. I found a local YMCA to walk in the pool and took a nice long hot shower. I went to an Indian restaurant and planned to look at the grocery store for dinners I could bring with me that didn't need to be cooked so I could test out hiking without my stove.

The next day my foot was feeling *so* much better. It may seem crazy that walking in a pool can help, but it's a fantastic therapy for me. I vowed to do more pool walks when I could fit them in. I continued to build upon my "Green Hat" list of ideas while hiking the next day.

I knew that I could make it if I focused on a small enough piece at one time—the next week, the next shelter, or just the next step if need be.

I finally figured out why I was having such a mental challenge. I was thinking, *I'm almost there. Just five hundred some more miles to go*, rather than my usual focus of just getting to the next town. Thinking this way was fine in the morning. But later in the day, when I was worn out from hiking over several mountains in the heat of the summer, I started to think, *What? 500 more miles! I can't do that! What the heck am I doing? My legs hurt!*

So, I decided that the secret was to *not* think about Katahdin. Yeah, it's only five hundred some miles, but that was enough to overload my little brain's mental circuits when it was taxed out trying to propel me up a hill late in the day. I changed my focus to thinking about getting to Manchester Center, which was forty miles ahead. Once there, I would pick a new target, maybe Rutland, Vermont, just another fifty miles. I knew I could do that.

This may seem simple, and it was. How do you eat an elephant? One bite at a time. The bigger insight was how much the mental aspect affected my journey. My father told me a story about a mountain climber friend who was all roped up trying to get across a scary section. Then another climber and his two kids came right by them with no ropes or anything. Dad told me, "If you think something is going to be difficult, then it will be. If you can get yourself to believe that you can do it, then anything's possible." I committed to remembering this *before* thinking about giving up.

That afternoon I came to a footbridge with a sign that said it was closed. I could see that it was sagging on one side, and I thought for a moment about trying to sneak across it before my better judgment kicked in. I headed upstream and found a wider spot to make it across where the water level was lower. The water was barely over my ankles, but this was the first stream I needed to ford, so I was a little anxious. I was carefully shuffling my feet across the last three or four feet of the stream where the water was faster and deeper when the sky opened up, and the rain came dumping down. As I took my last few steps across, I laughed because I was getting wet from the top and bottom at the same time.

I hiked without my raincoat, as it was warm enough to leave it behind in the car. When the temperatures are as warm as this day was, if you wear a raincoat, you'll still get wet from sweat, and I was doing everything I could at that point to lighten my pack. I arrived at the shelter and enjoyed talking with the fifteen other hikers as I made my dinner. It felt great to finally change out of my wet clothes and climb into my sleeping bag for the night.

The next day, after crossing the state line into Vermont, I climbed the Glastenbury Mountain fire tower and kept going all the way to the top even though I was scared stiff. As I made my way up, I told myself that plenty of other people had come up there, and it hadn't fallen down yet.

When I started feeling tired in the afternoons, I listened to audio recordings on my phone. This gave me something to think about other than how tired I was or how much my legs and feet were hurting. I didn't like using earbuds because they felt weird in my ears, and the cords got in my way. I played the audio on my iPhone out loud, but I was careful to turn it off when I saw or heard another hiker coming along. *The New York Times* audio digest helped me understand what was going on in the "real" world. I listened to a few different podcasts, audiobooks, and music using Spotify. I enjoyed getting recommendations from the app, something that didn't exist music-wise when I was growing up.

The Tim Ferris Podcast was one of my favorites. He was an interesting host who was able to interview and draw out information from his guests that made the show worth listening to. One topic of interest was on making daily goals easily attainable. His first example was for authors. "Don't try to write 2,000 words a day; just write two crappy pages, and if it's going well, then you can keep going and create more." He thought it was essential to have a goal to feel good about reaching every day. For example, he said, "If you want to start exercising, then set a goal to do just five minutes on the treadmill. Do that each day and then see what happens."

Then he mentioned the concept of "How can I make this easy?" He was talking about writing a book, but I thought, *how can I make completing the Appalachian Trail easy?*

After thinking this through, I became committed to hiking eight miles a day. If I felt good, I could go a little further—perhaps ten, but not more than about twelve miles in a day. I felt confident that I could do this and was reasonably sure that my leg could handle it. I wanted to try this in an effort to keep my foot and leg from bothering me so much.

The downside was that if I didn't hike as far, then I'll be out on the trail for a longer period of time, and I missed my wife a bunch. This seems to be the dichotomy that most hikers face. They want to get miles in to finish sooner while also making sure that they take the time to stop at the overlooks, talk with other hikers and enjoy the experience. My goals were to enjoy each day, complete the Appalachian Trail, and keep my body and spirit whole. I also wanted to see and hold my wife as soon as possible. I wanted the best of everything.

The next day started off with an easy four miles to a road crossing just before the climb up Stratton Mountain. I stopped in the parking lot and hung my shirt in the sun to dry off the morning's accumulated sweat. Thirty minutes later, I was heading up the hill and saw *Hestia* who was resting by the side of the trail. I first met her over 1,300 miles south of here.

The climb up Stratton Mountain wasn't too steep, but it seemed to go on and on in the afternoon heat. When I got to the top, I looked up at the fire tower, took a deep breath, and climbed up as I tried to control my fear of heights. At least the windows at the top had glass in them. This made hanging out up there easier for me than the open windows in the fire tower I had climbed the day before. The views at the top were spectacular. I took a few photos through the windows and then climbed down the stairs one flight to get some shots without the windows' reflection. I was afraid of being up so high and worried that the wind might cause me to drop my iPhone, so after getting a few photos, I came down quickly.

The Stratton Pond Shelter had a "no tenting" rule, so I set up my pad and sleeping bag on one of the wooden bunks. *Hestia* set up her tent inside the shelter on a double bunk while announcing what she was doing. Maybe she did this to give any other hikers a chance to object since putting up tents in shelters is frowned upon.

As I started to doze off, I heard a few people talking about hiking three-tenths of a mile down to the pond to see the sunset but figured I was too tired, and I didn't want any extra miles. I probably should have gone to see it. When I first started hiking the AT, I would always go out of my way to see a sunrise or a sunset. I wondered if I was getting too concerned about making it to Katahdin. I thought perhaps I should lighten up and enjoy the journey.

During the night, the mosquitos were biting, and I kept thinking about getting up to set up my tent inside the shelter.

As tired as I was, this seemed like it would take too much energy, and I made it through the night with just a few bites.

The following day at about noon, I stopped at Prospect Rock and met *Mudup* and *Tim*, who were hiking the Long Trail. They were willing to hike with me for the rest of the day. The miles slid by as the three of us walked and talked. At the trailhead, I met *Fugitive* and *Spider*. I offered to give them a ride to the outfitters since my car was there. *Fugitive* wanted to buy a set of Leki hiking poles just like the old pair I had in the car. Instead of purchasing new poles, he gave me $40 for my older Lekis, and we were both happy.

I had time to find a local pool and get some therapy by walking in chest-high water for forty-five minutes before heading to the Green Mountain Hostel. Jeff, the owner, was quite friendly. It was super clean, and everyone got a pint of Ben and Jerry's ice cream. I chose Chunky Monkey. It was so nice to be able to eat anything I wanted while hiking.

I liked Green Mountain Hostel so much that I decided to take a zero there. I shuttled my car north to Rutland, went walking in the pool again, played the piano, and sent a card to my wife to let her know how special she is to me. I was in the kitchen when I heard a familiar voice.

"Nate, is that you?"

Nate's a good friend and client of mine from North Carolina. We owned a 322-unit apartment complex together a number of years ago. He shared my passion for hiking and had completed most of the trail by hiking with a guided group; now he was finishing off some sections that he'd missed. Running into him in the hostel was surreal, like two different worlds colliding. We chatted for a while before wishing each other well and promising to get together once we'd finished our respective adventures.

The next morning, back on the trail, I thought about Nate. I had taught him to find passive investors to fund commercial real estate deals, and he's since developed an impressive portfolio of properties. Watching my clients succeed is akin to a father's pride, and I cherished the relationship we'd built. But as I trudged through the woods, I realized I'd failed to stay in touch with so many other clients of mine over the years. That's the problem (or blessing) with having so much time to think: I was discovering things I wished I'd done differently. I made a mental note to stay better connected with my clients going forward.

I moved on to contemplating reasons why my toes might be hurting so much on my good side. I realized I had developed the habit of scrunching my toes up with each step. If you can imagine trying to hold on to the trail by grabbing it with your toes, that's what I was doing. Perhaps this was because of the perilous terrain I had been hiking over lately. Once I figured this out, I immediately made a mental effort to stop doing it, and amazingly, within a few hours my toes and foot began feeling better.

Late in the afternoon, I came up a hill and was engulfed in the exquisite aroma of pine trees. This experience lasted for the next mile or so, including my time walking through two massive rock gardens. Hikers passing by over the years had piled rocks up into stacks. Each stack had as many as ten or twelve rocks balancing on top of each other. It was strange to see hundreds of stacks in one spot, all I could think of was *only on the Appalachian Trail*. I wasn't sure how to respond, so I added one more stack to each of the rock gardens just in case this was a required ritual that I didn't know about.

The blue-blazed trail to the shelter added another six-tenths in bonus miles for me at the end of the day. I could have kept going and found an unofficial spot along the trail to camp, but since I was hiking alone again, I thought it was essential to have some conversations with other people to help keep me sane. I met a dad who was out for the week with his twelve-year-old son. I told them that my father took me into the Canadian boundary waters on a canoe trip when I was ten. That's an experience that I've never forgotten.

It rained harder than any other time I could remember while being in my tent during the night. It was a little unsettling spending the night in the forest with lightning and thunder nearby, but at least my Zpacks Duplex kept me dry.

The following day at about 1 pm, I came to a road crossing where a restaurant was a half-mile down the road. I was eager to eat some real food. I hiked down the road, sticking my thumb out whenever a car came by to try and hitch a ride. Before long, I arrived at the restaurant, still on foot. I changed into a dry shirt and laid my sweat-soaked hiking shirt out along with my tent on the grass outside to dry in the sun. I started off with a chocolate shake, then had steak, mashed potatoes, another chocolate shake, and several diet coke refills. The waitress was nice enough to give me a ride back to the trail. When I arrived, I met a group of four hikers who were waiting for a taxi to take them into a hostel in town.

I was surprised that I didn't want to join them. That's what I would have done a few months ago. I used to jump at any chance to take a break from the trail, even if it was just overnight. I felt like I had gotten my pack weight down low enough, built up the strength in my legs, and finally turned the corner on the mental malaise that I'd been dealing with. I was beginning to enjoy my time on the trail again.

I sat around the fire at the shelter that night, talking with a diverse mix of hikers. There were NOBO and SOBO AT hikers as well as South and Northbound Long Trail hikers. It felt wonderful to sit on a nice log by the fire, eat my dinner, and connect with other folks who were on a journey similar to mine.

The Long Trail, which runs 273 miles through Vermont, is the oldest long-distance trail in the United States. It was constructed between 1910 and 1930 by the Green Mountain Club and served as an inspiration for the Appalachian Trail's development. It follows the same path as the AT for about a hundred miles. Interestingly, both the AT and the Long Trail are marked with white blazes.

I was having fun making my way up Mt. Killington over and around the many roots and rocks that were on the trail when it started to get dark, and the wind picked up as a storm was coming in. I found a spot just off the trail to pitch my tent and climbed in to wait out the storm. Since I had cell coverage, I made good use of my time to finish planning out my hike through the White Mountains in New Hampshire. I was concerned about hiking in the area above treeline. I wanted to have reservations at the mountain huts run by the Appalachian Mountain Club.

I was 140 miles from the Zealand Falls hut, so that would take me fourteen days if I averaged ten miles a day, plus I added a zero which meant I'd arrive there in fifteen days.

I'd heard that hikers tend to go slower through the White Mountains due to the terrain, so I figured on six or seven miles a day when going from one hut to the next. I also had to add the time I would be taking off to join my family for our vacation. I called, signed up as a member to get a discount, and made reservations at three of the huts. All the SOBOs had told me that the Whites can be extremely windy but are gorgeous.

Once the storm passed, I packed up my tent and hiked the rest of the way up to Cooper Mountain Shelter, which is near the top of Mt. Killington. I wanted to take the two-tenths of a mile side trail up to the top of the mountain to eat some real food at the lodge. The guidebook said the trail was rather steep, and it was correct. The trail was seriously straight up, so I had to put my poles up on my pack and use my hands and feet to clamber up the last stretch of trail.

The wind was blowing hard enough at the top that I had a difficult time walking. I made my way over the summit and then down to the lodge, where I purchased and ate a bunch of junk food and a nice cold Gatorade. I opened my pack to discover that the water bladder in my pack had been leaking for the last few days. I thought it was strange that my back was sweating enough to wet down the back of my legs each day!

I went into the bathroom and used the automated hand dryer to dry out my shirt and compression tights. I was the only hiker there, but plenty of tourists who had taken the ski lift to the top came in while I was drying my clothes out. I looked, felt, and probably smelled like a homeless person.

The morning's hike was quick and easy as it was mostly downhill. It felt nice to get back to my car, where I promptly changed out of my sweaty hiker clothes. I found a pool to walk in. Walking in the pool was pretty dull compared to hiking the AT, but I still enjoyed it, and it did wonders for my foot and leg.

I resupplied at the grocery store and sorted out my food on the top of my car while parked in front of the Yellow Deli Hiker Hostel. I really liked the place. The deli was uniquely furnished with curved tree branches or trunks that mold right into the restaurant seats. The people were friendly, and they had awesome root beer on tap!

Everyone who works there was involved in some sort of religion, something about the seven tribes or something like that. I've heard stories about hikers that end up working and living on one of their communal farms. I was also told that if you don't ask about it, they'll leave you alone, and I discovered this to be true.

The following day I walked past the turn-off where the Vermont Long Trail continues northward up to the Canadian border. As I mentioned earlier, the Long Trail was developed before the Appalachian Trail and uses the same white blazes for markings. I saw how easy it would be for someone hiking the AT to get confused and follow the Long Trail instead of the AT.

I stopped around dinner time to stay at a nice little flat spot I found in the woods. I realized that the cabin I was shooting for the next day was nine miles ahead, so I stopped there instead of pushing on to the next shelter. It was pretty isolated camping out alone in the woods, but that was where I ended up. I was proud of getting eight miles in on a day when I also spent three hours moving the car up the trail.

The next day was a series of climbs and descents made enjoyable by a smooth trail, some cooler weather, and a decent breeze. At 4:00 pm, I reached The Lookout, a private cabin where the owners allowed hikers to stay. I dried my clothes in the sun, climbed up to the rooftop deck to take in the 360-degree view, and then went into the cabin to enjoy a nap. I was so tired I fell asleep right on the wooden floor without bothering to blow up my air pad.

The next day was pretty hot. I stopped three different times to dry out my pack and shirt in the sun. This seemed pointless because I was soaked in sweat again by the time I went up the next hill. Despite this, drying out helped me feel a little more comfortable, and it was nice to stop for a twenty or thirty minute rest on such a hot day.

Getting water while hiking was becoming a little more challenging. Filling up by a shelter in the morning, I positioned my water holder to collect dribbles coming down from some moss in the center of a mostly dried-out stream bed. It took about fifteen minutes for me to collect two liters of water.

I was tired and hungry later in the day and wanted a place to sit down, take a break, and eat dinner. I decided to stop at a dirt road crossing to dry out my shirt in the sun while I ate. It felt strange to be sitting down on a dusty dirt road eating my dinner, but that's what I was doing. *Stumble Dwarf*, a SOBO, came by and told me that he had recently fallen in a creek and gotten scraped up a bit. He was a shorter guy, so he did look like a dwarf, and he had stumbled in a stream. Little things like this made each day interesting.

I had planned to hike up to the top of the next hill to camp, but about halfway up the mountain, I found a perfect campsite. It was flat and covered with pine needles. I set up my tent with the flaps up on both sides so I could cool off in the breeze coming up the hill.

In the morning, when I got to hiking again, I found the trail was nice to me, smooth with just a few ups and downs—a good day for this type of trail surface since it was pretty hot. I was happy to reach the bridge over the White River, where I saw other hikers jumping off the bridge down into the water below. I didn't know how well my leg would handle a long jump like that, so I decided to skip this AT tradition. Linda came over as I watched people jumping off the bridge and invited me over to their house to have a cold root beer and some meatball subs. It turned out that Linda and her husband Randy are trail angels that help over 1,000 hikers a year.

As I was contemplating how much further I was going to hike for the day, a storm front came through with fierce winds and a bit of rain. After the storm, *Long Shank*, a thru-hiker from six years ago, set up more trail magic out by the road, and I had some cookies, a hamburger, hotdog, and a few more things to drink.

Seven other hikers stopped and sat down to enjoy the trail magic. Rather than talking, I found it easier to just sit and listen to the ongoing conversations. I don't know if this was because I was tired from hiking or because I was a fair amount older than most of the other hikers. I decided to try to be more engaged in future conversations rather than indulging my introverted side.

That evening, I stayed in the top level of Linda and Randy's barn—or maybe it was a garage? I wasn't sure. I chose a bed close to a window thinking, *just in case I need to escape a fire.*

I wonder if this is because I was used to sleeping in shelters with one side open to the elements.

I got up early in the morning to hike during the cooler hours of the day, and it was quite pleasant after the previous day's cold front. There were quite a few trees and branches blown down on the trail from the previous day's storm. Luckily, I was on Linda and Randy's porch when the high winds came through.

Mid-morning, I saw a note on the ground that said. "Ground bees in ravine ahead, watch out." I moved along as fast as I could (which wasn't very fast) through the ravine and luckily didn't see any bees. I came out into West Hartford, Vermont, and followed the AT down Elm St. to find a cooler in front of a trail angel's house with a sign that said "Hikers, help yourself."

I had some banana bread that smelled and tasted heavenly. Wow, that tasted great after hiking all morning. In the cooler was a list of trail angels in the area that open up their homes to provide housing for thru-hikers. I called and talked with several and left some voice mail messages. Everyone I spoke with said they were full for the night.

I was excited to cross the Connecticut River and arrive in New Hampshire. Twelve states down and only two more to go! SOBOs told me that both New Hampshire and Maine would be rather hard. Once I got to Hanover, I got myself a treat —coffee gelato— and bought a merino wool shirt at the outfitters to replace the one I had been using, which was full of holes.

I walked down to the college parking lot where I had left my car and drove to a pool so that I could walk in the water for an hour. All of the trail angels that called me back said they were full for the night. So, I drove north to Glencliff, which is the next place I planned to leave my car anyway. I stayed at the Welcome Hikers Hostel with about twenty other friendly hikers and took a zero the next day. Only 442 miles to reach the top of Mt. Katahdin!

The following day I shuttled back to Hanover to continue my trek northward. I was dropped off on the corner of Main Street as the AT goes right through town there. I sat outside the Dirt Cowboy Café to enjoy an americano and a sweet roll while enjoying the fact that I was sitting at a café right on the Appalachian Trail.

I stopped that afternoon at Bill Akerly's house, the ice cream man. He recently died, but his son continued the tradition of giving out ice cream sandwiches to hikers for the year. By the time I started up Smarts Mountain, it was past 3:00 pm. I figured this was a good thing since the worst heat of the day was behind me. I set short-term targets as I made my way up the 2,100-foot climb.

Ok, I'm going to hike to the overlook that's nine tenths of a mile ahead. I told myself. *That's all I'm going to think about right now.*

As I listened to another Tim Ferriss podcast, he described breaking life down into two-week experiments. "You can do anything for two weeks," he advised. I thought this was a good way for me to break the rest of my hike into smaller pieces to wrap my mind around.

I stopped to rest again and had a quick dinner of tortillas with sharp cheddar cheese and pepperoni. This was my new dinner of late as I was hiking without my stove. It was faster to make and easier to clean up. On top of this, I slept better if I could eat at 5:00 or 6:00 rather than at 8:00 pm.

My granddaughter sent me a video where she's counting up to five. She's pretty cute, so I stopped to FaceTime with my daughter while sitting at an overlook with an outrageous view of New Hampshire. After starting hiking again, the mountain trail became steeper towards the top. The terrain was interesting; it had steeply sloped ledge rock with tree roots growing over it in places. I felt pretty good, most likely because the day was cooler, and I had taken it easy most of the day.

By the time I got to the top of the mountain, I had my headlamp on, and I walked over to check out the Ranger's cabin. Only one set of hiking poles was outside, so I figured I'd join the one person in the cabin for the night. I quietly opened the door and saw eight or ten hikers covering the floor area inside. I closed the door and looked around for someplace else to spend the night. I went over to the fire tower and shined my headlamp up into the night air. *Maybe I could sleep up there,* I thought, before deciding to take the more cautious approach of heading over to the tenting area. Another couple came in at 10:00 pm to join me. I fell asleep feeling proud of how I had covered thirteen miles in the heat for the day.

The next day I was surprised at how steep and rugged the trail going over Mount Cube was. It was a tough climb followed by a steep downhill trek. I noticed that some of the granite or marble-type rocks along the trail were wet while other rocks appeared dry. Another hiker suggested that there might be silicone in these rocks absorbing moisture from the air. That sounded like an interesting mystery, and I made a note to look into it later (although I still haven't done that).

At the end of the day, I found a campsite next to an old foundation made of fieldstones. It would be interesting to know the history of all the old stone walls and houses I had seen along the trail. I know that a family used to live and work there. Who were they? What was their story? What happened to them?

After spending another night at Hikers Welcome Hostel, I slackpacked from Kinsman Notch, heading back to Glencliff to go over Mt. Moosilauke headed southbound. The north side of Mt. Moosilauke can be somewhat treacherous. It has wooden steps added in places to help hikers make it up the smooth steep rock faces and a stream coursing down so close to the trail that in areas, the trail was wet from the water's spray.

Once I made it above treeline, I was rewarded with outstanding views. I also got to see a moose that I'd heard about. I'd been told that it was suffering from wasting disease and had been standing near the trail for the past week or so. When I got there, I could see the moose right on the trail about fifty feet ahead of me, and it didn't appear to be moving anytime soon. Other hikers avoided the moose by going off the trail, and I could hear them breaking branches off to the side of the trail as they made their way through the thick waist-high trees that grow at this altitude.

I wasn't comfortable going off-trail because I was worried about getting my injured foot caught in the branches. I also didn't want to damage the high-altitude terrain. You're supposed to stay on the trail, but I didn't know what the rules were for such a situation. I figured the right thing to do was either wait for the moose to move or turn around and go back down the mountain the way I'd just climbed up.

Instead of doing either of those, I inched my way forward towards the moose until I was within a few feet of it. The moose was facing away from me, and I could see that her back was covered with sores, flies, and ticks. I saw *Blue Beard* coming towards me from the other direction and asked him to take a photo. As I slipped by the left side of the moose, *Blue Beard* took my picture. It's a great photo, but I feel like I can't show it to anyone. I thought I believed in giving wild animals plenty of space, and now there I was standing right next to a moose.

After making my way down the almost-as-steep south side of Mt. Moosilauke, I walked out of the woods to see a motorcycle stopped in the road with a dog lying down near it. I thought the dog had been hit and went over to see if I could help out. Fortunately, it was just taking a nap in the middle of the road. The motorcyclist had stopped to get the dog out of the road and try to find the owner.

I mentioned that I was on my way to a nearby hostel. Despite my protests, I found myself leading the dog down the road using a rope that the motorcyclist provided. *This is great,* I thought, *I'm having a hard enough time hiking without becoming responsible for someone else's pet.* Fortunately, the motorcyclist found the dog's owner in an RV camped nearby along the stream, and I was able to turn the pup over to its rightful owner.

I decided to drop my car off at Crawford Notch that night and then shuttle down to a donation-based hostel that was in a guy's house in Lincoln, New Hampshire. It was past 7 pm by the time I arrived, and with my leg and the rest of my body hurting, I was in no mood to walk the half-mile into

ONLY WHEN I STEP ON IT

town to get dinner. I called around looking for a pizza place or *any* food place that could deliver, and I struck out. I tried using Uber—no luck.

Most hostels have some pasta or rice in the kitchen or at least something to eat in the hiker box. Still, all I found was an old refrigerator full of old-looking hiker leftovers. The bunks were full, so I put my tent up in the backyard and went down to the basement to do my laundry.

While waiting for my clothes to get washed, I opened my pack and pulled out one last tortilla along with a remaining single serving of peanut butter from my food bag. Hiker food like this tastes great when you're out in the woods but sitting there in the basement, not so good.

I looked around and found a shelf with a sign that said, "Free hiker food." I looked over some older-looking canned vegetables, but nothing looked good enough to eat. I opened a box of generic brand cheerios and ate a handful while pondering what to do for dinner. I slowly ate ten or twelve handfuls while coming to the realization that this, along with the tortilla I'd just eaten, was going to be my dinner for the night.

If I'd just waited until the following morning to move the car, then I'd have been able to drive someplace and get something to eat. That's one thing that I liked about bringing my car along with me. But for that one evening, no car, and no real dinner. I've mentioned before that to successfully complete the Appalachian Trail, you need to learn to "Embrace the suck." Perhaps my dinner that night qualifies for this.

I finished my laundry and retired to my tent, which was now surrounded by four or five other tents just a few feet

---

away. I tried to get to sleep, but other hikers were walking, talking, and making noise. I could hear the sounds of traffic, the nearby dryer vent, and the next-door neighbors talking loudly until almost midnight. It wasn't the most restful night I've had. I couldn't help but think how much more pleasant it would've been in the woods somewhere.

After a good day of hiking the next day, I finally stopped partway up the mountain by Eliza's Brook and was in my tent listening to the sound of the nearby falls. That was so much nicer.

17

AUGUST—MEETING WEIRD CHARACTERS

STRENGTH DOES NOT COME FROM
PHYSICAL CAPACITY. IT COMES
FROM AN INDOMITABLE WILL.

—MAHATMA GANDHI

The following day, my fingers were beginning to cramp up from holding onto the rock face in front of me. I hadn't seen anyone all day. I'd spent the entire morning clambering up the mountainous pile of rocks, using my hands and feet like a chimpanzee.

Now I tried and missed for the umpteenth time to swing

my leg up to a toe hold that would allow me to grab onto the tree root that was just beyond the reach of my right arm.

What the heck am I doing here? I can't do this!

The aching, burning sensations in my leg reminded me why I was there. I guess you could call it a mission. I was determined to heal myself.

I wanted to get moving so I could warm up. I'd been stuck here for half an hour.

I looked around, searched for other options, and finally decided to retreat down after finding none. Using my bum leg, I tried my best to feel around below for a place to step, but all I could find was the mountainside's smooth rock face.

And to think that a blind guy hiked the Appalachian Trail.

That's when the rain came pouring down.

I closed my eyes to keep out the rain and shut everything off so that I could think. I needed a few moments to come up with a solution.

Bingo. *That's the answer.*

Friction.

I read a book when I was sixteen about how to survive a motorcycle road bike accident. It said while you're sliding along the pavement at sixty miles per hour, you need to get as much of you as possible in contact with the road so that you can scrub off your speed. Your skin will grow back.

I knew that it was only five or six feet from where my feet were to the ledge below. So, I pushed my stomach, arms, and left leg into the side of the mountain, pulled up slightly on my hands, and moved my right leg from the rock I was standing on to stretch it down below me as far as possible.

And then I let go.

I wrapped my arms out, hugging the rock face as it slid by in an attempt to slow my fall. I made sure my right leg was first to absorb the hit before my injured side followed. I ended up crumpled up on the ledge below, a little scraped and bruised, but otherwise okay. I got up, brushed my shirt off, then moved off to one side to try another route.

When I finally reached the summit, the absurdity of all this caught up to me. *This is crazy. I can't do this—climbing up the side of this mountain like a monkey, and in the rain?* The problem was that now I was at the top. The only way out was to go down. So, turning around backward to face the mountain while descending, I carefully made my way down.

It was only down for a little way, because it wasn't long before I reached North Kinsman, which was another climb. Rocks, rock slabs, and more massive rock obstacles. I needed to make it to Crawford Notch by Thursday to fly home and join my wife and family for our annual beach vacation. I didn't realize that the White Mountains and all this steeper terrain started this far south on the trail. I thought I wouldn't hit climbs like this until I got to Crawford Notch.

I'd planned to average ten miles a day that week. With all the steep rocky climbs and descents, I found that it took me all day just to make it eight miles. I pushed it by hiking almost until dark, and I still sensed that I was getting behind. It was already dark when I stopped at a stealth site two-thirds of the way up to Liberty Springs Campsite and decided to call it a day. I was making it, but the Whites were kicking my booty.

The following day was another struggle for me as I made my way above treeline up over Mt. Lafayette. It started sprinkling, but it wasn't windy, so I could continue hiking without getting cold. I hunched under a rock to get a break from the rain while eating my lunch of peanut butter and tortilla, which tasted much better than it had the other night. Maybe it was the views that somehow improved the flavor.

Next, I climbed up and over Mt. Lincoln and then worked my way down into the saddle, which is the low point between two mountains before the final climb of the day up Mt. Garfield. The view from Mt. Garfield was so good that I decided to camp just below the peak to witness the sunset. At the end of the day, I looked back at the mountains I'd traversed and couldn't believe that I had made it up (and down) all of the steep climbs. I was looking forward to reaching Crawford Notch and having some time off with my family.

After spending the night at an unofficial site near the top of Mt. Garfield, I made my way down the steep trail, which appeared to also be a waterfall. I took my time and went slowly so as not to fall. At one point, I noticed a side trail that some hikers had created. It would get me away from the rocks with water flowing over them, and it appeared to be not quite as steep.

I started down the side trail but then decided to turn around and go back uphill to stay on the main trail. There were times over the past few days when I had almost fallen during a steep descent. If I were to fall, I wanted to make sure that I was on the main trail where someone might come by and find me. If I were to be injured and wasn't on the AT, then it could be days before anyone (my wife maybe?) missed me and made the call to send out a search party.

My wife had asked me before I started hiking down in Georgia, "If I don't hear from you, how long do I wait before calling out the search party?" I told her, "I don't know, maybe two or three days." Of course, this was back when I was trying to get my courage up to make it down a dirt path in the woods, not knowing that I'd be traversing down a crazy steep section that doubled as a waterfall.

I put my poles on my pack and made my way backwards down the side of the mountain, using my hands to hold onto the rocks. It did seem crazy to be going down stuff that was so steep I had to worry about where and when someone might find me if I should fall. I took my time and carefully checked to make sure each step was sound before putting all of my weight onto my leading leg.

Later that day, I stopped in at the Galehead Hut to get some snacks and soup. Despite trying to limit my time there, I stayed for almost an hour. While hiking that afternoon, I bumped into *Disfunkschwenal* again, a NOBO that I met down in Southern Virginia and then again while hiking with *Dr Fix-it* in Pennsylvania. It was nice to catch up with her as we made our way down to the Zealand Falls Hut, where I stayed for the night. I had a good dinner and enjoyed sleeping in the bunkhouse.

After an excellent breakfast, I headed downhill towards Crawford Notch the following day. The trail was flat much of the way, and I ended up getting there with plenty of time to make the drive to Portland, Maine, where I was catching a flight that evening. I was taking two weeks off from hiking to be with my family for our summer vacation at the beach. Then I would return to finish up the White Mountains and the rest of the trail before the summer was over.

The pain, numbness, and tingling sensations from my leg

and foot took a few days to calm down after the exertion I'd put out in the White Mountains. I put my body through a great deal the week before my vacation. Since I wasn't hiking every day while I was at the beach, I expected my body to stop hurting but was surprised to experience a fair amount of pain in my hip and leg.

I wondered, *if I'm barely walking, going a few blocks to the beach and back, why the heck is my body hurting so much?* A possible answer came to me late one night as I talked on the phone with my father.

"I'm going to work at getting rid of this limp I've developed," I said. Dad suggested a book he'd read called "Pain Free." I had a copy of this book at home that I'd bought a few years ago. I told Dad I was searching for a quick fix to my injuries back then, and that I'd skimmed through the book before tossing it aside. I remembered thinking *this is just a bunch of stupid exercises.*

I went on to explain how before I decided to hike the Appalachian Trail, I was looking for and wanted, expected, and insisted on finding some sort of miracle cure. I didn't care if it was an injection, a nerve block, or a pill I could take. I wanted something, anything—that would "fix" the damage from my shattered hip and associated nerve damage in my leg.

I told Dad how I admitted to myself while I was still in southern Virginia (three years to the day after my injury) that I would likely have to work at healing for the rest of my life. I was continuing on my healing journey by doing something about it myself. I got tired of expecting a doctor to come up with a miracle cure for me (although that still sounds really appealing). Dad agreed. If I could find a way back to a more normal body posture and gait, walking without limping, maybe this would allow my body to continue healing.

After relaxing at the beach with my family, I flew back to the Portland Airport and drove several hours to get back to the trail. The time off to rest up both physically and mentally was awesome. After being away for so long, I really enjoyed the time with my wife and kids. While hiking the trail, my daily contemplation has helped me to better appreciate all of the goodness I've been blessed with. My wife, kids, and grandkids are at the center of an incredible life. I was excited to continue northward on the trail the next day.

I spent some time the following morning at the Highland Center practicing walking on a nice flat floor without limping. I walked up and down the hallway doing my best to spend an equal amount of time on each leg. I worked at avoiding the limp and swing of my body back-and-forth. That's how I'd been walking ever since I got out of my wheelchair three years ago.

I went out front to hitch a ride the half-mile down to the trail and saw the shuttle bus waiting there. I decided to treat myself and pay the $19 fee, which was worth not having to embarrass myself by hitchhiking and hoping that someone would stop and pick up a 56-year-old man with a backpack.

I expected some mental resistance as part of getting back to hiking the trail. I tried my best to walk along without limping and did okay on the flat portion of the trail. However, once the uphill rocks started, I quickly forgot about this. I went through a series of mental gyrations as my leg and foot began bothering me. I wondered what the heck I was doing out there attempting to climb the White Mountains when I could be at home doing my deliberate walking back-and-forth in the living room. *Maybe I should just stay home and try and heal myself there.*

I kept going, of course, heading up the mountain, continuing my quest to hike the entire Appalachian Trail. At one point, it got steep enough that I took my poles off and put them on my pack before clambering up a vertical rocky section. I saw another steep section shortly after that, so I kept my poles on my pack. For the next 45 minutes, I made my way up the mountain using my feet and hands—at times pulling myself up and at other times walking along like a monkey on all fours.

I finally made the 6.4 miles to Mizpah Spring Hut. It took me almost eight hours of hiking. I think I was going slow because of the steepness and because it was my first day back on the trail. The hut staff, which appeared to be primarily college-age kids, is called "The Croo." They cooked up an excellent dinner for us. While eating dinner, I talked with four girls who were out in bad weather on Mount Washington the previous day.

They hiked in the rain from Madison Spring Hut up over Mount Washington and down to Lakes of The Clouds Hut in forty to fifty mile-an-hour winds with gusts as high as ninety-eight. Part of me was impressed by the fact that they were willing to take on this challenge, and another part of me was amazed that they went out in such bad weather. They made it, but if one of them had gotten injured or had wandered off the trail, they could've been in serious trouble. A hiker can get hypothermic quickly in conditions like that.

The next day I was to hike up over Mt. Pierce for a short day of less than five miles to Lakes of the Clouds hut. This would put me part way into the eleven-mile stretch above treeline and leave me with about ten miles to go the following day to get down below treeline where I could camp for the night.

As I lay in my bunk, I had trouble getting to sleep because I was apprehensive about the next section. First, I had never backpacked before going on this crazy trip. I obviously didn't have experience being above treeline other than during the short section over Mt. Lincoln the other day. I knew the weather could change quickly and read that you needed to hurry down the mountain to get to safety if a storm was coming. With my leg being injured, I was unable to hurry. I had my one limping-along speed, and that was about it. I mean, if a bus were about to hit me, I could get out of the way—mostly. I'd still take a grazing blow from the bumper.

To prepare, I carried most of my gear with me , including my tent, sleeping bag, wool shirt and pants, and my puffy down coat. Over the few weeks leading up to this section, I also prepared by reading a few books on my iPhone about the dangers of being on Mt. Washington. I started off with "Death on Mount Washington: Stories of Accidents and Foolhardiness on the Northeast's Highest Peak" and then read another called "The 129 people who've died in the White Mountains" or something like that.

That may have been a mistake.

I was feeling scared to death of what might happen to me, but there I was, six miles up the mountain planning to head up higher in the morning. *Would I follow the Appalachian Trail no matter where it goes just to have a chance to heal my leg?* I wondered. *Probably, yes.*

I took my time the following day enjoying breakfast. I then did some more deliberate walking back and forth in the big dining area to practice not limping. If I concentrate on it, I can see that I've already improved quite a bit. I finally rolled out at 10:30 and hiked my way north to the next hut, Lakes of The Clouds. The weather was stunning, with temperatures in the 50s, a nice breeze, and visibility clear to the horizon. It was fantastic to be up in the White Mountains, where the views were incredible. I felt so lucky to be able to do this.

Despite all of the concerns that kept me up the previous night, I did better mentally than I expected. There weren't any big hills, and I was hiking less than five miles. I was still having thoughts about the beach and *"what if I just stopped now"* contemplations, but much less of this was going on as compared to the day before. This area was well-traveled with mostly tourist-type hikers who were out for a few days making hut-to-hut trips. Most folks were friendly enough, but the camaraderie that's shared by thru-hikers was missing.

For example, when I arrived at the hut, there were two of us waiting in line to check-in. A group of three men I'll call *The Geezers* barged in the door and totally butted to the front of the line. *No worries,* I thought, *I'm on the AT, and I'm here to have a good time, no big deal.* I finally checked in and was pleased to see they had reserved a bottom bunk for me as I had requested so that I'd have an easier time getting in and out of bed with my damaged leg.

I went to Bunkroom #1 to put my pack down and see where I was going to sleep. I heard *The Geezers* starting to encroach on my bunk space. "Reserved for Peter? That sign's probably from years ago."

ONLY WHEN I STEP ON IT

"Actually, that's me, and yes, that's my bunk," I declared, glad that I had arrived in time to defend my spot. I wanted to wake up early to see the sunrise from the top of Mt. Washington. I didn't have a reservation at the next hut, so I planned to ask about work for stay. If you can get there at the right time and ask nicely, the Croo allows a few thru-hikers to help out with chores in exchange for food and a spot to sleep on the dining room floor.

If I couldn't get work for stay, then I would either need to hike three miles over Mt. Madison to reach the next campsite or hike six-tenths of a mile downhill on a side trail, which would be bonus miles—downhill and back up. I got my water and pack ready to go so that I could make an early exit in the morning.

After a nice dinner, I zipped over to the bunk room to get to sleep as early as possible. My plan was to wake up at five in the morning to get an early start on a long day of hiking and hopefully get to see the sunrise on top of Mt. Washington. I initially set the alarm on my phone but then realized I might wake up the other hikers in the bunkroom. So, I decided I'd do my best to get up without using the alarm.

One of the first things I learned on the AT is that you're expected to be quiet in campsites, shelters, and hostels after dark when other hikers are lying down or sleeping. The other etiquette to follow is to be cautious when using your headlamp so as to not shine your light directly at another hiker. Most headlamps have an option that allows you to see just fine in the dark using a red light that is much less intrusive.

Unfortunately, most of the hut-to-hut hikers in the White Mountains hadn't heard of this. You'd think that anyone with a tiny bit of common sense could figure out that waving a spotlight around at night in a small dark room might disturb the other occupants. However, *The Geezers,* who were my bunkmates that night, were absolutely clueless.

I had already settled in, read a few pages using Kindle on my phone, and was just falling asleep when four or five of these brain-dead morons came in with headlamps blazing. They were moving around, making more noise than a cabin full of rowdy ten-year-olds at summer camp. Then the person directly across the aisle from me pulled out a flashlight that was big enough to be used as a billy club, flipped it on full blast, and set it down on the bed, pointing right at me.

I really should have said something immediately, but I kept my mouth shut instead—probably because I don't like confrontation. I kept thinking, he's undoubtedly going to power that thing down any second, but he didn't. So as time went on, I found myself getting angrier and angrier. Then I realized I really shouldn't say anything. This was because even if I tried really hard to say, "Excuse me, Sir, could you do me a favor and please turn that off?" it would have come out sounding like "SHUT THAT @#$%ING THING OFF!"

I'm kind of weird that way. I don't speak up when I should, and then it builds up inside and comes out in a bad way, as you'll see in a moment. The next thing I remember (not counting the snoring episode that lasted several hours) was when the person above me climbed down without using the ladder and stepped on my bad leg. I jerked up and banged my head on the bunk above me.

As I lay there nursing the bump on my head and my throbbing leg, I looked at my watch to see that it was two in the morning. Next (and I'm definitely NOT making this up), the same guy who just stepped on my leg turned his headlamp on. He was using the top power searchlight setting—and moved within eight inches of my face with the light pointing right at me! It may have been my imagination, but I could swear I felt my face warming up like I was in an interrogation room.

Once again, I really should have said something. That would have been a better move than what I did. I wasn't sure if this crazy moment was the result of complete stupidity or if this was a retaliatory move from *The Geezer*, who had tried to move in and take over my bottom bunk spot earlier in the day. *Is he threatening me?* I thought. *Oh, I can see now that he's looking for the bunny slippers that he put under my bunk in the spot where MY stuff was before he shoved all of my gear over into the corner.*

I hope you can see that I'd had it by this point. In hindsight, I would have been better off moving from the bunk room to go sleep on the dining room floor with the work-for-stay thru-hikers. But instead, I did something that I'm, uh, not so proud of, but I did it, and you're here to read about my adventure, so here goes.

I figured the heck with it. I AM going to set my alarm for 5:00 am. And then, (this is the part that's hard to write) I turned the volume ALL THE WAY UP.

What comes next wasn't my best self.

When my alarm went off at 5:00 am, I took my time. I mean *really* took my *sweet time* turning it off. Everyone else, all of the noisy light shiners and especially the jerk that shined the light right in my face, were *nice* and awake. And I will admit that this *did* give me somewhat of a thrill.

I moved quickly to get outside and head up Mt. Washington before one of my roommates decided to joust with me. The early morning light that was creeping over the summit of Mt. Washington painted pastel colors on the lakes, mountains, and sky as I made my way up the trail.

By the time I made it to the top of Mt. Washington, it had turned into a clear, windless day with views as far as I could see. I checked out the museum and gift shop, bought a breakfast sandwich, and joined the crowd gathering for the Mt. Washington Summit Bicycle Race. I noticed that some thru-hikers had stealth camped underneath the cog railway platform for the night.

I hung around to see the first wave of finishers come across the line and even got a photo with the race winner, Eneas Freyre. I took a selfie with the summit sign and headed northward down the mountain. As I made my way down the mountain, I crossed the tracks and noticed a puff of black smoke off to the west. I sat down on a rock with a few other hikers to wait and was rewarded with a view of the steam-powered cog railway puffing and chugging up the hill.

I'd heard about another tradition on the AT and figured I'd never get another chance to give it a try. So, I stood upon a rock and mooned the train as it went by. I kept my grey camo compression tights on, so I got a laugh from the other hikers but didn't break any laws that I know of.

My parents rode this cog railway up Mt. Washington in 1954 on their honeymoon. I found out later that the steam-powered train only makes one trip a day while all the other trains are powered by diesel. The diesel trains use eighteen gallons of gas to climb the mountain, while the steam-powered version uses an entire ton of coal to make it to the top.

I thought about my parents as I made my way down Mt. Washington. The day remained clear with a cool breeze and blue skies as far as I could see. I skirted around Mt. Clay, followed another part of the AT around the top of Mt. Jefferson, over Adams Five and Mt. Sam Adams, and past Mt. Quincy Adams. I finally arrived tired and worn out at Madison Springs Hut. I was thrilled when they agreed to let me do work-for-stay. Getting work for stay can be tricky. They only take a few hikers, and you have to ask them at the right time. If you get there too early, I've heard that they'll tell you to keep moving on. I don't know if the time varies, but it was about 4:30 pm when I asked them. While waiting for the paid guests to finish dinner, I sat outside talking with *Slope Turtle* and *Mr. Tuxedo,* who were my workmates for the evening.

I got to scrub pots and pans in exchange for dinner and a spot for the night on the dining room floor. I was glad they let me do work-for-stay because I was too worn out to make it over Mount Madison, and I really didn't want to have to hike another six-tenths of a mile down a side trail down to a camping area (and then a second six-tenths of a mile back up).

When I left the hut the following day, it was just fifty feet before the trail headed straight up Mount Madison. I managed to make my way up several obstacles that I call "Rock puzzles." Each time I asked myself, *how can I get up that?* Closer to the top of the mountain, the trail turned into a boulder field. It was as if a fleet of colossal dump trucks dumped out tons of rocks ranging in size from baseballs to small tables. Instead of an obvious path, there were simply cairns—triangular piles of rocks that marked the trail's general direction.

I found walking on this type of surface difficult for two reasons. First, it was hard to find a flat place to rest my injured foot. Each rock was angled differently, and the side pointing up might be flat, an edge, or even a point. The other thing is that due to my poor balance on my left side, and perhaps my age, I felt like I was constantly in danger of falling. The ongoing precariousness of watching every single place I put my foot was tiring. I had to adjust to compensate when I started to lose my balance. This wore me out both physically and mentally.

At the top of Mount Madison, I was greeted with 40 to 50 mph wind gusts. I took a few photos and then quickly headed down the other side, thinking of how nice it would feel to get below treeline and be out of the wind. The trail roller coastered its way down the ridgeline going over many smaller summits, each one covered in similar boulder fields for me to traverse. When I finally made it down past treeline, I was relieved to be out of the wind, and the trail was much smoother.

After a steep descent through the woods, I stopped to eat my lunch while processing more erroneous thoughts of quitting my hike. *This is nuts. This is not fun. What am I doing hiking such treacherous terrain?* I thought as I sat there looking at a house-sized boulder across the trail from me. *Honey Buns, Jokester,* and a few other hikers joined me in taking a rest after the trek over Madison. They were contemplating taking a shortcut trail that wasn't part of the Appalachian Trail down to Route 16.

"It's about two miles shorter than the AT, but I'm sure I'll end up walking at least two miles when I'm in town," said *Jokester*. *Honey Buns* wanted to stay on the AT, and they went back and forth trying to decide which way to go. I suggested that if they do skip two miles, then they'll need to walk an extra two miles. "Sometime in the next year," I added, "and for it to count, you'll need to be thinking about the AT and have a few pages of the guidebook in your pocket."

Jokester laughed and then added, "Yeah, and if anyone asks where you're going, you have to say Katahdin." I felt better after joking around with them and made my way down the (longer) official Appalachian Trail. After a few miles, I was rewarded with a section called Old Jackson Road, which was primarily smooth, wide, and gently sloped downhill. I made it to my car at Pinkham Notch and drove to White Mountain Lodge (now called Rattle River Lodge and Hostel) in Gorham to spend the night. The hostel was clean and well-run, and they served stuffed French toast for breakfast.

I was going to take a zero the following day, but after discovering that I could take the ski lift down from the top of Wildcat Mountain, I elected to hike up the super steep trail with just a fanny pack holding my cell phone, a small bottle of juice, and half of a Rueben sandwich. I met Tom, a rather fit section hiker, who would hike up the mountain and then meet his wife at the top of the gondola. She wanted to skip the steep climb by taking the gondola up. Tom was in great shape from 48 years of rowing, but was willing to slow down so that I could keep up with him.

It was great to make my way up without my pack's weight. Because I was busy talking with Tom, I made it up an extremely steep section and over Wildcat Peak E to reach the summit. I did all this without thinking too much about just how steep the mountain really was. At the top, I waited for the next gondola and stepped in, finishing my hike for the day after doing just three miles. When the wind picked up, it blew the gondola from side to side, and I was a little nervous. Other than that, it was fun to ride down the mountain. My plan was to take the gondola back up the next day and continue my hike northward.

At the bottom, I met *Trotter*, a 64-year-old NOBO who was at the end of her rope. She'd also taken the gondola down. She'd had it with all the steep climbs, rocks, and technical sections in this part of the trail.

"I'm going to skip the rough sections and go up to Andover. Can you drive me there? I'll pay for your gas," she asked.

"I'm sorry, but that's several hours round trip, and I have stuff I need to get done this afternoon," I responded. "I'll give you a ride anywhere you want here in town. I could take you to the bus station."

"No. You should skip up to Andover with me. This is a horrible part of the trail. Why don't you just skip this hard part? You can always come back and do it later."

"Uh... No thanks, I really don't want to skip any parts of the trail." I ended up dropping *Trotter* off at a campground where she knew some other people. She thanked me for the ride, but the scowl on her face revealed her irritation.

The following day, I got a ride to the gondola and rode up Wildcat Mountain to continue my adventure. It was another clear day. I was able to look across the valley to see Mt. Washington, where I was a few days ago. When I got off the gondola, I walked over to find the northbound trailhead.

It wasn't quite straight up, but it did look intimidating. *Trotter* had mentioned something about this the day before. Perhaps that's why she decided to skip this part of the trail and jump ahead to Maine. I slowly clambered up the steep section and then went up and over Wildcat Peak D, Wildcat Peak C, and Wildcat Peak A. I'm not sure what happened to Wildcat Peak B.

Then, I carefully made my way down the steep descent to Carter Hut. As I walked up to the hut, I was greeted with "Hi, *Flash 52*, how are you doing?" It was *Smiley*, a NOBO that I had met a few days ago at Madison Springs Hut. The dinner the Croo made for us that night hit the spot, and, thankfully, the bunkhouse was less exciting (and much quieter) than my experience at Lakes of the Clouds Hut.

The climb up to Carter Dome the following day, while steep, wasn't hard because the trail didn't have any technical sections. The steep parts had been improved by trail maintainers, who've worked diligently cutting and moving rocks to create a staircase-like experience. I can't imagine how many hundreds of hours of time and effort this took. Hats off to the thirty-one different volunteer hiking clubs that participate in maintaining and keeping the trail open.

I'd been struggling lately. The views were incredible, and I should have been really enjoying this part of my hike. However, I was so worn down that it was hard to keep going. I just wanted to be done. So, I thought about this dynamic. *I'm in a breathtaking wilderness that I might never experience again after this adventure is over, and I'm not having a good time?*

The guidebook mentioned a stealth site near the top of Mt. Moriah, so I turned left onto a spur trail that led to the top of the mountain. I came to a rock ledge that went pretty much straight up. I had to wedge myself up by pushing off the sides of a three-foot gap. I wasn't sure if I could make it up or not because my left foot was lousy at getting a grip on the narrow cracks in the rock face. Despite having one foot that didn't work very well, I kept trying for twenty minutes or so and finally managed to make it up.

I passed the site referenced in the guidebook, tucked away under some pine trees and continued up to the summit. A rock dome rising above the terrain provided 360-degree views. Looking out at the surrounding mountains, I decided I wanted to cowboy camp up right there under the stars.

I blew up my sleeping pad and centered it on a flat spot in the middle of the dome that was about the same size as the air mattress. The dome sloped off gradually on all sides for about ten feet before dropping straight down. So, I'd have to be careful not to roll off. If the weather got bad, I didn't want to go back down the trail and the steep ledge in the dark, so I liked the idea of having the site nearby as a retreat if needed.

As the sun started going down, the western sky lit up with breathtaking shades of yellow, orange, and red. I took pictures with my phone, but it wasn't the same. The camera couldn't capture the immenseness of the wilderness, the feelings of being surrounded by mountain ranges as far as I could see, of being out there, embracing the moment. As the sun retreated below the horizon, the sky gradually darkened, and one by one, the stars slowly blinked on. It was pitch-black out, and I could see the Milky Way. It was glorious!

Life was good. I just needed to remember to enjoy it.

It was wonderful to wake up and see the sun come up from the comfort of my warm sleeping bag. It was just another six miles to hike down past the Rattle River Shelter and then follow an old fire road to reach the road in Gorham. I turned left and walked 100 yards to reach the White Mountain Lodge. They were nice enough to offer me a left-over breakfast burrito even though I stayed at the Notch Inn Hotel because it had a pool I could walk in.

By the time I shuttled my car up to Grafton Notch the following day and got started hiking, it was almost noon, so I didn't expect to go far. I was going to stay at the Trident Col Campsite but decided to skip it when I saw it was two-tenths of a mile off the trail. Earlier in my trip several months ago, I'd hike over to a shelter without thinking about it. I preferred to stay in shelters and enjoyed the companionship of hanging out with other hikers.

At this point, I was so worn out that I had to pass on hiking any extra miles, even if it was just two-tenths of a mile to the shelter (and another two-tenths back). I walked a half-mile further north on the trail instead and found an excellent stealth site where I could stay for the night. Once I was in my tent, it felt nice to be sleeping in the woods again.

The next day my hike took me past Dream Lake, Gentian Pond, and then up and over the difficult Mt. Success. I took my time and stopped to rest a few times on the way up. It was a tough climb, but not nearly as difficult as the White Mountains were. I planned to make it to Maine that day, but when I came across a nice looking place to camp at 6:30 pm, I decided to quit and call it a day.

I woke up the next morning and was excited because I would finally get to Maine! Ten minutes after starting out, I came to a sign marking New Hampshire and Maine's border. It was only 270 miles from there to Mt. Katahdin. This was the last of fourteen states on the Appalachian Trail, and the SOBOs had all been telling me that Maine was gorgeous.

It was 2:30 in the afternoon when I stopped for a snack at Full Goose Shelter before heading down the mountain toward the famous Mahoosuc Notch. This narrow Notch with cliffs on both sides is filled with boulders as big as the size of a house. It's called the hardest or the most fun mile on the entire Appalachian Trail, depending on your viewpoint. You have to make your way around, over, or in some places, under this mile-long jumble of rocks.

Halfway down the hill, I caught up to *Twinkle Toe*, a seventy-two-year-old lady from New York. She was carefully but steadily making her way down to the Notch. I decided to stick with her for the next mile to make sure she didn't have any trouble making it through. Once we started into Mahoosuc Notch, it was nice to have two of us exploring and trying out various routes. One choice that looked like the right way to go might lead you to another obstacle that appeared impossible or simply too dangerous for either of us to try. Then we'd have to turn back and try another route.

We tried different routes and took turns saying, "This looks like a better way to go over here." After two hours of this, it became clear that *Twinkle Toe's* slow pace was pushing us dangerously close to the end of the day. I move pretty darn slow myself, so I really mean it when I say someone's moving slowly. I kept looking at my watch, thinking *I've got to be out of the Notch by nightfall* but was worried about her making it through by herself. Each time I thought, *I need to go faster,* I'd take a step or two forward but then stop and turn back to wait again for *Twinkle Toe* to catch up to me.

We were two-thirds of the way through the Notch when it got so dark that we had to turn on our headlamps. Then the thunder started rumbling overhead. Before long, there were a few big drops of rain plunking down around us. We needed to get out of the Notch, and quick, but it's pretty hard to hurry when you're trying to find a safe way through an obstacle course like that. I noticed a spot barely big enough for my tent, and I thought about camping right there in the Notch so that I could get my tent up before it really started raining.

I thought for a moment and decided the storm might flood that spot. Besides that, dang it, I felt obligated at this point to get *Twinkle Toe* safely to the campsite on the north end of the Notch even though I hadn't promised her anything. I was just hiking with her. It's kind of like finding a stray cat; once you feed it, you're on the hook for whatever that cat needs until you can find someone else to take it. It was close to an hour later when we finally made it through the Notch and began looking for the campsite.

The rain was steadily coming down, and I was ready to call it a night. I saw the glow of a tent off to the side of the AT but couldn't see an entrance to a trail that went over that way. So, we kept going. When the pathway started climbing uphill ten minutes later, I thought we had gone past the campsite. I checked the FarOut App and confirmed my suspicions.

We turned around to backtrack and finally found an unmarked, overgrown trail that led us to the campsite. I guess there wasn't a sign since it wasn't an official campsite even though it was big enough for a dozen or more tents. As I started to put up my tent, the rain gods turned the faucets on, and the water began pouring down in earnest. I got inside, blew up my sleeping pad, changed into a dry set of clothes, and climbed into my sleeping bag for what I thought was the end of a challenging day.

At three in the morning, I woke up to see that someone was outside my tent. "Hey, *Flash 52*, can I share your tent?" I turned on my headlamp to see *Twinkle Toe* out in the rain. "I'm all wet, shivering, and I'm freezing," she said. She explained that she hadn't set up her hammock correctly in the rain.

"Sure, come on in," I said, moving my stuff out of the way to make room for her. I gave her my sleeping pad to insulate her from the ground. I then unzipped my sleeping bag to be used as a blanket over both of us. She was able to warm up and went to sleep while I did my best to try and catch a few winks lying on the ground using my puffy coat as a pillow.

About an hour later, the rain stopped, and I saw another hiker with their headlamp on. They were up and about doing something. I didn't know what they were doing for sure but based on the time of night, my best guess would be they needed a potty break.

"HEY!...

"HAAAAAAY!...

I was yanked out of my sleep-deprived haze. I came to full alert and realized that *Twinkle Toe* was yelling at the top of her lungs out of *my tent*.

"GET THE #$%K AWAY FROM MY STUFF!!!!

"THAT'S MINE!

"GET THE #$%K AWAY FROM IT!!!!"

I had hiked almost 2,000 miles on the Appalachian Trail by this point. I'd seen nothing but goodwill from one hiker to another. We all looked out for each other. I hadn't heard of anyone ever taking another hiker's stuff. (That is, unless you count the tent that *Dr Fix-it* left behind at a campsite that we were never able to find again.)

"I don't think anyone's messing with your gear," I suggested. *And I really wish you'd stop yelling obscenities from inside my tent.*

As I lay back down on the hard ground, I told myself, *this is just another part of my adventure that I can write about in my book someday.* Then I made a fervent wish for the morning light to arrive as soon as possible.

Once my unexpected guest got up and left that morning, I tried to get back to sleep for a while before packing up and starting up Mahoosuc Arm, which is a 1,600-foot climb over the course of just a mile and a half. I had heard from other hikers that this was a real doozy. The trail led me up a series of seventy-five to one-hundred-foot-long slabs of rock tilted upward at forty-five degrees—or worse—in various places. At first, I tried to walk up the face, but when I attempted it, my boots let go, resulting in either a slide back down or a fall followed by a slide back down.

In some places, I was able to find some rough spots that gave the soles of my boot enough traction to slowly advance my way up. In other places I had to make my way up the edges. I had to find a tree root to step on with one foot while using my hands to hold onto smaller trees that were right next to the trail. Most of the trees at the edge of the trail had been pulled on by numerous hikers over time. Their roots reminded me of loose teeth that've been wiggled and are ready to be pulled out. This thought didn't inspire much confidence. So, I took my time searching for teeth that I hoped wouldn't pop out and send me reeling back down the mountain.

By the way, David Miller, author of "AWOL on the Appalachian Trail" came up with this loose tooth analogy. It fits the situation so well that I simply can't find a better way to explain it. After stopping to rest a few times on the way up, I finally made it to the top. I enjoyed hiking down past Speck Pond, which was wind-blown with whitecaps. I stopped at the shelter to eat lunch while talking with several hikers, including *Twinkle Toe,* who had her sleeping bag and other gear hung up in the breeze to dry out. She thanked me for helping her through Mahoosuc Notch, but neither of us mentioned last night's excitement.

Before long, I bid everyone farewell and headed up and over Speck Mountain. There were some steep hands-and-feet climbing sections towards the top where the wind was reasonably strong. I had a hard time holding on. I'd guess that the gusts were about 70 mph. After making it over the summit, the trail became friendlier, and I made my way down to Grafton Notch where I was pleasantly surprised to see my car patiently waiting for me.

I drove up to The Cabin Hostel, where I spent the night. I had a great breakfast the following day. The Cabin was run by *Honey* and *Bear*, who were kind and loving folks. We had blueberry pancakes (with more blueberries on top), real maple syrup, eggs, potatoes (with other good stuff cooked in), biscuits, melons, orange juice, coffee, and (this lets you know you are in Maine) baked beans!

Each summer, my parents would load up my six siblings and I into our Suburban and drive three days to get to Maine from Illinois. This was for our summer vacation at my grandparent's dairy farm along the Kennebec River. My grandfather would play his harmonica, and we'd sing songs like "Beans for breakfast—breakfast—breakfast... beans for dinnah—dinnah—dinnah, beans for suppa, down on the old Bragg Farm!"

I decided to try using just my fanny pack again for the day. I brought my cell phone, a quarter roll of TP (just in case), a bottle of Gatorade, water treatment pills, a few protein bars, and some peanut M&Ms. On the way up Mt. Baldpate, I met Cary, a section hiker from Madison, Wisconsin. He was willing to slow down to my pace, and I enjoyed having someone to talk with. It kept me from thinking about all the steps I needed to take to climb the mountain. He was a journalist of sorts and was interested in my story.

Before long... Presto! I was at the top of the first peak, and it had incredible views. Maine really is beautiful. Traveling without my pack, I found the hiking fun for a change. The trail included several ladders and even one section where you had to hold onto a rope to get down a steeply slanted area. The last few miles were a nice dirt path, and I called The Cabin to pick me up at the trailhead. Earl, also known as *Bear*, was there within five minutes of my arrival. He was nice enough to stop at the corner store in Andover so that I could get a root beer float to hold me over for dinner. And wow, what a feast. *Honey* had cooked up a storm, including homemade brownies with moose tracks ice cream on top.

Honey and *Bear* had been running this hostel for twenty-two years. It was apparent that they still loved what they did and really enjoyed helping out all of the hikers. Unfortunately, *Bear* died in 2018. *Honey* continues to run the hostel along with assistance from a reluctantly famous former thru-hiker who wished to remain anonymous.

My muscles were sore in the morning, and it was raining outside. I decided to take a zero and rest up a bit. *Honey* was going to visit her sister in Rangeley and offered to help me shuttle my car up there. On the drive north, I noticed that Maine appeared to be more remote than any other state I had driven in along the Appalachian Trail. I didn't see a single gas station, food place, or any other type of business during the hour-long drive. All I saw were a few houses, some camps, and miles and miles of bumpy road lined with forest on both sides.

In Rangeley I found an excellent physical therapy center with a heated therapy pool. I was the only one in the pool and enjoyed walking in the water while listening to some soothing music they put on for me. After that, I ran into the IGA grocery store to resupply my food. Then I left my car at the Farmhouse Inn Hostel and caught a ride back to The Cabin with *Honey* after she was done seeing her sister.

I enjoyed listening to *Honey's* stories during the ride back to Andover, including how she met her husband, Earl, on a hiking trip twenty-two years earlier. She was now eighty years old and has hiked up Mt. Washington once a year for many years, including this one. The dining room was packed with other hikers surrounding a massive family-style dinner with all the fixings plus ice cream with brownies for dessert. I could see photos signed by well-known hikers such as Earl Shaffer and Warren Doyle on the walls.

The next day I traversed a ten-mile section while going southbound to make it easier for The Cabin to pick me up at the end of the day. In the morning, I bumped into Cary and

Kirsten at the trailhead, whom I had met up on Mt. Baldpate a few days earlier. They slowed down a bit, and I did my best to speed up a notch so that I could hike with them for most of the day. I shared some of my funnier hiking adventures with Cary to help spice up his journalistic pursuits.

We knocked out the bigger climbs in the morning and were rewarded with a relatively easy downhill trail towards the end of the day. I was so much—SO MUCH—happier hiking on trails like this than the rocky boulder fields that I had to traverse while in the White Mountains. I found that even a tough obstacle or steep uphill section was now easier for me because I reminded myself that *this is better than the Whites.*

Speaking of stories that spice things up, the reluctantly famous helper from The Cabin picked us up at the end of the day. I'll refer to her as *Thumper.* I don't want to give away too much here, but Cary asked if she was *Bismarck's* hiking partner, and she said, "Yes, but I don't want to talk about it." I learned that *Bismarck* was actually James T. Hammes, a famous fugitive who was hiding out on the Appalachian Trail. He also spent part of each year at The Cabin with *Honey* and *Bear.*

In 2009, Hammes was asked to report to his employer's beverage bottling company headquarters in Cincinnati, Ohio, to answer questions about a possible fraud scheme inside the company. As the company's controller, Hammes handled all his business division's vendor accounts and payments. He was interviewed by the FBI that day and repeatedly denied any knowledge of the fraud. But shortly after he left the company's headquarters, the forty-six-year-old Hammes disappeared, leaving his wife and a child behind without even saying goodbye.

Hammes disappeared in plain sight, spending much of the next six years on the Appalachian Trail as *Bismarck*, a likable hiker with a full beard. *Honey* and *Bear* described him as "One of the nicest people we've ever met." He was later charged with embezzling more than $8.7 million from his employer over the course of eleven years. In 2014, a hiker who'd spent time with *Bismarck* on the trail "recognized his eyes" while watching a rerun of *American Greed* and called the FBI. They caught up with *Bismarck* in 2015 at the hiker trail days celebration in Damascus, Virginia. A federal judge sentenced Hammes to eight years in prison and ordered him to pay nearly $8 million in restitution.

18

SEPTEMBER—A DIFFERENT ENDING

HEALING IS A MATTER OF
TIME AND OPPORTUNITY

—THE PROPHET

The following morning, I had a final, big breakfast with all the fixings at The Cabin before reluctantly saying goodbye to *Honey* and *Bear*. More than any other place I stayed on the trail, I felt so welcomed and cared for that it was hard to leave this hostel. I had initially planned to take a day and a half to hike the next 13 miles, but when I noticed there weren't any big hills and the trail was reasonably smooth, I decided to see if I could make it to Rangeley in one day.

By the time I ate breakfast, packed up, and got a ride with Honey out to the trail, it was 9:30 am—a late start for me if I was going to make thirteen miles at my slower pace. I tried to walk purposefully without rushing. I found that if I hurried too much, it wore my injured leg out, making it hurt more, which ended up slowing me down overall.

I did make sure to limit any stops that I made. When I sat down for a snack, I looked at my watch and made sure I was moving again within five to ten minutes. I skipped the several views I went by and even walked right by a shelter that was just a hundred yards off the trail. I knew that if I stopped at the shelter, I'd probably meet another hiker and end up talking for an extra twenty minutes, time that I didn't have that day.

I managed to make it thirteen miles by moving steadily along. While I did say "Hi" to everyone I met, it was more like, "Hi, beautiful day, isn't it? Have a nice hike!" while I kept moving. As I walked along, I thought back to how things were when I first started hiking last year down in Georgia. I stopped off at every viewpoint and signed the logbooks in every shelter. I realized that had changed. I now had one focus: to finish. I was still enjoying my adventure, but I couldn't wait to get back home.

I went to the Farmhouse Inn Hostel and discovered that it was full that night. While I was trying to check-in, *Optimistic Dreamer* was dropped off after going to the hospital. He had a cast on his ankle, which resulted from a nasty fall on the trail. I met him almost a year ago when he was going southbound in Virginia. I had stayed in touch with him long enough to know that he had made it all the way to Springer Mountain. Then he hiked the Florida Trail down and back before returning to hike the AT northbound this year.

I slept in my tent with a few other hikers in a field behind the hostel. I was glad I decided to camp further back in the field because a group from a wedding rented out the bunkhouse and talked loudly out on the back porch until after midnight. The next day, I would get up early and go walk in the physical therapy center pool, which was just a few miles away.

After going to the pool, I was soon back out on the trail. The climb up Mt. Saddleback wasn't too technical, for the most part, but it took most of the day to reach the top. I did find a few places while climbing the mountain that were challenging to get up and over. A few months ago, I would have taken one look at these obstacles and thought, *What the heck? How in the world do they expect me to get over that?* After successfully traversing numerous difficult portions of the trail, I just looked for a way to get up and over each obstacle without slipping or falling. I no longer spent any mental energy trying to figure out *why* the trail goes over some of the stuff that it does.

The top of Mt. Saddleback was open, above treeline with mostly flat ledge-type rock to walk on. The sky was clear, and I had terrific views that stretched out for miles all around me. I sat down by the summit sign and had my cold dinner of tortillas, pepperoni, and cheese. As I waited for the sun to go down, I said "hi" to a family with young kids that came by, and then two southbound girls came by looking for the trail down to the ski slope.

"I think it's on that next peak to the south," I suggested. "Do you have a headlamp?"

"Oh, yes, we have headlamps. Our parents are waiting for us," came the reply. I thought that perhaps their parents would be worried until they made it down the hill in the dark.

As dusk arrived and it started getting darker, I scouted around to find a spot out of the wind where I could spend the night. I rolled out my pad on the lee side of a big rock, perfect for blocking the wind. The only downside was that it was right by the trail. I had such a good time sleeping cowboy style on Mt. Moriah last week that I wanted to try it again. It became completely dark, and the stars were out, thousands of them. *Wow!* I saw a falling star and made a wish that I might soon be home in my wife's arms.

By morning time, my sleeping bag had slid down into the middle of the trail, and a passing hiker had to step over me. My goal had been to be up and out in the morning before anyone came by. Sleeping on the trail is not considered good hiker etiquette. Overnight my sleeping bag had gotten wet from condensation. There's probably a way to look at the humidity and dew point to predict when I could get away with sleeping under the stars without this effect, but I hadn't figured it out yet.

I packed up everything except my sleeping bag and then folded it in half before strapping it to the top of my pack so that it could dry out as I hiked. The trail dropped down steeply into a saddle as I made my way over to the next peak called The Horn. There were several places where I had to be careful not to fall. I also saw the metal ladder that a south bounder had mentioned yesterday. "I saw my first ladder," he had said.

Hmm... that means I'm climbing my last ladder on the trail—I hope!

I made my way up The Horn and then Saddleback Junior before coming to Poplar Ridge Shelter. This is the last place that anyone saw Gerry Largay, also known as *Inchworm*, a retired nurse from Tennessee who tragically got lost along the Appalachian Trail in 2013. She was a sixty-six-year-old flip-flop hiker who had started out heading north from Harper's Ferry in April. She'd had a hiking companion, *June Lee*, who was with her until June 30th, when *June* had to go home for a family emergency.

There's a photo of *Inchworm* in front of this shelter the morning she went missing. She had a big smile on her face and a survival whistle hanging from the front of her pack. Her husband George had planned to pick her up at a road crossing twenty-one miles north at the end of the next day. When *Inchworm* didn't arrive, he figured she'd been delayed by a rainstorm and would be there the following day. When *Inchworm* didn't show up the following morning, George called the police. Search parties were assembled and over the next ten days, the trail and surrounding areas were searched. GPS tracking indicated approximately one mile on each side of the trail was well covered; however, *Inchworm* was not found.

It turned out that she had apparently stepped off the trail to go to the bathroom and gotten lost in the area where the spruce growth is particularly thick, even by Maine woods standards. She was reported to have a poor sense of direction. She had gotten anxious or flustered in previous situations when she wasn't sure which way to go.

Finally, after two years, some forest surveyors happened upon her body. From notes left in her journal and text messages on her phone, it appeared that she had climbed to higher ground in an attempt to get a cell signal so she could text her husband. It seemed that she set up her tent to await rescue in a location that was about one mile off the trail.

She had sat in her tent waiting for help that never came (although searchers had come within a hundred yards of her location). No one knows why she didn't use the whistle on the front of her pack. It's possible that she did blow it, but not when searchers were close enough to hear it. I made the mistake of digging around on the internet to find a photo of what her tent looked like when they found her.

As I hiked through the area, I looked at how closely spaced the trees were while thinking about *Inchworm*. I found it unsettling to walk through those old woods. I wish I hadn't seen the picture of her tent flat on the ground. I couldn't get that image out of my head. In the afternoon, I walked down to Oberton Stream and up to the Spaulding Mountain Lean-to, where I spent the night with three day-hikers and a late-starting SOBO.

The following day I got up and moved out early. I had several mountains to get over, and I wanted to make it to Stratton in time for my 6:00 pm shuttle pickup. I used the same strategy that I did the other day to stay moving: take quick timed breaks, don't take any side trails to see the views. Getting my miles in had become a priority at this point in my journey.

Towards the end of the day, the trail improved from steep to not-as-steep and then finally into a pleasing slight downhill. This was a welcome sight and helped keep me on time even though I was getting tired. I came around a bend and was surprised to see that someone had arranged sticks to spell out "2000 Miles." For the first time that day, I sat down without worrying about time going by and felt a wave of emotion wash over me.

It had been eighteen months and three days since I started on this journey from the top of Springer Mountain in Georgia. At the time, I didn't know if I'd be able to make it through the first day, much less make my way 2,000 miles up and over hundreds of mountains on my way to Maine. I did know that if I didn't find a way to have some semblance of control and heal myself, then my life was going to be pretty much over.

I'm not talking suicide here. That's not for me, as I've already shared. What I'm talking about is living with chronic pain. Over the past four and a half years, I've met so many people who live every day with ongoing debilitating pain. When you have an elephant sitting on your foot, it's impossible to think of anything else.

The pain slowly takes over the neurons in your brain until you're left with one blasting non-stop thought in your head. *Stop! Stop! Stop! I want the pain to stop!* It's like a blaring car horn that won't shut itself off. So, whether you try to distract yourself with pain pills or by binge-watching *Breaking Bad,* you can't get away from it. It's always there, slowly eating away at your soul.

The tears flowed down my face as I thought about every time I had struggled over the past eighteen months. There were times when my leg hurt so much that I didn't know if I could keep going. I knew that if I didn't hike this trail, then I'd end up living the rest of my life here in body, but not in spirit. I'd be mentally checked out permanently as that was the only way for me to flee from the pain.

I was shaking, sobbing uncontrollably. I had made it.

I made it 2,000 miles.

Don't get me wrong here. I still had a long way to go. But I felt that if I could hike 2,000 miles, I could finish all 2,189 miles of the Appalachian Trail. That's an elevation gain equal to hiking from sea level up to the top of Mount Everest and back down sixteen times. For the first time in four years, six months, and three days, I finally realized that I could do this.

I *could* heal myself.

The following day I took a zero to recover from something I had tried. When I hiked up Mt. Saddleback a few days earlier, I tested out the "no shirt" method that I'd seen some of the twenty-something (male) hikers use. The idea was to keep my shirt dry and avoid sweating by leaving it off.

Well, I succeeded at keeping my shirt dry. The problem was my pack rubbed my skin during the day to create several rashy, raw spots, with the worst one on my shoulder and several around my middle section where the pack belt sat. I wanted to let my damaged areas heal and get something from the store to treat them. *What should I ask for? Maybe some diaper rash cream?*

It's all just another part of the adventure, I told myself. While it may not look like it, I was trying to be extra careful at this point to make sure that some minor issues like this rash didn't worsen to make it difficult for me to finish the last 189 miles. Since I wasn't hiking that day, I took care of resupplying my food and moved the car up to Caratunk. I liked the therapy pool in Rangeley and walked in it again that afternoon.

That night I stayed at the Sterling Inn in Caratunk to be near the trailhead where I parked my car. I wasn't too hungry at dinner time, so I grabbed a can of baked beans from my car trunk and a root beer from the fridge to have, along with a slice of pizza that *Outback* offered me. That's not much of a meal but compared to pepperoni, cheese, and tortillas, it was actually pretty good.

In the morning, the Sterling Inn shuttled me down to Stratton to continue my northward hike. It was almost 10:30 by the time I started up the trail and I warmed up with a few flat miles before heading up South Horn Mountain. My leg felt good after walking in the therapy pool the day before, and the trail was decent—not too steep or rocky, just steadily up.

I'd been looking forward to getting these last 4,000-foot mountains before Katahdin out of the way for several weeks. Yet I found myself feeling like I was spending my last day with an old friend. *What…? No more big mountains to climb?*

I made my way up and over South Horn as I enjoyed the views and then found myself buffeted by wind and fog as I reached the top of Bigelow West Peak. The summit of the mountain poked up into the sky, looking like the back of a brontosaurus. Going over all of this by myself in the wind and the fog had me a little worried. Once again, I thought, *what the heck am I doing up here?*

Once I made it over the other side and down below treeline, I could get out of the wind, relax, and take a deep breath. Within another 20 minutes, I arrived at the campsite I'd been headed for. I took a photo of the caretaker's map showing where the tent pads, privy, and two different water sources were. I hiked around looking for the first water source, but the trails I found didn't seem to match the map. It started to get dark at this point, so I turned on my headlamp, went back to where I started, and then headed down another trail to find the other water source.

It was a dripping spring with a puddle below it that I could get a few liters of water from. I had to push the bugs and some pine needles out of the way before using the bottom of a plastic soda bottle that I used as a water scoop for situations like this. I decided to skip the wooden tent platforms and instead found a place on the ground to set up my tent. I hadn't used a platform yet, it had just started to rain, and I didn't want to try and figure out how to use a platform in the dark. It was nice to be in my tent with the sound of the rain coming down. I was happy to have made it eight miles up a decent-sized mountain after getting a late start.

I first noticed a weird sensation about a month and a half earlier while lying half-awake in my tent. That morning, along with most mornings since then, I experienced a fluttering sensation in my stomach that felt like a wave of fear washing over me when I first started to wake up. I had never felt this way before, so I dealt with it the best way I knew how. I tried to ignore it.

This method obviously didn't work, as each morning, the sensation grew a little stronger until it felt like it pinned me down to the ground. It felt like fear, but I wasn't sure what I was afraid of. Maybe it was anxiety or possibly a panic attack? I heard of people having panic attacks, but I had never had them before, so how would I know?

It would happen right when I would first wake up and realize that I was in my tent out on the Appalachian Trail. I felt overwhelmed. It was a combination of sadness and thoughts of "what the heck am I doing out here?" and a hefty dose of "I can't do this." After having these sensations in the early hours for the past month or so, I knew that it would pass, and I'd feel better in a few minutes. But it was weird.

I made it this far hiking the Appalachian Trail, so I was confident that I could continue and most likely even successfully finish my hike. It was almost as though my fears snuck in during that moment of semi-consciousness when I hadn't quite fired up the "I'm doing this no matter what" part of my brain.

I knocked out one last 4,000-foot peak first thing in the morning. I then enjoyed a decent trail that guided me gradually downhill throughout the afternoon. I heard there was trail magic ahead at East Flagstaff Road. When I arrived, I met some Maine Appalachian Trail Club members who were putting on their annual four-day trail magic fest. I had two root beers, some potato chips, chocolate cake, and a couple of hamburgers. Perfect!

I enjoyed talking with hiking club members and other hikers who stopped by to enjoy the food and drink. I got to meet *Guthook*, the guy who created the FarOut app that I used to show me where I was on the trail. He was a nice guy who was camera shy when I tried to take a photo with him. I guess he didn't want his face out on the internet.

I was tempted to tent nearby and wake up in the morning to sample their breakfast offerings but instead decided to get a few more miles in towards Katahdin. About a mile before reaching my intended target—a campsite on a hill above the lake—I stepped out on the sandy beach of Flagstaff Lake. It was gorgeous, and there was a perfectly flat spot on the sand with no rocks where I could set up my tent, so that's what I did.

As the sun went down over the lake, I heard the sound of waves lapping against the shore. This, combined with the haunting calls of loons on the water, made this an ethereal experience. This was an exceptional place to camp—so calm and beautiful. I tried to let it all soak in. At the same time, part of me was *so tired* of hiking that I just *wanted it to be over*. I sensed that someday in the future, I would long to be back on that sandy shore, looking up at the stars and listening to the call of the loons.

The sound of my alarm going off at 5:00 am the following day got me up and moving. I wanted to get my miles in so I could have a shorter hike to the Kennebec River the following day. The trail had just a few small hills, smooth dirt, and the usual rocks and roots combo. I felt relatively good deciding mid-afternoon to try and make it to Harrison's Pierce Pond Sporting Camp. I needed to give my dragging spirits a boost. Not to mention I wanted to try out their semi-famous twelve-pancake breakfast.

As I got within an hour of the camp, the trail took me right over the Pierce Pond Dam, which appeared to be three or four feet high. It also appeared to be made out of spare lumber. Really. A motley array of various boards, logs, and rocks were all held together by old wagon spikes. It's been there for a long time, though, so it must be built well enough to hold back the water.

When I took the side trail to the Sporting Camp, I noticed that various parts were used to create a makeshift bridge across a low wet area. I could see that old boards, logs, branches, and even forklift pallets were used to make up the bridge over to the camp. The camp itself was nice enough, operated by a guy named Tim, who'd run it for the last thirty years. He told me that the Appalachian Trail in Maine was initially designed to go from one sporting camp to the next before being rerouted to stay away from commerce and civilization.

Sporting camps provide lodging, meals, and guide service for hunting, fishing, and outdoor recreation. At this point, you can easily reach only two sporting camps from the AT: Harrison's Pierce Pond Sporting Camp and White House Landing in the 100 Mile Wilderness.

I tried out the piano in the community area, but it was so badly out of tune that it was hard for me to play. I thought about when I first decided to learn to play, thirteen years prior in Maui at an annual retreat that I put on for my consulting clients. Beverly Sallee played grand piano on stage as she gave her presentation on leadership. She was explaining what she'd heard so many people tell her.

"That sounds great, Beverly," she said as her hands gracefully ran up and down the keyboard. "I want to play just like that."

"Oh, you want to play like this?" More graceful arpeggios up and down the keyboard from her fingertips. "Then you need to start out like this—with three fingers, playing the notes C- D—E," (as she demonstrates playing three notes going up), "And then back down like this, E—D—C."

"Oh, I don't want to play like that. I want to play just like you do."

"Then you need to start out with these three notes..." (She demonstrates the three simple notes again.)

I had always wanted to play piano but figured it must be hard to learn. When I heard Beverly's story, I thought, what the heck, I can start off by playing three notes. I'm going to play the piano. Then I challenged myself by boasting to my clients that I'd play the piano on stage for them the following year. I started with the basics, just like Beverly suggested. I took lessons, practiced every day, and played a duet with Beverly at the event a year later. However, I will admit that I was incredibly nervous. I've continued to play over the years and hope to improve enough to be able to knock out informal performances.

I've discovered that almost anything you want to do in life can be broken down into basics that you can learn and eventually master. The problem is that, just like the person in Beverly's story, most people want the end result without putting in the work and effort that it takes to get there.

I spent the night at the camp in a rustic-looking cabin stocked with two queen beds but without blankets, electricity, or heating. I pulled out my sleeping bag for covers and lit the oil lamp to read a *People* magazine from seventeen years earlier that was on the table. It felt nice to stretch out across a large bed, as my sleeping pad was only twenty inches wide. And it was nice to be inside and out of the rain. I was proud of that day. At 16.2 miles, it had been my longest day yet on the Appalachian Trail. I felt good!

I sprung out of bed the next day when Tim clanged

the breakfast bell right outside my door. I chatted with five other hikers, some of whom had camped up at Pierce Pond and hiked down earlier in the morning just to be there for breakfast. I was stuffed after eating just half of Tim's famous twelve pancake breakfast. He went out of his way to take care of us, was super friendly, and made a wonderful host.

After breakfast, I put my pack on, walked back across the makeshift pallet bridge to the trail, and then turned downhill to hike four miles to get to the Kennebec River. I was about halfway there when I heard a crack of thunder, and the sky got dark. Really dark. Even though it was 10:00 in the morning, it was dark enough that I considered getting my headlamp out. Then the skies opened up, and the rain gods poured down on me.

Since I knew that I'd be in my car within an hour or so, I didn't bother stopping to put up my tent in an attempt to stay dry. Once the rain slowed down to a drizzle, I did make a quick stop to wring out my shirt so that it wasn't sopping wet. In my continuing quest to keep my pack weight down, I had left my raincoat behind in my car. Fortunately, it wasn't too cold out, and as long as I kept moving, I was able to stay warm.

When I reached the river, three other hikers were waiting ahead of me to take the canoe ferry across the Kennebec. This is the only ferry located along the entire 2,189-mile Appalachian Trail. Trying to cross this wide river without using the ferry is highly discouraged because the water level and volume can change rapidly due to unannounced upstream water releases from a dam.

In 1985, a NOBO, Alice Ference, drowned while attempting to ford the Kennebec River at this crossing.

After this, the Appalachian Trail Conservancy first published instructions for fording the river and then switched gears. They advised hikers *not* to ford the river while offering them a free alternative — the canoe ferry.

Since I was soaking wet, I cooled off quickly while waiting for my turn. I watched as the ferryman dropped off the other hikers and paddled back across the river to give me my first canoe ride in many years. The ferryman, Greg Caruso, told me that I was the 2,067th hiker he'd taken across the river so far that year.

I told Greg about my father, who had grown up in nearby Waterville. He had built canoes for most of his life as a hobby, and the two of us had spent plenty of time together in canoes on rivers and lakes while I was growing up. Once I made it across, I was freezing, so I hurried up to the parking lot where I'd left my car a few days before.

The hikers who'd crossed the river ahead of me were trying to hitch a ride by the side of the road. I gave them a lift to a nearby restaurant before heading north to my next parking spot—Shaw's Hostel in Monson, Maine. I decided to spend the night there at Shaw's and then shuttle back down to Caratunk in the morning.

Despite being tired, I did find time to play their piano (which was in tune) and visit the Appalachian Trail Information Center. This newly added location is designed to help prepare and educate thru-hikers about entering Baxter State Park, home of Mt. Katahdin. Percy Baxter donated the land for the park to the State of Maine with the stipulation that it would be kept primarily undeveloped and wild as a priority over making it easily accessible to the public.

As a result of this, Baxter Park has rules and guidelines that differ from and are stricter than many other parts of the trail. In 2015 Scott Jurek, after breaking the speed record for hiking the Appalachian Trail, was accused of drinking champagne, littering, and bringing an oversized group to the summit of Mt. Katahdin, all violations of park rules. Considered civil violations under Maine law, each offense carried a fine of up to $1,000. Jurek later agreed to a plea deal, pled guilty to one of the charges, and was fined $500.

I've heard other hikers say that Jurek boasted it was worth $500 for him to do what he wanted rather than follow the rules. Now, for the first time ever, Baxter State Park is setting limits on how many thru-hikers can access the park each year. While the published limits are now higher than the current number of annual hikers, this could be an issue for future thru-hikers. Once again, to quote what I've heard on the trail, "Thank you, Scott Jurek."

> *"Man is born to die. His works are short-lived. Buildings crumble, mountains decay, wealth vanishes. Above all, Katahdin in all its glory forever shall remain the mount of the people of Maine."*
>
> —Percival Baxter

The following afternoon the sun brightened up the forest, along with my mood. Because it was cooler in the low 60s, I didn't sweat all day. I met several other hikers, including *Will*, who was in his 60s. I say I'm not competitive, but I noticed I was trying to stay in front of the other hikers. Everyone eventually went past me at some point.

While I stopped for dinner, I called Joanna.

"I'm ready to go home, I'm so tired, and the rest of the trail isn't going to be any different. What's the use?"

She said, "It sounds like you're really tired out, but you've come this far. You really need to finish it, Honey. I think if you stop now, you'll wish later that you'd stuck with it to the end." I agreed with her and thanked her (for the hundredth time) for all of her support. I needed to find a way to enjoy the last two weeks of my adventure.

In the afternoon, I made my way up Pleasant Pond Mountain and finally made it to the top. I looked to the Northeast in an attempt to spot Mt. Katahdin, but I couldn't tell if it was out there or not. The trail going down the other side wasn't too steep, making it easier to work my way downhill. I experimented hiking without the knee brace on my right side (my good side).

I had worn the brace ever since my knee started hyper-extending, or bending backward, in Southern Virginia. I recently started carrying the brace in my pack. This allowed me to bend my knee and climb easier while keeping the brace on hand in the event my knee acted up again. I finally decided since I was carrying the weight, I should probably keep wearing it—the knee brace made for interesting conversations. When people saw me limping up to a shelter, they noticed the large brace on my knee, and they'd ask me how my knee was doing.

"My knee is feeling great today," I'd say while thinking, *Yeah, my knee on that side is fine, but my foot on the other side is killing me.*

The FarOut app had comments from other hikers about stealth camping locations. These are often just a flat clear spot along the trail where other hikers have spent the night. My target for the day was to reach one of these spots just past a power line up the trail in another few miles.

When it started to get dark, I noticed it was 7:00 PM, right when I expected daylight to run out. I spied a clear flat spot about seventy-five feet off the trail and decided to stop for the night. I had stopped a few hours before to eat my dinner of tortillas, cheese, and pepperoni. I put up my tent, hung my food bag, and lay down to sleep within thirty minutes of arriving. It was dark and quiet outside, so I knew I'd sleep well.

I've taught people how to get started investing in real estate for most of my work career. I had to learn how to speak in front of large groups to teach the various seminars we used to put on around the country. Many years ago, while teaching a workshop in California, I started to get nervous and feel anxious, similar to the way I had been feeling before I woke up. I stepped down from the two-foot-high stage to be closer to my audience—I did this at times to connect with folks.

Once I stepped down from the stage, my anxiety went away. I finished teaching the point that I was on, but needed to put the next overhead sheet onto the projector. I stepped back up on the stage and was overwhelmed with—you got it—a crazy case of nervous anxiety again. I flipped the next overhead on the projector and moved back down off the stage. Once I was down on the floor again, my nerves subsided. When I went back up on stage, I thought my voice was going to tighten up so much that I wouldn't be able to talk.

I had been speaking to large groups for years and never had a problem like this before. So, I did what I've advised my clients to do when they get nervous talking to a property owner or a commercial real estate broker. Just tell everyone about it. I stopped for a moment and told everyone that I was struggling for some reason with getting nervous. I said, "I'm not sure what's causing this, but perhaps you could help me get through it."

The crazy thing about this is that once I brought it up, the problem disappeared immediately. While I was hiking, I opened up to share the story about my morning anxiety along with a few online followers, just as I've shared with you here in this book. And then—presto!—right after opening up and revealing this fear, I was back to feeling fine. Is that because I told you about it, initially in my journal and now in this book? All I can say is that's weird.

The following day, that nagging sensation of feeling overwhelmed and anxious when first awakening was finally gone.

It used to take me an hour to get going in the morning, no matter how much I hurried. Over the past few weeks, I was able to pack up in just under thirty minutes. To be fair, this didn't include the stretches and ankle rotations I did for my leg and foot while waking up. But I was in a hurry to get to Katahdin, so maybe that was why I got a faster start these days.

After hiking a few miles, I ran into *Will*, staying at the campsite just past the power line that I was hoping to reach the day before. I tended to compare the spot where I camped to other places that I could have camped instead. I walked by and said good morning to *Will* while evaluating *my* tent site as the better of the two locations.

I stopped at the top of Moxie Bald Mountain and looked out across the beautiful countryside. A thought came into my head: *Alone. Sadness. Hmm... what's that about?* I realized that being way out in the wild of Maine—with those beautiful views—was sad in a way. It wasn't that I was lonely. I was fine, really. It was just that it was so beautiful it would be great to have my wife or kids there to enjoy it with me. I could take photos or videos, but there was no way I could capture the essence of the experience.

From the top of Moxie Bald, I looked to the Northeast to try and see Mt. Katahdin again. I couldn't see anything that looked like the big mountain, so I started down the other side. As the trail swung around the east side of the mountain, I walked along a flat rock path. I looked up and realized that Katahdin was straight ahead in front of me.

"There it is!" I shouted out to no one in particular. After all these miles and telling everyone I met that I was headed to Mt. Katahdin, I finally had it within my sights. For the first time, I felt as if I was being pulled along the trail rather than pushing myself to take each step.

At the end of the day, I stopped just before crossing a stream that I planned to wade across in the morning. I found a nice campsite there and made a campfire while thinking this might be the last fire I got to enjoy along the trail. It grew dark, and the fire died down into glowing red embers. I couldn't believe I had made it over fourteen miles in one day! I made better progress when I didn't have to go up and down big mountains.

The following day I prepared to ford the stream that had been described by SOBO's as "knee deep." Most thru-hikers end up having to ford at least four or five streams, but I was lucky it had been a dry year. Besides getting my feet a little wet one time, I hadn't had to wade across any streams before getting to this water crossing.

The Maine Appalachian Trail Club provided a thick rope for hikers to hold onto while fording the stream. I could see that it was tied to a large tree on each side of the stream, stretching across the water like an oversized clothesline. I had watched some YouTube videos, so I knew a little bit about how to cross streams. I took my pack off, moved all of my gear inside my trash bag liner, and then sealed it off with a handy little piece of Velcro that I had.

I put my pack back on but left the belt clips undone so that I could take care of the first thing you're supposed to do if you fall in the water while crossing—ditch your pack. While I understood this was to keep me from becoming part of a news story about "Injured Hiker Makes it 2,000 Miles Then Drowns," and I didn't disagree with this advice, the idea of "ditching" my pack went directly against the relationship I'd developed with my hiking gear.

I had walked all this way with everything I needed in my pack. That is, if you don't count all the resupplies and extra gear I had on hand in the car to swap out when I needed it. But you get the idea. I pretty much kept my pack within eyesight, especially after learning that bears sometimes steal hiker's packs and waltz off into the woods.

And that overwhelmed, anxious feeling that I was dealing with in the morning? The only way I could reassure myself I'd be okay was by telling myself that if something happened to me—like getting wet and cold from falling in a river—I could hole up in the safety of my tent and sleeping bag to await rescue.

Of course, I couldn't help but think about this as I reached up to grab the rope and take my first step into the water flowing by in front of me. I pulled my foot back out of the water, stepped back from the edge of the stream, and let go of the rope, telling myself, *I can't do this*. Well, I mean, I could, but if I fell in the water while I was all by myself and I lost my pack, then I would probably be screwed. Sure, chances were that another hiker might come by and save me from hypothermia, but I certainly couldn't count on that.

I explored along the bank upstream, looking for rocks I could step on or a place where a tree had fallen across the stream that I could use as a bridge. I went as far as I could go before the brush got so thick that I couldn't continue and then turned around. I went the other way downstream and eventually found a place where I could step on rocks and cross the stream without getting my feet wet.

I was happy to get past this obstacle. Still, I was a little disappointed when I realized I'd subconsciously been looking forward to experiencing wading across a water crossing like this. Now I didn't get to do it. I thought about this and realized that my disappointment came from comparing myself to an ideal vision I had of a completely healed version of myself, boldly striding across rivers with no concerns about falling because of the lousy balance I have on my left side.

I had read books and seen movies about other hikers and imagined myself doing everything exactly as they did. The truth was that for this hike (and most other things in life), we have to find our own way.

In the afternoon, I practiced looking at the trail with new eyes. I asked myself, "What would this feel like if this was my very first day hiking the Appalachian Trail?" I was doing this in an attempt to enjoy this last part of my journey rather than being so focused on getting it done that I didn't have a good time. With my leg feeling stronger, I was able to go a little further than planned each day, and I ended up making it to Monson in three days instead of four. I planned to reward myself by taking a zero the next day to rest up before tackling the 100 Mile Wilderness.

I stayed at Shaw's Hostel again, along with at least twenty other hikers. Shaw's, run by former thru-hikers *Poet* and *Hippy Chick*, is well-known for quite a few things. For one thing, it's the last stop before heading into the 100 Mile Wilderness. It's also known for having a great breakfast, including plenty of eggs, bacon, and pancakes stacked up into cairns, just like the stacks of rocks that mark the trail above treeline.

Shaw's operates as a hostel, has an extensive outfitter barn, and a complete selection of hiker resupplies. *Poet* helps both NOBO's heading into the 100 Mile Wilderness and SOBO's coming out of the 100 Mile Wilderness. He gives advice, makes repairs to gear, and as you might guess from his trail name, he's a remarkable poet. While I didn't get a poem written by him, several other hikers expressed admiration for the poems he'd written for them. *Poet* did fix the broken tent pole for that other little tent of mine.

Shaw's also provides food resupply drops at two different spots in the 100 Mile Wilderness. While taking a zero to rest up, I figured out how much food I needed to carry in my pack over the next few days. I decided to start off with three days of food, which would allow me to get up and over the largest mountains in the 100 Mile Wilderness while keeping my weight down. I packed up a box of food for Shaw's to deliver to me on a private logging road about thirty miles north. At seventy bucks, it seemed a little steep for the food drop. Still, I figured it was worth it to help me keep my weight down, and besides, I had paid that much or more to shuttle drivers that helped me leave my car at different locations all along the trail.

I also mailed myself a box of food and my raincoat to White House Landing, a sporting camp that offers to pick up hikers in their boat seventy miles into the 100 Mile Wilderness. I had debated whether to carry my raincoat with me. The weather forecast looked okay, and even if it rained, it shouldn't get cold enough that I'd need my raincoat, at least not until I got to Mt. Katahdin. That's why I shipped it ahead to White House Landing. I got my pack weight at this point down to fifteen pounds, which was pretty light when you consider that when I started my hike in Georgia, it weighed thirty-six pounds.

I was still eating tortillas, pepperoni, and cheese for dinner so as not to have to carry my stove and the fuel to power it. I had lost weight as I made my way north from Georgia by either buying lighter gear or getting rid of things that I learned I could get by without. I purchased a lighter weight sleeping bag, air mattress, down coat, tent, and even a new backpack.

I discovered I could get by without numerous things I found I didn't need. This included rain pants, leg gators, a blow-up pillow, mini-iPad (I read books on my phone), knife (didn't ever use it), shaving stuff, camp shoes, a big medical kit, extra rope, pen, pencil, a paper journal, and any extra clothes besides one dry set to wear at night.

Some of this, such as the iPad and the blow-up pillow, were easy to get by without. After realizing that it weighed less than a single paperback book, I bought the iPad, but after hiking for a few weeks, I realized that I was too tired to read at night. Besides, I could use the Kindle app on my phone to read if I wanted to. So, I got rid of the iPad. I thought I'd need a pillow to be able to sleep at night, which was why I started out with a blow-up pillow. After a while on the trail, you learn how to use things for multiple purposes. For example, I realized I could use my down coat as a pillow.

Then I found that I really didn't even need a pillow once I got used to it. The other thing is that each item you carry with you not only adds a bit more weight to your pack, but it's one more thing for you to look after, to have to store away and keep track of. My leg gators were a good example of this. I had a big pair of gators that were helpful when hiking in the snow down in Tennessee. The smaller nylon gators that I had are supposed to keep dirt and rocks out of your boots. But they didn't work. By using them, I had two more things to keep track of, to make sure I didn't lose, to take off at night and put back on in the morning.

If I could get by without something, I'd save the extra weight and have the extra time and energy from not having to deal with one more thing. But this bare-boned approach contributed to my worries about heading off into the 100 Mile Wilderness the next day. This area of the Appalachian Trail is generally considered the wildest section of the trail.

It is regarded as one of the most challenging to navigate and traverse.

I hiked light so that it would be easier for me to make it, but I needed to balance that against making sure I was not putting myself at risk. Take the medical kit that I got rid of, for example. I might need it at some point. My medical supplies at this point were limited. I had some duct tape wrapped around my hiking poles, some white sports tape I used for taping hot spots or blisters on my toes, a sewing needle and floss, and a few Band-Aids.

On most other parts of the trail, I figured that if I got injured and needed medical attention, another hiker would be coming by before long, and they surely wouldn't be so stupid as to be out hiking the Appalachian Trail without a complete medical kit, would they? In most places on the AT, it wasn't too far to get to a road crossing where you could get some help if you needed it.

Way up in Maine, in the 100 Mile Wilderness, I wasn't so sure about that. In fact, I knew that there were just a few private logging roads that cross the trail. If I were to get hurt, I couldn't count on another hiker coming by to help me. My biggest fear was that if I didn't have my raincoat, the weather turned colder, and it started to rain, I'd have to hole up in my tent to stay warm. Not a big issue for a day or two, but it wouldn't be long before I'd run out of food.

Chances were decent that another hiker would come by. Still, when you're in a wilderness area, it's different than asking someone for an extra Snickers bar when you're at a hostel. Each person needs to be self-sufficient because they will need the food they have to make it through the 100 Mile Wilderness themselves.

Despite thinking all of this through, I checked the weather report one last time and then mailed my raincoat ahead up the trail. My pack was ready for me to grab it and go in the morning. I had three days of food and just the basics that had gotten me this far. I was used to hiking light and hoped that this didn't cause any issues during this final 100 mile stretch before getting to Mt. Katahdin.

When I opened my eyes the following day, that overwhelming sense of anxiety was back. It started in the center of my stomach and blossomed out to engulf my entire body while I focused on taking some slow, deep breaths telling myself that I was okay. I was right there in the bunkroom of the hostel. Everything was all okay. It subsided after a few minutes, but the experience didn't help bolster the confidence that I was trying to work up before heading off into the 100 Mile Wilderness.

I gathered my stuff together and headed downstairs for another great breakfast with all the fixings, including *Poet's* pancake cairns. My pack was ready to go from the day before, but I ended up taking some time to upload some files for an old work project and played a few last songs on the piano.

By the time *Poet* dropped a few other hikers and me off at the trailhead, it was already 10:30 AM. I thought that a late start would be fine until I pulled up my schedule and saw that I'd planned on making it thirteen miles that day. That probably wasn't going to happen. I stepped into the woods and was greeted with this ominous warning.

APPALACHIAN TRAIL
CAUTION

THERE ARE NO PLACES TO OBTAIN
SUPPLIES OR GET HELP UNTIL
ABOL BRIDGE 100 MILES NORTH. DO NOT
ATTEMPT THIS SECTION UNLESS YOU
HAVE A MINIMUM OF 10 DAYS SUPPLIES
AND ARE FULLY EQUIPPED. THIS IS THE
LONGEST WILDERNESS SECTION OF THE
ENTIRE AT AND ITS DIFFICULTY SHOULD
NOT BE UNDERESTIMATED

GOOD HIKING

M.A.T.C.

Well, that wasn't exactly true. I would get a resupply drop from Shaw's in thirty miles and then another resupply box that I shipped to White House Landing, which was seventy miles from here.

As I headed off into the 100 Mile Wilderness, I enjoyed views of North Pond while hiking past, and I also stopped off to check out Little Wilson Falls. This is a spectacular waterfall with perfectly carved out steps that look like part of a giant staircase for the water to cascade down from one step to the next. I imagined that it looked even more impressive in a year that's not as dry as this one with considerably more water pouring down the face of the mountain.

I sat down to eat a protein bar while thinking about how long the water had been rushing over these steps. Undoubtedly hundreds of years, probably thousands, perhaps even millions of years, this waterfall had been there. I was there at just this one moment in time to enjoy the experience, feeling and hearing thousands of gallons of water smashing down into each step. I took some photos and a few videos, knowing that once again, I couldn't come close to capturing the actual experience. Then I got up, swung my pack onto my back, picked up my hiking poles, and headed up the trail.

The day's terrain included some minor ups and downs along with a steady supply of traditional Maine roots laced across the surface of the trail. I could only make it nine miles by the time it was getting dark. I found a flat spot on a side trail called the Big Wilson Tote Road and decided to tent there for the night while hoping that no one would be night hiking on the side trail since I was completely blocking it.

It was already getting dark when I set up my tent. By the time I ate my usual dinner of tortillas, pepperoni, and sharp cheddar cheese, it was pitch black out. Like really seriously dark. I know that I should have turned on my headlamp and gone out to put my food bag up for the night. But I was dead tired from hiking all day and wasn't up for the extra effort that it takes to find a tree limb and make multiple attempts at throwing the rope in the air and all of that.

Some hikers had told me they wouldn't always put their food up in a bear bag. One hiker said, "I hiked the entire trail and slept with my food in my tent every night and never had a problem." From what I had seen, most hikers do follow the written guidelines. All food items and anything with a smell like toothpaste should be put where a bear can't get to it.

Many of the shelters down south had bear cables where you can clip your food bag onto a line and pull it up high above the ground for the night. Other campsites and shelters have tall metal poles called bear poles. You use another long pole attached by a chain that allows you to lift your food bag up onto a hook at the top of the bear pole. Other shelters have bear boxes to protect your food bag for the night. They look like big metal toolboxes you might see in the back of a pickup truck.

Of course, you can always hang your food bag from a tree limb, which is recommended for situations like this night when I was out in the middle of nowhere. The idea is to find a branch that will allow you to get the food bag at least twelve feet off the ground and six feet away from any trees. I've heard stories about bears that are smart enough to scratch all the trees around a bear bag until they end up snagging and breaking the rope where you've tied it off to a tree. They can be pretty smart, for a bear at least.

You'd think that after hiking all this way from Georgia, I'd know enough to take care of my food bag. When you consider that one of my biggest fears was having to hole up in my tent to avoid weather and running out of food, I'd be determined enough to go hang my dang food bag. But nope. I figured I'd be fine for this one night with my food bag in the tent.

In the middle of the night, I woke up to a loud snap. *What was that?*

Then I heard another "Crack!"

When you're out in the woods at night, there are plenty

of sounds. You can listen to the wind sliding through the treetops, various noises from different animals, maybe even the soothing sound of a stream or water flowing nearby. This was a different sort of noise, one that got my attention.

"Snap!" There it was again. Sounding like it was getting closer.

There's a big difference from when you're out in the wild listening to the ordinary sounds compared to hearing that distinct sound that's made when something BIG steps on a branch. Well, let's just say that my heart rate went through the roof. *Um… maybe it's a squirrel…* I tried convincing myself.

"CRACK!" even louder. *That's one heck of a giant squirrel…. Perhaps it's a huge squirrel pretending to be a bear…. Maybe it's a person who's slowly sneaking up on my tent… Whoa! That's even more frightening! Okay, don't think about that… it's a bear… no…. it's a—maybe it's a deer—a big deer… sneaking up on me in my tent… Ahhhhhgh!!!*

I'm amazed at how the human mind works in crazy situations like this where there is no good answer, just like when the doctors crushed the nerve in my leg three and a half years ago. This shot the pain level in my head on a scale of 1 to 10 up to 200. My brain had to find a way to deal with that. I can recall some sort of stacking sequence, like sorting chunks of the pain together as if they were Lego pieces in my head.

So, here's what I worked out during that night. I figured that it might be a deer, an elk, or perhaps a moose. Why not? As long as I was making up stuff, it could be a moose. I actually wanted to see a moose—a nice live healthy one—although not necessarily inside my tent.

Or it could be a bear.

If it is a bear and this bear decides to join me for dinner or even take a bite of me for dinner, then there's really not much I could do about it at that point. My Cuben Fiber tent was good at keeping the rain out, but it certainly won't do much of anything to slow down a bear. I can't jump up and run for two reasons. First off, I can walk, but I certainly can't run. The other thing is that I can't step on anything with my left foot unless I have my boots on. Even though my nerve was damaged up in my hip, it's mostly my foot that hurts. It's so sensitive that stepping on a tiny little pebble or stick or anything, like a lamp cord on a hardwood floor, sends me through the roof.

Now, as I'm explaining this to you afterward, I'm thinking, well Peter, maybe if you had a bear chasing you... and it was like... growling... and maybe even swiping its paws at you... I bet that would get you moving pretty fast, wouldn't it?

But I didn't think about that. For some reason I didn't even consider putting my boots on. I didn't consider yelling or even turning my headlamp on. I don't know why. I just didn't think of it. I lay there resigned to the situation, feeling like there wasn't anything that I could do about it. Either the bear was going to get me, or it wasn't. Once I accepted my fate, I noticed my heart rate and breathing began to slow back down. At least I'd go out pursuing my dream of healing myself. I can imagine the headlines...

"Injured Hiker Gets Eaten by Bear."

As bad as that might be to experience, you have to admit that it would make a great story after I was gone. "*Flash 52* didn't make it to Mt. Katahdin, but wow... his story went viral... look how many views he has on YouTube."

Sometimes my quest to find humor in every situation goes beyond the boundaries of common sense and decency. So, if you find this last bit distasteful, I apologize. Hopefully, the bear would say that his dinner was delicious. By the way, after hearing a few more snaps and cracks, it was all quiet, and I fell back asleep.

The following day, the first order of business was figuring out how to get across the Big Wilson Stream. I should probably mention that what they call a stream up in Maine is called a river anywhere else in the country. From the sandy bank, I estimated that the stream was at least sixty feet across and perhaps two or three feet deep in places.

Like the last stream, this crossing also had a rope stretched across for hikers to hold onto. Before using the rope, I searched upstream and then downstream to see if I could avoid going in the water by walking across a fallen tree or stepping on some rocks. I didn't find a place that would work. This stream was broader and had more water in it than the last crossing, so it looked like I'd have to ford it.

I sat down to wait, hoping another hiker might come along to help me across or at the very least sound the alarm if I lost my footing and fell in. While waiting, I prepared to cross by getting my footwear ready. I understand that some hikers go barefoot, but this wasn't an option for me due to my sensitive foot, as I couldn't step on rocks without my boots on.

Many hikers will take off their hiking boots when fording a stream and wear camp shoes, which are typically a pair of Crocs. I'd tried out using Crocs as camp shoes when I was down in Georgia, but I kept stepping out of my left shoe because my foot muscles didn't work well enough to keep the shoe on. So, I wore my hiking boots all day until I was ready to go to sleep. This was one of many things that I eliminated to keep my pack weight down.

I took my boots off and removed both my outer wool socks and my Injinji sock liners. Then I pulled my Superfeet insoles out and put my bare feet back into my hiking boots. Then my socks, insoles, and all the other gear that was usually attached to the outside of my pack were sealed up inside the trash bag liner to keep everything dry if I fell in the water. I also strapped one of my hiking poles to the outside of the pack since I'd be using one hand to hold on to the rope as I forded the stream.

A half-hour went by, and no other hikers had shown up. I didn't want to wait all day, and besides, I needed to be making my way through the 100 Mile Wilderness. I put on my pack, made sure to leave the belt unbuckled, reached up with one hand to hold onto the rope, and carefully stepped out into the water.

I took my time and carefully planted my pole ahead of each step. While I could see the bottom of the stream, I found it challenging to find solid footing because the rocks were slippery, and the moving water made it hard to see where each rock was. I securely planted my pole and felt my way with each foot over to the next step. This was easier to do with my right foot than on my injured side.

The water was only knee-deep, but the fast current and slippery rocks on the bottom made me uneasy. I was relieved when I safely made it across. While climbing up the far bank, I thought, *it would be cool to have a video of myself making this crossing*. I'd need to clip my phone to a tree overlooking the stream and then go back out into the water at least halfway to get a decent shot.

I looked back across the water and, in one of my wiser moments, decided that getting a video wasn't worth the additional risk. Especially when you consider that I'd just cleared an obstacle I'd been so worried about. This was definitely a task that would have been easier or safer with someone else nearby, but I was hiking on my own. I made it work.

I sat down on a big tree root to put the insoles back into my boots and put my socks on. I put the Gore-Tex waterproof socks over the top of my hiking socks. This allowed me to put my feet back into my soaking wet boots without getting my socks wet. Pretty cool, huh?

The trail that day included a few mountains to go over, and it was later in the day when I made it to the top of Barren Mountain. I laid out my shirt to dry in the breeze and called my wife to check in with her. She really is extraordinary, supporting me as I made my way along this journey. I found a decent spot right by the trail to camp in the small saddle between Barren Mountain and the next mountain coming up.

The next day I had a challenging hike with several climbs up and down a series of numbered Chairback Mountains and Columbus Mountain. I focused on moving along at a slow but steady pace. I reminded myself to breathe slowly and deeply when going uphill. I felt surprisingly good at this point and was pleased to have made it over the worst of the mountains in the 100 Mile Wilderness.

I arrived at the Katahdin Ironworks road with forty-five minutes to spare for my 6:00 pm food drop from Shaw's. I sat down to wait, and within the next fifteen minutes, several large logging trucks rumbled past, kicking up dust from what appeared to be a well-built gravel road. I understand there's a $15 fee to access this private logging road, which I'm sure contributes to the $70 cost that Shaw's charges for a food drop.

Restorer arrived a few minutes later and sat down to chat with me while I was waiting. He asked if I had a cold six-pack of beer coming with my food, and I told him I wasn't into drinking beer but had asked them to bring me a root beer. I was really looking forward to this after a long day of hiking. AJ arrived right on time. He lifted the box with my resupplies out of the truck along with a cooler. When I opened the cooler, I saw a can of Budweiser surrounded by ice instead of the root beer I was expecting. I gave the can of beer to *Restorer,* and he was pleased to do his part by consuming it.

Getting a food drop thirty miles into the 100 Mile Wilderness allowed me to carry a lighter load over the more demanding mountainous section. It was comforting to have my resupply and be heading north into hopefully easier terrain. *Restorer* and I set up our tents right by the trail about a half-mile north from the road, along with two other NOBOs.

Being "out there" in the 100 Mile Wilderness mentally challenged me. The following day, I had to deal with that panic attack thing again. It started out small, then morphed into a robust amount of overwhelm combined with anxiety before a good-sized dose of outright fear gripped me in its jaws. *What the heck am I doing out here? I can't do this.* I tried to come up with logical ideas to reassure myself that I'd be alright. After taking some deep breaths, it finally passed, and I was okay.

I spent the day climbing up and down more mountains, including White Cap, the last prominent peak before

Katahdin. I had heard from some SOBOs that the trail was easier here than the mountains I'd gone over the day before, and I was pleased to find this was true. While there were plenty of ups and downs, the trail wasn't too steep or technical. I tried to make up a few miles that I lost by getting a late start into the 100 Mile Wilderness a few mornings earlier. At the end of the day, I was thrilled to have hiked almost thirteen miles over such challenging terrain. I slept in a shelter for the first time in several months. There were two other NOBOs there, and it was nice to have some company.

Without any big mountains to go over the next day, I took advantage of the terrain by moving along at a steady pace. By midafternoon I was still feeling strong, which is unusual for me. Maybe after hiking all this way, my legs were actually getting a little stronger. At about 4:30, I was walking through an old-growth forest with massive trees that reached all the way to the sky when I noticed a black-looking something off in the woods to my right. Then, something, due perhaps to an ancient instinct, a dose of caution, or both of these combined with a dash of hopefulness caused me to stop in my tracks and think:

Bear?

Before I go any further, I should probably let you know that I reacted exactly like this at least once a day since I first started hiking. When you're out in the woods where bears are known to prowl around, you can't help but keep an eye out for them. You'd be surprised at how many times I stared at what I thought was a bear. I'd even imagine seeing some movement before realizing it was just another fallen tree, a shadow, or a rock or whatever.

So, when this black thing moved a couple of feet, I took a deep breath, dropped my pack on the ground, and dug out my glasses so I could get a better view and figure out what it was. *Oh, my goodness! It was a moose, a BIG moose.* No antlers, so that made it a female moose. I took a few photos and then started taking a video while quietly narrating like I was filming for National Geographic or something.

"Here comes the moose… it's walking towards the trail… and it's turning towards me…. (voice gets quieter) … here it comes… uh…. I'm backing up now..."

I turned my video camera off and hobbled back the way I came to put some distance between the moose and me. When I stopped to look back, I could see the moose standing in the middle of the trail looking at me. Having a large wild animal coming toward me increased my heart rate substantially, so I headed further south to increase the distance between us.

Unlike the nearly dead moose I saw on the top of Mt. Moosilauke a month ago, this moose appeared quite lively. It looked to be a few feet taller than my full height of 5' 9" (if I stand up straight and have my hiking boots on).

I was happy to see a moose, thrilled, actually. Now that I saw it, I was good with checking off the "saw a moose" box and moving on. Unfortunately, the moose was still standing there right on the trail, and I needed to get by to reach my campsite, so I could have dinner and go to sleep.

I headed off the side of the trail about 150 feet and then turned northward, paralleling the trail so that I could get around the moose without bothering it. In most places along the trail, I'd be completely hidden in the undergrowth. But there were just a few twigs and some ferns on the ground in this old-growth forest. This meant there was nothing to keep the moose from eyeballing me as I made my way Yogi Bear style, scurrying from one tree to the next in a lousy attempt to discreetly slip past.

As I got up within 100 feet of the point where I'd planned to slip by the moose, it suddenly started walking... well... it was faster than walking... let's just say it marched... yeah... it *quickly* marched right at me. I picked it up a notch and hobbled along faster (which isn't fast, mind you) from tree to tree. The moose adjusted her path to track directly toward me even though I was moving even faster—well, as fast as I could with my injured leg!

As the moose came closer, I didn't have much time to think through my options. I looked up at the tree I was hiding behind and knew for sure that climbing up there was out of the picture, and when I glanced back at the moose, there it came, looking like it was prancing now. *Wow, what big hoofs you have there, my lady!*

All I could picture was me trying to race around the tree faster than this moose could reach out and take a bite out of me. That's how my mind worked. In hindsight, I don't think that a moose is likely to bite you, yet when that big moose mouth got within five feet from me, I hollered, "HeeYaw! HeeYaw!" Then I shouted out "Leave Me Alone!" for good measure (just in case the moose understood English). I may have even clacked my hiking poles. It's hard to remember with all of the excitement.

The moose startled and did a half-turn away from me for a few steps before turning back to look at me again. I retreated back the way I had come since the moose had angled over to block the path I'd planned on taking to get by. Once I was back on the trail, I headed further south to increase my moose buffer and give my heart rate a chance to settle down again.

I couldn't see the moose at this point, so I sat down on a log and took some deep breaths to calm down. After waiting five or ten minutes without seeing anything, I started back up the trail, taking five or six steps at a time. I then stopped to look and listen everywhere for the moose. I'd made it pretty far down the trail when I heard something off to my left. I looked over to see her 50 feet away, looking directly at me.

We locked eyes and stared each other down. Meanwhile, my feet were taking me up the trail at an ever-increasing rate. In fact, I don't think I'd ever hiked this quickly before. I kept glancing back as I made my way up and over a slight rise in the trail. I continued to hike in "Get away from moose" mode for another ten minutes before slowing back down to my normal pace.

After another half mile, I met some other hikers who had set up camp next to the trail. I spilled out my story in rapid-fire format, realizing that I probably sounded a little manic. Freaked out would describe it pretty well. I texted a few details to one of my daughters, who used to live in Alaska, and she asked,

Did you check the ears? If moose ears are back it's aggressive.

I replied,

Nope—forgot to check the ears...

I didn't know anything about checking ears. Even if I did, I probably wouldn't have seen the moose's ears when they are so much smaller than that big set of hooves, and of course, that oversized moose mouth that was coming right at me. I had plenty of energy to hike another few miles before finding a spot right by a stream to set up my tent for the night. I had wanted to see a healthy moose, and I was able to finally check that off my list. *Whew!*

I'd just completed my highest mileage day so far, perhaps because of all the adrenaline I got from seeing that big moose. I made it almost sixteen miles, and I was still feeling fine the following day. My foot was a little stiff, but it wasn't hurting too badly. I decided to switch gears and take my time hiking for the day since it was only another ten miles to my next destination, White House Landing.

That afternoon, while walking along the trail, I looked through the trees to see parts of Lake Pemdumcook sparkling blue in the mid-day sun. I turned onto a short path towards the lake and discovered a sandy beach where a gentle percussion of windblown waves was lapping against the shore. I looked out across the lake and then turned northward to see the most incredible view of Mt. Katahdin.

It looked like the opening screen of an Imax movie in full Technicolor—but it was real. It was more than real. That may sound strange to you, but if you'd started out on a journey like this, and each and every day, you thought about making it to Katahdin—and then you just look up to see it there, like, "TAA DAA! Here I am, and I look absolutely magnificent!" It's hard to explain how I felt about this. I mean it's a mountain, a big pile of rocks, right?

The name Katahdin comes from the Penobscot Indians who named it in reference to its high altitude. Katahdin translates to "The Greatest Mountain." For the Penobscot

Tribe, Katahdin represented the beginning of life, a place of birth and spiritual enlightenment.

For me, and I sensed other hikers felt this way as well, Mt. Katahdin had a magical essence. Sure, it was special because it's the summit, the peak, the exclamation point at the end of a northbound hike. But it's so much more than that. Over the past few weeks, I slowly transitioned from pushing myself along the trail to the point where I could now feel Katahdin steadily pulling me northward into her arms.

That afternoon I walked up to a handwritten sign that instructed folks like me to walk two-tenths of a mile over to a small dock on the lake. "Call us on your cell phone, and we'll pick you up with our boat." By following this fun and different process, I got a ride in a boat to reach White House Landing, an old sporting camp that operates much like a hostel along the AT.

Bill and his wife Linda made me and a few other hikers hamburgers for dinner, after which I lay in a hammock that looked out over the lake as the sun slowly set. I'd learned to tell time by looking at the sun by this point. Out in the woods, I could look at the sky each day, and know how much time was left before the sun went down. This was probably helped out by the digital watch on my wrist, but it was one more connection with nature that I enjoyed anew.

I opened up the box I'd shipped to the sporting camp to resupply my food and pulled out my raincoat so that I'd have it for the next few days, as well as for when I climbed Mt. Katahdin. Like many of the bunkhouses along the trail, the White House Landing was a little rustic. The camp was off the electric grid and used a combination of solar and generators to produce the power they needed. Unfortunately, the generator running that evening to boost the batteries back up was right outside our door. Put me back out in the woods, in my little tent, and I'd quit complaining.

The last part of the 100 Mile Wilderness didn't have many elevation changes to deal with, so the next day was relatively easy. At the top of the one small hill I climbed, I noticed a note under a rock. It said, "The view is totally worth it!" So, I took the side trail over to see another beautiful vista of the ever-magical Mt. Katahdin.

Later in the day, the trail followed Rainbow Stream, which had numerous cascades and delightful waterfalls. I must have been spoiled. I'd seen so many waterfalls lately that I didn't even stop to take pictures of any of them. At most, I'd pause for thirty seconds to enjoy the experience of seeing and hearing the white water rushing by before continuing my hike.

I made it another fifteen miles for the day, an easy day for most hikers, but this was a great distance for me. I arrived at the shelter just as the last bit of daylight disappeared through the trees. "Looks like a full house," I said as I looked in to see a solid row of sleeping bags and pads. "Yup, it's full," came an answer from the shadows. So, I went up the hill, found a level spot, and set up my tent before coming back down to join the group sitting around a healthy-looking fire in front of the shelter.

I knew that this could very well be the last fireside chat of my journey. I soaked it all in and fully appreciated the pleasure of sitting out in the woods talking with friendly strangers. We watched the campfire flames dance back and forth under the moonlight shining through the trees.

I pulled out my dinner of tortillas and pepperoni. I tried my best to enjoy it while gazing longingly at the versions of chili or macaroni and cheese that were being consumed by my campmates. I was getting a little tired of pepperoni for dinner but, what the heck, I hopefully only had a few days left to enjoy fine hiking cuisine like this.

I retired to the safety of my tent up the hill from the shelter. While reading a book on my iPhone, I noticed a mouse scurrying up the outside of my tent. A quick flip of my wrist sent this intruder flying through the air to an unknown landing spot out in the pine needles. If I excluded mosquitoes, I could claim that I'd seen more mice during my hike than any other animal.

The next day I put it in high gear, taking hardly any breaks as I traversed the relatively flat, friendly terrain. I was able to knock out another fifteen-mile day. This got me almost to Baxter State Park a day earlier than I had planned. I was ready and raring to finish this thing up.

I don't know why I did this, but at Abol Bridge Campground, I paid $81 for "one or two people" to sleep in what was described as a bunkroom. I thought that I might find another hiker to split this with (which I didn't), and I also pictured the bunkroom as similar to other places on the trail. I envisioned a place with room for ten or twelve hikers to sleep along with the opportunity to hang out and talk with each other.

Instead, I was given the keys to "Number 4," which looked pretty much like a tool shed to me. It had three bunk beds inside, but nothing else: no chairs, no tables, no lights, and no electricity or heat. I tried to console myself by thinking at least I could hang my tent up to dry out and be indoors for the night.

The campground did have an okay (but not great) restaurant where I managed to eat twice before closing time at 7:00 pm. After that, I was alone in a freezing cold toolshed that was pretending to be a bunkhouse. I went over to the camp bathroom building and used the shaving supplies I purchased at the store to clear off several weeks of facial hair that I'd built up. Joanna would be meeting me at the bottom of Mt. Katahdin in a few days, and I didn't want to scare her off.

I was set to hike into Baxter State Park the next day so that I'd be at the base of Mt. Katahdin and ready to summit the following day, as long as the weather cooperated. I had planned to reach Katahdin Stream Campground and then take the AT Lodge shuttle into Millinocket. I realized that I could get an earlier start hiking up Katahdin if I camped at The Birches thru-hiker shelter instead. That was my new plan. Despite my funky accommodations in the tool shed, it felt great to be there.

The following morning, I walked over, entered Baxter State Park, and signed the list to reserve a spot at The Birches Shelter. It was a beautiful day with a primarily flat, smooth trail through the Park and a few lovely waterfalls that I stopped to enjoy. That afternoon another NOBO told me to turn off on a short side trail to see Daisey Pond.

The view of Katahdin from the pond was amazing. I had fun setting the timer on my phone and then clumping my way out onto the dock to try and get there in time to pose as if I was deep in thought, gazing up at her majesty, Mt. Katahdin. I ended up, of course, with about twenty shots of me not quite there yet, along with one or two photos in which I finally made it.

Blueberry Crisp, Mogly, and I stopped in at the ranger's station to get our climbing permits, and I was northbound hiker number 984 for the year. We asked about the weather forecast, and the ranger informed us that the next day looked like it was going to be a little windy but clear. She explained that the forecast only applied to the mountain base and that conditions up at higher altitudes could be dramatically different. She said, "Be prepared to turn around. People have died up there."

I thanked her for her advice and offered to buy two firewood packs if someone else would agree to carry them over to our shelter. *Blueberry Crisp* said, "I'm not paying for firewood, but if you want to buy it, I'll carry it." We all walked over to The Birches Shelter, got a nice fire going, and each of us made dinner. We were sitting around the fire, savoring our last night on the trail, and there was a gentle breeze coming through the trees. The temperature was perfect. Suddenly, a big guy with a headlamp walked up and said, "Park Ranger. You all got a permit for that fire?"

"Uh, no sir... I didn't know we needed one," I responded.

"You sure do. That's a $30 fine for each one of you around the fire."

It was dead quiet as the impact of this was sinking in. Here we were relishing this last moment... and now this?

"Tell you what... I'm going to write up a warning, but don't let it happen again."

He let us sit with that for another moment before saying, "Naw! I'm just kidding—this place has way too many rules. I wouldn't be surprised if they did fine you for something like that." Turned out he was just another thru-hiker. Well, I must say, he had me going on that one.

Hikers complain about how Baxter State Park is run differently than the rest of the trail. I didn't really mind that Katahdin had rules. Percival Baxter bought up a bunch of land and donated it to the State of Maine to create the Park. I was okay with any conditions that were placed upon the thru-hikers (and on me, as I wasn't technically a thru-hiker). After coming this far along, I hope you can forgive me for pretending to be one. The fire died down, and it was getting cold, so I went to bed with dreams of sugar plums and climbing Mt. Katahdin dancing through my head.

To keep my pack weight as low as possible lately, I had my lighter summer sleeping bag. It weighed a pound and a half less than my winter sleeping bag, but I was concerned about making it all the way to Katahdin without getting cold. That night, I slept wearing a pair of heavy wool socks, my puffy down jacket, and a wool cap. I also zipped my sleeping bag all the way up and then pulled the drawstring tight, leaving only my nose exposed to the night air. This trapped my body heat in and kept me warm enough to make it through the night.

I was up before my alarm went off at 5:00 am. I was excited to get an early start on the five-mile hike up Mt. Katahdin. The AT follows the Hunt Trail, which starts out easy enough, but the trail began climbing in earnest after a mile or two. The wind, which was calm when I started out in the morning, seemed to gradually increase the further up I went. I wondered if this would be the best day for me to summit. I could easily wait until the next day if I needed to. You're only allowed to spend one night at the Birches Shelter in the Park. Still, I could wait for a better-looking day if required by shuttling out to the AT Lodge in Millinocket.

Several groups of people passed me that morning, including a few thru-hikers with family members who'd joined them for this last day of their 2,189-mile journey. I'll admit that a part of me wished I had some family members or at least another hiker to accompany me during this ascent of what appeared to be an ominous peak. Other than having *Dr Fix-it* with me for part of my journey, I'd made it most of the way on my own. While I'd have been less worried if I had someone to hike with, I was going to get this done.

As the mountain trail carried me upward, the temperature gradually dropped with a corresponding increase in wind speed. *Barefoot* came by with a few family members accompanying him, including his mother. As you may have guessed from his trail name, he wasn't wearing any shoes. I heard his mother say, "I don't know why you can't put some shoes on. It's freezing out here. You're going to get frostbite."

As they went by me and moved ahead up the trail, I heard *Barefoot* say, "That's the whole point, mom. It's who I am...I can't just put on shoes all of a sudden." I stopped and took off my pack to get out my down coat, wool hat, and raincoat (I was *so* happy to have that with me) and then pressed onward. I reached a point where I had to stow my hiking poles up on my pack and began climbing hand and feet over giant boulders. I went up a short section and stepped out from the leeward side of a boulder, only to be hit with a frigid blast of air that almost knocked me off my feet.

Wow... this isn't looking so good. Shortly after that, I noticed a steady procession of people coming back down the mountain.

Several of them, including a few of *Barefoot's* family members, told me, "This is way too cold; I'm not going up there."

Then, I came to a place where the only way to get up was to grab a piece of strategically placed rebar and swing my leg up onto the top of a ledge. I tried, again and again, to make it up but didn't have the strength in my injured leg to get it up onto the ledge. I held firm onto the rebar and paused for a moment to think while the wind swirled around me.

I was frustrated, worn out, scared, and angry. *What the heck? Here I am. I've come all this way, and now I can't make it past this spot? Why can't I have someone,* anyone, *here to help me? Why do I have to do all of this by myself?*

This, of course, wasn't a situation that "they" or "the world" had somehow dumped on top of me. I had chosen to go on this journey on my own despite the pleas many months ago from my wife and kids for me to wait until I could find someone to hike with. I was the one who had insisted on pushing along despite all the pain, the stiffness I felt each morning, the incredible loneliness and isolation. Don't get me wrong, the adventure had been outstanding. I had seen mountain vistas, met terrific people, and had the satisfaction of working on overcoming this seemingly impossible challenge of healing my leg.

By sharing this part of my life with you, I'd changed. During the process I'd learned to lighten up and reveal more of my feelings, more of what was really going on in my head. You've made it all this way with me, so I'm going to go out on a limb to open up and reveal my secret weapon to you.

Are you ready? (don't tell anyone…)

Anger.

Yup. Anger at myself for being stupid enough to get hurt on a motorcycle when I already knew better. Anger at being out here doing this on my own. This may be hard to understand, but it was self-imposed anger. I grew up in a big family with seven kids. So much was going on that despite growing up surrounded by loving parents and siblings, I developed an emotional hunger for attention. Much of my life has been a strange mix of, "Look what I'm doing now," combined with "No one cares, no one's going to help, I'll just do it myself."

I've used this anger as fuel to power my way through numerous challenges. I'm not saying that this is healthy or right. Walking the trail allowed me to finally see this part of my life. Until this moment, I thought that I had walked all of that off and left it somewhere behind me. I'm going to summarize my journey in one word:

Acceptance.

Accepting my injury. Accepting that I do have value. Accepting that I don't have to do crazy things like hike the Appalachian Trail to get the attention I've always so desperately felt I needed.

I can't believe I'm sharing this with you.

Anyway… anger redirected can be a powerful force. I'm not recommending this as a useful or particularly healthy strategy. I'm just telling you what my superpower is.

Another blast of wind brought me back to my senses, and I took a deep breath before taking another shot at getting past this obstacle. I held onto the rebar with my right hand and grabbed the side of my leg with my left arm. Then using all of the (not so great) muscles I could summon in my injured leg, along with a boost from my arm pulling up my knee, I gave it a mighty UMPH! and my leg was up on the ledge!

I then reached my left hand over to the rebar and pulled up with both hands. Using all of my strength, I slowly... slowly... inched myself up onto the ledge, all the while thinking that if I fell, it wouldn't be pretty. I then flattened myself out and did a half roll to move in from the edge. *Whew... I made it.* I was unsure how I'd get back down, but I wasn't going to worry about that until later.

I climbed up an exposed ridgeline and made my way over, around, and in-between various boulders as if I were climbing up a Stegosaurus's back. The wind was really howling. I guessed that it was gusting at around sixty or seventy miles-per-hour. Despite feeling quite exposed, I continued making my way up, climbing slowly.

More people passed me heading back down. A girlfriend and father of a thru-hiker said, "We're not dressed for this cold weather," leaving the NOBO to continue on by himself. I could feel and see fine sleet blowing sideways across the mountain, and I was starting to notice places where ice was beginning to build upon the rocks.

With all this wind and now the sleet, I really would have felt better if I had someone to hike with me for the day, for moral support, to give me a boost, if I needed it, and to be there in case I slipped and fell. *Well, I've made it this far mostly on my own,* I thought while wishing that my old hiking buddy *Dr Fix-it* were with me.

A bit further up, I met *Mogly* coming down the mountain. He had spent the previous evening in the shelter with me. Shouting so that I could hear him over the sound of the wind, he told me that he'd already made it to the top and then said, "It's pretty bad up there. It gets quite a bit worse than right here; in fact, I was blown off my feet at one point in the flatlands up there."

"Should I turn around?"

"No, you can make it. Just take your time and go slow," he advised. I made it up to the flatlands and went by Thoreau's Spring, which appeared to be a tiny little trickle of water coming out from under a big rock. I had another mile or so to go across the flatlands and managed to make my way across without getting knocked off my feet. The sleet was coming sideways across the mountain now, hitting me like a shower of tiny little bees that melted the instant they hit my face. I was cold and miserable yet determined to make it to the top.

And I finally did.

For the past year and a half, I'd dreamed of a sunny day on top of Mt. Katahdin. I expected to spend hours soaking in the celebration and congratulating other hikers who'd made the same journey. Any thoughts I had of hiking back down the Knife Edge Trail disappeared into the mist. Everything was obscured except for the wooden summit sign and a dozen or so day hikers who were taking photos and enjoying being at the top of Maine's highest mountain.

I was thrilled to have made it to the top, but due to the wind and sleet, I'd had all I could take of the bone soaking cold. I desperately wanted to get off the mountaintop and back down to complete the journey that I had started 19 months earlier. I had enough energy to get the job done but felt mentally worn thin from months on end of hiking up and over challenges that should have been beyond my capabilities.

I took some quick photos with the summit sign and then grabbed my hiking poles to head back down the trail.

Heading back across the flatlands, I was cold and uncomfortable in the fierce wind. I wanted to make it below treeline as soon as possible. It had taken six hours to get to the top, and I knew I had another five or six hours to go to complete the day. I hurried along and turned onto the Abol Trail near Thoreau's Spring. I knew that the Abol Trail was steep but doable. Going down this way would spare me the challenge of making it back down over the obstacles I'd struggled with on the Hunt Trail while climbing earlier in the day.

As I progressed down the Abol Trail, the wind became less and less piercing by degrees as I made my way lower and lower down the rockslide. I felt frozen both physically and mentally, so every bit of wind that diminished was welcomed.

Once I was out of the worst of the wind, I found a spot behind a large rock that offered shelter from the remaining gusts and sat down to eat my lunch. I ate my usual fare of tortillas and peanut butter, and the sun broke through the clouds. I began to sort through the emotions swirling in my head like the wind atop the mountain.

It was starting to sink in. I'd achieved my goal of hiking the entire Appalachian Trail. But my inner purpose, the thing that had driven me up and down 2,189 miles of mountains through rain, fog, sweat, rocks, sleet, and snow—was my belief that if I hiked 2,000 miles, then my leg would HAVE to be healed.

As I took a few more Advil, I looked down at the worn-out boot on my left foot. I realized that my foot and leg were still hurting. Unless a miracle happened on the way down, they would still be hurting the next day, and the day after that.

On the positive side, I'd been able to discard the brace I'd worn for most of the trail a few hundred miles ago. My leg and foot were undoubtedly stronger, and my balance was getting a little better. But after over 2,000 miles of pushing myself, brutally at times, my freaking leg hadn't healed itself!

As I put my pack back on, grabbed my poles, and began making my way down the trail, I knew that I needed to find a way for all of this to make sense. I didn't want the adventure of my lifetime to be spoiled because of my crazy expectation that somehow hiking 2,000 miles would fix my foot.

By this time, the clouds had lifted somewhat, and the sun was peeking through here and there. I looked out at the beautiful vista of lakes that stretched across the landscape, clear to the horizon. I tried to soak in every bit of the experience, knowing that this was the last day of an incredibly long journey.

About an hour later, after I'd made my way down the rockslide and was below treeline, I met *Jackson*, a section hiker who walked with me for a bit. He said, "Oh my goodness, you're limping. Does your foot hurt?

"Only when I step on it," I said, laughing at my own joke. I told him how I was injured three and a half years ago and that I'd just completed the Appalachian Trail. He seemed impressed.

"Wow! That's amazing. You hiked the entire Appalachian Trail—congratulations! And to think you did it with a BUM LEG!"

He then moved on down the trail as I limped along behind him, unable to keep up with his faster pace. I thought, *Dang it, he's right. My hope, my dream, my mission of healing myself by reaching the top of Mt. Katahdin isn't going to come true.*

As much as I wanted to find a way to heal my leg, I hadn't reached my goal yet. I'd been persistently hiking for a total of eleven months while thinking the entire way, *"The Appalachian Trail is healing me. All I have to do is get to Katahdin."* I admitted to myself that this problem was even bigger than I imagined. As much as I wanted to find a way to make it happen through brute effort, I guess that not everything in life can be forced. Perhaps nothing can really be forced or pushed through in life. I thought about how much I wanted to be healed before I started my hike.

I ran through and processed all of the emotions that I'd felt each day as my foot hurt and hurt and hurt, yet somehow, I'd found a way to keep moving, to hike through it. I thought about how I'd broken the trail down into day-by-day sections to keep myself from quitting when the idea of going hundreds of miles further was simply overwhelming.

I realized that I was like most people. Anytime I wanted something or needed to make a change, I'd want it to happen right then or the next day at the latest. But life doesn't work like that. You pick a direction and start walking towards your goal. And something magical happens when you take that first step. As I did here on this journey, by starting in the direction of your dreams, you claim responsibility for your life. You're no longer drifting in the current, letting life and other people dictate the path you're on. Ideally, you'll have enough persistence and determination to stay on track, no matter how far you have to travel to make your dreams come true.

By deciding to hike the Appalachian Trail alone, I transformed myself from a person who was waiting for someone else to fix all my problems into someone who's willing to grab the reins and say, "Giddy up!"

This voyage was absolutely the right place for me to begin healing myself. Sure, I wanted to be completely healed by this point. Don't most of our goals take longer than we expect? I continued down the Abol trail, thinking about how far I'd come. I'd gone from sitting on the sofa in constant pain, taking handfuls of pills, and watching Netflix to distract my mind from the pain to where I was now. Sure, my foot and leg still bothered me, but I'd gotten so much better.

I'd lost an extra 25 pounds of weight that I didn't need. My leg muscles were finally getting close to the same size, and I could hike 15 miles without much pain or having to think about my leg for every second of the day. So, there's no question that I'd gotten better. And sure, I admitted to myself that I still had a long way left to go.

In most cases, you can't or won't get everything you want overnight, but you can choose the path you're going to follow. And by choosing your own path, you can become who you're meant to be, making your way through the long journey that we call life.

I had to learn to nurture myself by hiking shorter distances, bringing my car, walking in pools, and getting lighter gear. After doing this, I could see that hiking was the perfect physical and mental therapy for me. When I got up in the morning, I didn't have to think about what I would do each day. I knew that I needed to walk another eight to twelve miles. All I had to do was follow the white blazes and make sure that I was headed north.

When I got tired in the afternoon, I could stop and rest, but I didn't have the luxury of plopping back down on the sofa, which is exactly what I'd have done if I were still at home. I had to keep going. When I struggled to make it up another mountain, I knew my two choices were to give up and go home or to keep going no matter what. Giving up meant resigning myself to a life filled with pain. Pain that was likely to never get better.

As impressive and as hard as this journey may seem to you, I don't want you to think that I'm some kind of a saint or something. Please understand that choosing to hike was simply the easier choice for me. As hard as this adventure was, it was easier than the alternative, which was doing nothing and living a lifetime of never-ending pain.

I really am so much better than I was before. I'm hopeful that I can continue to (slowly) get better. I can confidently tell you that anything you or I really want to do can be accomplished if you just break it down into bite-sized pieces that you can handle each day.

Your best life is waiting for you right now; all you need to do is reach out and grab it.

When I heard a car starting in the campground, I could tell that I was almost to the bottom of the mountain. I stopped to brush my teeth and ran my fingers through my knotted hair. I walked another hundred yards, came around a turn, and saw my beautiful wife standing there waiting for me. I grabbed her in an embrace and held on like I was never going to let go.

She had flown into Bangor and driven up into Baxter State Park earlier in the day. She brought along a special friend of mine that one of my daughters got for me when I was first injured. It's a little white teddy bear wearing a red shirt that says, "Get Well Soon!"

She brought out a bottle of champagne to celebrate (she wasn't aware this violated park rules). I talked her into huddling inside an empty campsite shelter where we enjoyed a secretive victory toast. Joanna drove us down the long dirt road heading out of the park to 5 Lakes Lodge Bed and Breakfast on Lake Pemdumcook where she had booked a room for us. After an elegant dinner with a few other couples, we went out back to sit on the porch. Looking across the lake, we could see the late day sun starting to fade on Mt. Katahdin, standing there proudly, now and forever.

My kids surprised me with a video that tells the story of my injury and healing on the Appalachian Trail. You can see this video and photographs of my journey by going to: OnlyWhenIStepOnIt.com

EPILOGUE

In the days that followed, I felt like a fish out of water. My wife drove me over to Monson to retrieve my car, which was parked at Shaw's Hostel. I entered our home address into my phone and was surprised to see that it was over ten hours to get home to Maryland. My car had followed me up the trail in tiny little jumps as I had moved it from one trailhead to the next over the past eight months.

After leaving Monson, I stopped to see my brother and his family in central Maine. From there it was a nine-hour drive home to Annapolis, Maryland. Normally, I would never drive nine hours. Ugh! Just the thought of it would put me to sleep. With airfare so cheap these days, I tend to fly when I'm going somewhere. But there I was with this car of mine, all the way up in Maine.

I thought about it for a moment and decided that if I could spend 10 or 12 hours each day hiking up and over mountains, rocks, roots, and mud, then I could easily sit in a car and make the drive home all in one shot. So that's what I did.

Once I got home, it seemed strange to be done hiking the trail. I missed the simple routine of having one goal each day: to walk another 10 or 12 miles. I missed the serenity of walking through the woods and the reassuring sounds of insects in the forest at night.

I had adjusted to life moving along at one or two miles an hour and didn't want to be pushed back into the fast-moving stream of regular daily life in a small city. We went out to dinner a few nights later, and my wife was driving us over the Severn River Bridge. I felt like I was hurtling along at 90 miles per hour. I shouted out, "Slow down! Slow down! You're going too fast!"

"Peter, I'm going the speed limit."

"Really? It feels like we're flying."

I thought about different ways to continue with my physical training regimen. I could walk five miles a day, but that would take a bunch of time. I tried riding my bike down into Annapolis for several weeks. The big picture is that I slowly became more adjusted to being done with the trail. While I did a fair amount of walking, the amount of physical activity decreased over time for me.

The first month or so off the trail, my foot and leg seemed to bother me more than when I was hiking. I no longer had the daily task of pushing myself up and over the mountain of the day as a focus to keep me from thinking about how much my leg was hurting.

As part of my never-ending optimism, I expected that once I rested up for a few months, my leg would be completely healed. Four or five months later, I realized that the pain in my leg was bothering me enough to interfere with getting any productive work done. I'd been doing one-on-one consulting, helping clients with their commercial real estate projects.

I was fine when I was on the phone going through a potential property with a client but otherwise found myself migrating back to my old habit of watching Netflix to distract myself from the pain in my leg. After some research, I decided to go to a pain treatment practice at University of Maryland. After filling out a bunch of forms and waiting over a month, I finally got in to see a doctor. I told the doctor about my injury and how I had hiked the Appalachian Trail in an effort to heal myself. I let her know that the pain was still bothering me and wanted to know what she might recommend.

"Oh, you probably need a spinal cord stimulator," she said. "Let me take a look at your foot."

I took off my left shoe and sock and pulled my pants leg up so she could see my foot.

"Yup, that's classic CRPS... a spinal cord stimulator will definitely help you with that. There are a few things we'll need to do so that you can have the surgery."

First off, let me just say that I had spent the last four years wondering why in the heck my leg kept hurting me. I was initially told by my doctors that the nerve in my leg had been damaged, and once the nerve grew back, I would be better. Nerves only regenerate at about one millimeter per month. This meant that it would take about three years for the nerve to grow back. There I was at four years after my injury, and while my leg was getting better (hiking the Appalachian Trail definitely helped!) I was still dealing with ongoing pain issues.

"What did you say?" I asked.

"Oh, it's CRPS, and I think that we can help you with that."

"Wait a minute, I'm going to write that down. C. R. P. S.—what does that stand for?"

"It's Complex Regional Pain Syndrome," the doctor replied before moving ahead with scheduling an appointment for me to see a Psychiatrist. "It's a requirement before I can give you the final approval for the spinal cord stimulator."

Ok, timeout. A few background items I should explain to you.

First off, I don't like surgery, so I'll do almost anything I can to avoid it. A spinal cord stimulator had been suggested to me about two and a half years ago. My response then was to finally quit taking the opioid pain medications I was on, cold turkey style. I didn't want to go to the extreme of having something implanted in my body without really knowing how much pain I was actually dealing with. The end result was my pain levels actually went down when I got off Oxycontin. I ended up passing on the surgery and deciding three months later to hike the Appalachian Trail.

I thought about all of this and told the doctor that I didn't want any surgery. I asked her what my other options were.

"You could try Lyrica."

Lyrica was initially developed as an anticonvulsant and has been found to help with nerve pain. So, I took Lyrica for the next year or so, but the critical part is what I discovered when I got home later that day.

I looked online to see what I could find out about Complex Regional Pain Syndrome (CRPS). There's no known cure for CRPS, but a combination of physical treatments, medication, and psychological support can help manage the symptoms. Still, some people experience continuous pain despite treatment.

Complex Regional Pain Syndrome (CRPS) is a form of chronic pain that usually affects an arm or a leg. CRPS typically develops after an injury, surgery, stroke, or heart attack. The pain is out of proportion to the severity of the initial injury. The big picture is that my brain has gotten stuck in a loop where it expects my foot to keep hurting, which makes my foot hurt, which then reinforces the loop. That's a simplified explanation, but it's the easiest way that I've been able to wrap my head around CRPS.

Signs and symptoms of Complex Regional Pain Syndrome include:

- Continuous burning or throbbing pain, usually in your arm, leg, hand, or foot
- Sensitivity to touch or cold (that's why I needed foot warmers)
- Swelling of the painful area
- Changes in skin temperature (My left foot is 10 degrees colder than my right foot!)
- Changes in skin color (gets red or pinkish, and is worse when I first get up)
- Joint stiffness, swelling and damage
- Muscle spasms, tremors, weakness, and atrophy— This makes it hard to control the limb
- Decreased ability to move the affected body part (because it hurts and it's weaker)

Symptoms may change over time and vary from person to person. Pain, swelling, redness, noticeable changes in temperature, and hypersensitivity (particularly to cold and touch) usually occur first. Over time, the affected limb can become cold and pale. It may undergo skin and nail changes as well as muscle spasms and tightening. Once these changes occur, the condition is often irreversible.

I've learned more about this condition, including attending seminars and consulting with specialists. In my case, I think it was caused by the over-sensitization of my central nervous system each time my pain levels shot up to the moon. There's also research that indicates long-term use of opioid medications (I was on Oxycontin for 18 months) can irritate and inflame the glial cells. These are packed in tightly around the nerves in your body. I understand that once the glial cells get irritated, they can cause the nerves to become inflamed.

I, of course, don't accept that CRPS is incurable. I've been to CRPS support groups where I've met people with an arm or other body part that they haven't moved in years. And it's not a pretty sight. I could tell that they were suffering from incredible pain. Nerve pain is strange in that while it hurts, if you don't move, it gets worse. My understanding is that remaining stationary makes everything tighten up even more. And the tighter you are—the more you allow your brain to *fight* against the pain—the worse it's going to hurt.

Once I discovered the persistent pain in my leg was caused by CRPS, I realized the only way to have a chance at overcoming this condition (which people claim there's no cure for) was to keep moving and exercising even though it can hurt like crazy.

Hiking the Appalachian Trail was perfect for me. I was stupidly stubborn enough to think that my leg would somehow be magically healed once I completed the entire AT. But isn't that what we all want? Just take this one pill, do this one particular exercise, wave this magic wand, and then presto! All of your troubles will just disappear.

Discovering that I can work at and make progress on overcoming something as strong and as stubborn as CRPS while hiking the Appalachian Trail was huge for me. Although I didn't know that it was CRPS at the time, the challenge of having to walk eight or ten miles a day was perfect for me. Hiking and stretching loosen things up to counteract the ongoing constricting and tightening process. If one leg hurts, a person will naturally favor their stronger side and use the injured side less frequently. Exercising or doing physical therapy of any type helps offset the weakening and atrophy caused by CRPS.

So as much as I wanted to experience a magical walk to Katahdin, at this point, six months after finishing my hike, I wasn't healed completely. I still had a long way to go. But hiking the Appalachian Trail put me back in control of my life. I could do something to heal myself rather than hoping and waiting for a doctor or a magic pill to take the pain away.

The following year on June 8th, I flew up to Portland, Maine to reunite with *Dr Fix-it*. He was finishing up his section hike of the Appalachian Trail and had asked me to accompany him through the White Mountains. He picked me up at the airport and drove over to Crawford Notch in New Hampshire. I spent the night in a pop-up tent mounted on top of "Leti," a hiking van that he had purchased after hiking with me two years before. Leti was a better-organized version of my car with plenty of food, hiking supplies, and assorted hiking gear. *Dr Fix-it* had outfitted the van with a bed in the back, which makes an incognito place to sleep while parking in a "no camping" area such as the lot we were in.

The pop-up tent on the top, on the other hand, was like a big flag announcing, "Somebody's camping over here." The following morning, I was awoken by a friendly ranger who said, "That's quite a nice contraption you've got thay-a." (He was from Maine.) He was super friendly, and didn't even threaten to write me a ticket, simply saying, "You can't camp here, ok?"

Over the next seven days, we made our way north along the Appalachian Trail, stopping to stay mainly at the Appalachian Mountain Club huts along the way. *Dr Fix-it* said that my balance and hiking speed had improved considerably from the last time we had hiked together. I know I'm continuing to make progress with recovering from my injury. Still, at this point, it was happening so slowly over time that it was hard for me to notice.

We had near-perfect weather with views as far as you could see from the top of Mt. Washington and the Presidentials. I was able to keep my pack light by eating breakfast and dinner at the huts. I'd also occasionally take an extra helping of bread or dessert from the evening meal that found its way into my pack for the following day's lunch on the trail. While I can't say with any certainty whether this violated any of their rules, I didn't see anything posted that expressly prohibited it.

I thoroughly enjoyed my time with *Dr Fix-it*. He has this fantastic ability to share one story after another about his life experiences with the depth, expression, and passion that you'd expect from a keynote speaker. Actually, he is a speaker, one of many things that the two of us share in common. We finally arrived at the Rattle River Lodge and Hostel near Gorham and took a shuttle back over to Crawford Notch to get "Leti", which I've been told, stands for "light at the end of the tunnel." I'm not sure how it stands for that, but as with all thing's *Dr Fix-it*, a bit of intrigue and mystery is par for the course.

Dr Fix-it gave me a ride back over to the Portland Airport where I picked up a rental car. I wanted to see if I could redo my summit of Mt. Katahdin. When I completed hiking the AT, I had hoped to experience a happy, joyful time on top of the mountain. I wanted to replace the frenzied, frozen exclamation point that I'd experienced on the last day of my hike with something more enjoyable. I stopped for a few days to stay at my brother's house in Sidney, right along the Kennebec River. I was able to monitor the weather and talk to a pleasant park ranger on the phone, which helped me plan my second ascent of Mt. Katahdin.

When I explained I wanted to hike the Knife Edge, he suggested starting at Roaring Brook Campground. He told me how to hike a loop up and over the Knife Edge, then back down along the Chimney Pond Trail. He said I could stay in the bunkhouse at the base of the mountain, allowing me to get an early start. After checking the weather one last time, I reserved my spot and drove up to Baxter State Park the next day.

I got up the following day and quickly dressed in the cold air. When I stopped at the ranger station to sign the trail register I could see that I was first on the list for the day, with a departure time of 5:20 am. I made my way up the trail and, noticing low-hanging clouds above me, whispered a plea for clear skies up on the mountain for the day. As I climbed, the clouds seemed to rise above me, providing magnificent views out across the shaded valley below.

By the time I made it to Pamola Peak, I had climbed up into a fog but figured I'd keep going since I was about halfway to the summit. I came to "The Chimney," a three-sided chute that headed straight down into a notch in the ridge. It looked impossible to get down without using a rope. As I sat down to consider my options, the wind picked up and started clearing some of the fog away. I'd read about this and thought I'd be able to push my back against one side and my feet against the other, but The Chimney was too wide for that maneuver to work.

I eventually got up my courage and managed to get down by holding on with my fingertips and using the side of my boots to grip onto various ridges and cracks on the rock faces. When I made it to the bottom, I let out a sigh of relief, realizing that I'd been holding my breath the entire way down.

The Knife Edge had an impressive drop-off on each side, probably at least a few thousand feet from what I could see. This wasn't a problem for the first two-thirds of the Knife Edge. The trail at the top varied in width from ten to twenty feet. It had rocks protruding up that I could hold onto with my hands while clambering along. The wind had cleared the clouds away by this time, and the view was amazing.

Then I got to a section where the trail narrowed to two or three feet wide. If you imagine a sidewalk running from the top of one skyscraper to another, it was sort of like that. The difference was that while the sides didn't drop off straight down, they were steep enough that if you fell, you'd undoubtedly keep moving until you reached the bottom.

Have I mentioned that I'm afraid of heights?

That said, I'd made it this far and wasn't about to turn

back. I told myself that all I had to do was shimmy across on my hands and knees. As long as I stayed right in the center and the wind didn't blow me off, I figured I'd be fine. I took a deep breath and crawled on my hands and knees like a baby until I made it to the other side. One hundred yards further, there was another narrow section, except it was a little longer. While going across that portion, I made the mistake of turning my head for a brief moment to look down at Chimney Pond to my right side. The view was gorgeous and spectacular, superimposed with a massive dose of fear. I obviously made it across, but that image remains seared into my head to this very day.

After another thirty minutes of clambering along, I finally made it to the sign that indicated Mt. Katahdin's summit. It seemed strange to arrive coming from this direction. When I was up there two years before, I couldn't see the Knife Edge as it was completely enshrouded in fog. The mountaintop today was sunny and warm with a festive atmosphere enhanced by 30 or 40 other hikers talking, celebrating, taking photos, and eating their lunches. I congratulated thru-hikers as they arrived at the end of their long Appalachian Trail journey. I also took another "victory" photo standing on top of the sign with my poles in the air.

Then it was time to go down. I took a different trail that led to a long steep rockslide. This was really steep, so I took my time, stopping partway to refill my water in a spot where it trickled out amongst the rocks. Once down the rockslide, the trail appeared to level out, although it was still taking me downhill. When I arrived at Chimney Pond, I realized this was the spot that my parents and six siblings had hiked up to forty years ago. Back then, it was a fun hike up to a pond. Dad seemed impressed at the time, but I didn't understand what all the fuss was about. At age ten, one pond is like any other.

After hiking the Appalachian Trail and learning to love and appreciate the wilderness, I now looked out at Chimney Pond with a different set of eyes. This was pure, pristine, picture-postcard-perfect wilderness. The mirrored surface showcased trees growing on the other side of the pond surrounded by the mountain backdrop. The water, while crystal clear, seemed to bring alive the colors reflecting on its surface. I looked up in awe at the Knife Edge stretching across the sky above. I sat down and spent the next hour soaking in and appreciating the incredible beauty and wonder that was spread out like a banquet in front of me. It was the same spot I'd seen as a kid, but now it meant something to me.

I didn't want to leave but knew that I should get moving to make it back down before nightfall. On the Chimney Pond Trail, I was able to "rock hop" which is where you traverse across the top of the rocks by stepping from one rock to the next. This is an easy thing for most hikers to do, but I was unable to do this while I was hiking the Appalachian Trail. I didn't have the balance or control in my left foot to manage landing on the tops of rocks at different angles. Instead of rock hopping, I had to slowly make my way around or over the rocks, staying primarily on the ground.

I had conquered the Knife Edge. I'd gotten to enjoy the sunny day on top of Mt. Katahdin that I'd dreamed about. I fell in love with Chimney Pond. Now I was on top of the rocks, moving along faster than I'd ever hiked before. It was an amazing, beautiful day.

Over the next few years, I continued to walk in the pool, stretch my leg out and ride my bike. I was determined more than ever to heal my leg and foot completely. I wanted to be able to walk straight again rather than to hobble along, looking like someone who'd been seriously injured. I discovered while grocery shopping that it was easier for me to walk by holding onto the shopping cart. I could stand upright and work on improving my gait.

I wondered what I could get to hold onto while I was out walking. A rollator, a walker with wheels on it, would do the job, but I didn't like using a cane, much less a walker or rollator. So, I figured with our new grandkids arriving, we'd need a baby stroller. I could use that to hold onto while going out for my walks. Without a baby to weigh it down, the stroller would pop a wheelie. To fix this, I put a box of my real estate books in it and started pushing the stroller up and down our street while walking Snickers, my pet Yorkie.

My son thought this was hilarious and suggested that I wear a wig and carry a purse to complete the ensemble. Of course, the neighbors were curious, and one by one, they all asked what was in the box. I didn't care if I looked silly or not. I wanted to learn to walk straight. I wanted to be healed, so much so that I pushed that darn baby carriage up and down the street for several more years.

I've just "Celebrated" the eighth anniversary of my injury as of this writing. While it may sound crazy to celebrate such a traumatic event, my life was transformed on that day. I went from moving along one path to take an unexpected fork in the road that led to my hiking the Appalachian Trail. This resulted in healing myself physically while also helping me figure out how to follow my true passion in life.

At this point, I'm happy to say that I'm no longer in pain every day. I've progressed to where I still have some stiffness, and my foot feels numb and tingly at times. I still do stretches, squats, leg lifts, and ride my bicycle every day. I'm still working on improving my balance. It's gotten better, but I'm still clumsy on my left side. This bothers me, yet over time I've gotten used to it. I roll my foot on a ball to loosen it up and wrap a heating blanket around my foot while I'm working. I also walk in a therapy pool three times a week as this continues to help build my strength and somehow makes my foot feel better for three or four days afterward.

> I feel like I'm still walking to
> Katahdin. And I'm ok with that.

I realized on my eighth anniversary that I was waiting to be completely healed so that I could finish this book with a happy fairy-tale-like ending. I wanted to be able to say, "I wasn't healed on top of Mt. Katahdin, but now I'm all better." The biggest challenge I've had over the past year is the disappointment I feel when I realize (for the hundredth time) that I'm not entirely healed. You see, there are times when I faithfully stick to my daily schedule, and my foot starts feeling pretty darn good. "*Wow... I'm finally healed up,*" I tell myself, despite having been down this road before. Then I cut back on stretching, going to the pool, and bike riding. *"Why take the time to do all that stuff if I'm completely healed?"*

Then after cutting back on all the things that keep my leg feeling better, my foot starts hurting, and the pain persistently climbs up my leg, almost as if saying, *"I'm still here… you can't get rid of me!"*

I found myself getting a bit depressed at times over all of this. I was continuing to push myself to get better. I realized that my rules were "I won't be content until I'm completely healed." And then I remembered what I discovered while hiking the Appalachian Trail.

Acceptance.

I can't change any part of my long, painful journey, nor would I even if I could. It's been a glorious adventure. By learning to accept and live the best I can with the hand I've been dealt, I've discovered something that's been elusive for most of my life.

Happiness.

The truth is that while I continue to slowly improve, my foot and leg still bother me at times. I finally realized that I could continue fighting against this or simply accept it. The moment I realized this, I felt a reassuring calmness flow through my entire being. I'm ok looking awkward when I walk. I'm ok with my foot hurting a bit at times. Sure, I still want to get better. But from this point forward, I'm going to enjoy each and every day, each moment in time, knowing that I'm doing the best I can.

After all, it's not what happens to you. It's what you do about it.

A NOTE TO YOU, THE READER:

Thank you for following along on my journey. As part of writing this book, I hope to create enough of a connection with you to encourage you to improve your life. You certainly don't have to hike the Appalachian Trail, although you'll have a blast if you do.

I hope I've provided you with some motivation or at least a respite from the day-to-day challenges that you may be dealing with.

COULD YOU PLEASE DO ME A SMALL FAVOR?

I put my heart and soul into completing this hike and figuring out how to heal from a traumatic injury. I spent hundreds of hours writing this book, edited it six times (with plenty of help), got the cover just right after testing two other versions, plus a bunch of other behind the scenes stuff. It's been a massive project that's taken me five years to complete. This book means a lot to me as it's my way to reach out to help, motivate, and inspire greatness in you and other readers.

Can you take a moment right now to leave your heartfelt comments on Amazon? Your review will help someone who hasn't read the book yet know what you liked about it and why they should take their time to read it. I love getting honest feedback and will read every single review including yours. Reviews make a HUGE difference to authors— Writing a review is the very best way to help me out :)

To post your review of Only When I Step On It, please go to: **review.OnlyWhenIStepOnIt.com**

Your feedback lets me know that all of my efforts to hike 2,189 miles thru the woods, up and over mountains, and sharing my story was worth it.

In addition to this, please recommend Only When I Step On It to several of your friends or post a note on social media. This will help me encourage and inspire as many people as possible.

Finally, if you know of anyone who's struggling with chronic pain, please send their name and address to my email below and I'll ship them a copy of this book. I'm so thankful to have you as a reader and I appreciate your help.

CONNECTING WITH THE AUTHOR

Peter Conti is an inspiring, entertaining keynote speaker and podcast guest. He also enjoys using Zoom to attend book club meetings to answer questions and share further details and stories about his Appalachian Trail adventure. You can contact him at Peter@AdversityPress.com

RESOURCES

A Walk in The Woods
Bill Bryson

This was the book that planted the idea of hiking the Appalachian Trail in my head many years ago. I love his personal anecdotes as well as the history of the trail. The encounters with Stephen Katz and other characters make this one hard to put down.

Katahdin or Bust: Increasing Your Odds of Enjoying Hiking and Backpacking
Gail Hinshaw

This book by the one and only Dr Fix-it shows you how to solve the problem of how to keep your feet, legs, and the rest of your body from failing if you're in your 50's, 60's, or 70's. It's also chock full of ideas, tips, and revolutionary strategies that will make your hike easier and more enjoyable at any age. Reading this book will make you much more likely to succeed rather than fail just like 80 percent of thru hikers do.

AWOL on the Appalachian Trail

David Miller

If you've ever wondered what it would be like to leave your job and family behind to knock out an Appalachian Trail thru-hike, then read this book. The way David described his experience on the trail and the people he met led to my decision to try hiking the trail myself.

Commercial Real Estate Investing for Dummies

Peter Conti

Despite the lack of hiking trails in this book it will lead you to an exciting adventure in commercial real estate. You can get a *free* copy (just pay shipping) by going to PetersFreeBook.com

APPALACHIAN TRAIL HIKING CLUBS

'm so thankful for all of the volunteers and organizations who've helped to create, improve, and keep up the Appalachian Trail over the years. Without all of you and your efforts I wouldn't be able to enjoy one of the nicest stretches of wilderness in our country. Thank you very much.

Here's a list of the affiliated trail maintenance clubs from South to North:

- Georgia Appalachian Trail Club
- Nantahala Hiking Club
- Smoky Mountains Hiking Club
- Carolina Mountain Club
- Tennessee Eastman Hiking and Canoeing Club
- Mt. Rogers Appalachian Trail Club
- Piedmont Appalachian Trail Hikers
- Outdoor Club of Virginia Tech
- Roanoke Appalachian Trail Club
- Natural Bridge Appalachian Trail Club
- Tidewater Appalachian Trail Club
- Old Dominion Appalachian Trail Club
- Potomac Appalachian Trail Club
- Mountain Club of Maryland
- Cumberland Valley Appalachian Trail Club
- York Hiking Club

- Susquehanna Appalachian Trail Club
- Blue Mountain Eagle Climbing Club
- Allentown Hiking Club
- Philadelphia Trail Club
- AMC-Delaware Valley Chapter
- Batona Hiking Club
- Wilmington Trail Club
- New York—New Jersey Trail Conference
- AMC-Connecticut Chapter
- AMC-Berkshire Chapter
- Green Mountain Club
- Dartmouth Outing Club
- Randolph Mountain Club
- Appalachian Mountain Club (AMC)
- Maine Appalachian Trail Club

The Appalachian Trail Conservancy (ATC) reported in a recent year, a record-breaking 6,827 volunteers contributed approximately 272,477 hours to maintaining and protecting the AT. Since the ATC began collecting reports in 1983, individuals have contributed more than 5 million hours to the AT. That's amazing.

A special thanks goes to Najdan Mancic who patiently worked with me to create the book cover, interior layout, and even this cool line drawing of Mt. Katahdin shown above. You can find Najdan at iskonbookdesign.com